LESLEY GARRETT

Notes from a Small Soprano

This book is dedicated to my parents, Derek and Margaret Garrett, who not only gave me life but taught me, through their example, how to make the most of it; to Vivien Pike who taught me to sing and Joy Mammen who taught me to sing with my soul; and, lastly, to Peter, Jeremy and Chloe, who have taught me what love really means.

Contents

———•———

Preface

———•———

When it comes to music I'm with Duke Ellington who said there are only two kinds: good and bad. That, as much as anything else, is what attracts me to Lesley Garrett. She moves effortlessly through musical styles giving as much devotion to a melody by Kern as she does to an aria by Puccini.

She is a maverick and an endearing one. She proves the adage you can take the girl out of Yorkshire but you can't take Yorkshire out of the girl. Much has been made of the 'Diva from Doncaster'. It is used in an almost derogatory fashion, as if opera and South Yorkshire were contradictory terms. In fact, that part of the world is synonymous with good music.

Were it not for the brass bands of the north country (I was going to say 'Yorkshire' but I have to admit that Lancashire has produced a fair share) many symphony orchestras would be short of a player or two. The industrial revolution not only spawned mills, shipyards and mines, it also produced people who took music seriously and made a very significant contribution to British culture.

I lived in a pit village near where Lesley Garrett was born and, like her, grew up to the sound of music. If we stood outside the Miners' Welfare on a Sunday morning we could hear the Grimethorpe Brass Band rehearsing in an upstairs room. The *Messiah* was not just a treat reserved for religious festivals but an ever-present glory. In our village of five thousand souls there were at least four versions each year.

I loved the *Messiah* but hated the ritual of attending which meant we were attired in our Sunday best, scrubbed clean as a doorstep and buffed like guardsmen's boots. Smelling of Brylcreem and carbolic soap we perched on church pews while being exalted and purified by Handel's music. That, at least, was the intention. Truth be told there was much illicit enjoyment to be had watching the tenor who almost always had a wobbly adams apple, and the soprano who more often than not had a bosom which was ample, heaving and full of dark promise for a pubescent youth.

Any child brought up in that kind of society would have to be tone-deaf not to understand that music wasn't just a background noise but something to love and respect through a lifetime. Lesley Garrett was lucky in that she came from a family of performers. As you read her book you come to believe in the presence of a musical gene. From the day she was born she was destined to be a singer. It wasn't a career, it was a vocation.

If her musical talent was genetic I suspect the rest was

shaped by the clay of her native Yorkshire. She is a strong, independent woman – sometimes wilful, oft-times vulnerable, because that is what people are like where she comes from.

She shuns the carapace of stardom that separates the celebrity from the public because where she grew up they are severe on people who forget where they came from.

She knows what she wants but, more importantly, she knows who she is. In the rarefied and illusory world of opera it is easy to sidestep reality, to assume another persona. Lesley's greatest gifts are both uncommon talent and the common touch. She sings for the people while remaining one of them.

Hers is a fascinating story of a life that will one day make a marvellous musical. The good news is that there is more to come. Her story has far from run its course. What we have so far is inspiring and entertaining enough to hope she is now at work on Volume Two.

Moreover her confirmation that, as the great Duke said, there are only two kinds of music is a major contribution to the niggling border disputes that deter so many people from enjoying all the riches on offer.

Here's a good idea:

Dame Lesley Garrett, Minister for Music. What would they make of that in Doncaster?

Michael Parkinson
March 2000

Prologue

The last twelve months had been among the best and worst in my life. And now my beloved Nanan, my father's mother, was dead. She was my last surviving grandparent and her passing meant not just the loss of a woman I had loved for forty years, but the end of an era, the drawing of a line under yet another branch of my huge and colourful family tree.

She had been ill for such a long time, but I had hoped to see her just once more. I didn't quite make it and she died while I was on the train from London to Yorkshire. They had taken her away by the time I reached the house, but the essence of her remained. The familiar smell of baby powder and warm tea still lingered in the air though I sensed it was fading as I stood beside her empty yet still warm bed and wept. I was born in this bed, as my father had been before me.

Other smells returned like childhood ghosts to haunt

me; my father coming home in his huge greatcoat with its shiny silver buttons, smelling of smoke and steam and work, the stench of the ash-midden in the backyard, sweet apples baking in Nanny's kitchen, Grandad's hands after he had filled his pipe.

I had never seen the point of writing down the story of my life – I was too busy living it. Now I realised that I was ready to make a start. This book is the result: not so much the story of where I have been but where I came from.

Chapter 1

——————

Small Beginnings

Just outside the small town of Thorne in South Yorkshire lies the little hamlet of Waterside. It had once been a bustling port on the river Don, handling cargo and passengers *en route* for the great cities of Hull, Sheffield and even London. Steam ships and sailing barges moored at the quayside where an ancient bonded warehouse stood, next to the Old John Bull pub. At one end of the quay was a long, straight lane where gangs of burly sailors stretched and wound their ropes. At the other end sat a row of solid red-brick cottages, home to the dock workers and shipwrights and their families. In the middle of the nineteenth century the railways came to Thorne and the river traffic dwindled to a trickle. With disuse, the river itself began to silt up until the big ships could no longer pass. One by one, the dockers left, leaving their machinery to rust and the buildings to sink into damp decay. Ultimately, the meander was dammed at each end and a channel cut to provide a new, straight course for the Don. Waterside's decline was now complete. Lying isolated on the banks of a man-made ox-bow lake, it was a port no more. A few families remained, but it was a closed, inward-looking (some local gossips muttered 'in-bred') community, fearing and feared by outsiders from the town. This was not a place where a young, newly married couple would choose to set up home and raise a family but that is exactly what Derek and Margaret Garrett did. They came here because nobody else wanted to and that made it cheap enough for them to afford. And so it was that I arrived, just five days old, at Number 9 Waterside.

My mother was born Margaret Wall, the youngest daughter of Colin and Elizabeth Wall. Colin came originally from Wath upon Dearn near Sheffield. There were eight children in his family, which, while common enough in those days, was a remarkable feat on his mother's part for she had only one breast. Whether this was a result of surgery, trauma or an accident of nature no one seems to know, but she nevertheless successfully nursed her eight babies with this one, massive, cyclops-like breast that had somehow gravitated over time to the middle of her chest. Colin grew up thinking one breast was the norm, until one day he saw a woman washing herself at the pump in the backyard. Shocked by the sight of a normal bosom, he rushed home to tell his mum of the neighbour's terrible abnormality.

Colin was a small, delicate boy with a chronically weak chest, who caused his parents much anxiety. Fresh air was believed to be the only remedy for his condition and for many years he was made to sleep out of doors when the weather was fine and with his bedroom window wide open when it was not. It was obvious he would never be fit enough to work in the colliery like his father or in any of the heavy industries on which the area's prosperity depended. Somehow his parents hit upon an ingenious solution to the problem of how he was to earn a living – he would be put to the piano. There was only one obstacle to this imaginative scheme. Although the family owned a piano – practically everyone thereabouts had one in the front room – no one in the family could play and professional lessons were way beyond their means. So my great-grandfather went to the library and borrowed a book. He mastered the first lesson and then taught it to his son who would be expected to practise for hours every day. There was no time for playing with the other children and Colin was forbidden to play cricket with the local boys for fear that he might damage his hands. His musical education continued in this way for many years and, slowly but surely, the apprentice surpassed his master. Colin became not just a competent player, but an exceptional one.

On the wall above my piano now is a photograph of a young Colin Wall in cap and gown proudly holding his certificate from the London College of Music. Hanging next to it is a photograph of me receiving the Honorary Fellowship of the Royal Academy of Music. I wish he had lived long enough to see it – I know he would have been so proud of me, though to my mind his achievement was the greater one.

Grandad Wall made a good living playing the piano with

a small orchestra in cinemas in and around Sheffield. They accompanied the silent movies six days a week and on Sunday, when film shows were forbidden, they would take the stage and play concerts to packed houses. They covered a wide range of repertoire, thanks to the local library, which stocked full sets of orchestral parts for hundreds of classical works. This seems extraordinary nowadays, when only specialised (and expensive) commercial organisations can provide such a service. But it is one small example of just how important music was to local communities then, when all music was popular music.

At the age of twenty-two he met and fell deeply in love with Elizabeth Mellars, the fifteen-year-old daughter of a travelling showman. They enjoyed a long, chaste courtship, accompanied at all times by a Miss Shipton. This redoubtable lady was horrified when my grandparents' engagement was, at last, announced. Whilst everyone else concerned had believed her to have been acting as a chaperone, she had assumed for five years that Colin had been courting her.

When the talkies came to town, cinema pianists became redundant, practically overnight. The depression was at its height and work was scarce, but with a wife and children now to support, work had to be found. Grandfather Wall did what many have done before and since. Just like Norman Tebbit's dad, he got on his bike. Day after day he cycled in ever increasing circles around Wath until he found a job playing piano in the White Hart Hotel in Thorne.

Accustomed to the grandeur and formality of the picture

houses, with their well-dressed and well-behaved clientele, this was a dreadful come-down for him. He had sacrificed his childhood to become a professional musician and now he was playing for the turns in a smoke-filled, beer-stinking pub. To make the best of a bad job he took to starting work early and playing his own favourite concertos and overtures to the all but empty bar. In time, word spread of these impromptu recitals and they became a draw, attracting a new clientele who came primarily to hear him play. When war broke out in 1939, Grandad, too old for active service, volunteered to work in the shipyards where the blow-torch he held all day crippled his hands. Despite this, he still managed to carry on playing at the White Hart, his audience now swelled by airmen from the local RAF bases.

Margaret, my mother, had a very difficult childhood. She had two older sisters and was the youngest child until her brother, Colin, was born on VJ night, fourteen years later. It was a strict, formal household, and although she was deeply loved and well cared for there was little room for physical warmth or affection. At the age of six she developed an uncontrollable tic, which was eventually diagnosed as St Vitus's Dance (the modern medical term is Sydenham's Chorea). The only treatment available at the time was complete rest, total quiet and a foul-tasting vitamin cereal called Bemax. She was to spend years away from school, with long stretches alone in her room, before the condition resolved itself. Such a regime would be ghastly for any child but for Margaret, who was a particularly active and high-spirited little girl, it must have been torture. When she emerged from her enforced seclusion she made up for lost time. At school she studied hard and soon caught up with the other children in her class. Outside school she ran wild with the local lads, revelling in the freedom to be out in the fresh air again. At the age of ten she won a scholarship to Thorne Grammar School where she excelled in all subjects, though music and sport were her real loves. It was sport that was to bring her into contact with Derek Garrett.

Derek lived just around the corner with his younger brother and sister and parents Arthur and Kathleen. Kathleen (née Appleton) was the daughter of a Nottingham coal miner, a huge mountain of a man, feared for his strength and his hot temper. As a girl, she had helped her mother in her little cottage industry of sewing miners' shirts and selling them, for a few pennies, door to door. Arthur Garrett was a railway booking clerk, and this clean, safe, indoor job made him something of a catch. They married in 1928 and Derek was born two years later, followed by Arleen in 1933 and Fayne in 1940. Arthur was called up soon after war broke out and disappeared off to various camps around the British Isles, managing by chance to avoid being sent overseas until 1945 when, two days after the end of hostilities, he was finally dispatched to Germany.

Like many women of her generation, Kathleen was left to manage as best she could. And, like many, she managed remarkably well. Wartime brought hardship and fear but it also brought a degree of freedom and independence hitherto unknown. To help make ends meet, she took in lodgers and when space became short she swapped her little council house for a slightly larger one. More lodgers followed, bringing in more money, and she moved again and again until, by 1946, she arrived at 70 North Eastern Road. For reasons best known to herself, Kathleen never bothered to warn Arthur of these moves and he became resigned to arriving home on leave to find his old house occupied by strangers. He would have to go round the neighbours, knocking on doors until he found out where his wife and family were living.

Derek and his chums played cricket on a little patch of land just behind Margaret's house and they were forever knocking their ball into the Wall garden. Margaret was always eager to retrieve it and at long last was invited to join the game. She was drawn to the impetuous, energetic Derek and they became close friends. She spent hours at his home where the warm, lively, noisy Garrett clan made her feel relaxed and welcome. It was a striking contrast to the serious, restrained atmosphere of her own home just a few streets away. Under the stern discipline of her father, Margaret had become an accomplished pianist and was doing exceptionally well at school, both in academic work and on the sports field. Physical Education College and a career were within her reach, but the bond with Derek, who had left school at fifteen and was working in his uncle's bakery, proved irresistible. Despite passing her School Certificate with flying colours, and in the face of violent opposition from her father, she turned her back on school and took a job at the bakery too.

When Derek was called up to do his National Service in the Royal Air Force, Margaret enrolled as a student nurse. She relished the work and the studying that went with it, but when she was moved to the children's ward she found the suffering of her young patients too much to bear. She abandoned her nursing career and returned home to become a booking clerk at Thorne North Station. My parents were married in Thorne Parish Church in 1951, and when Derek came out of the Air Force the following year he joined the railway as a Signalman, Second Class. He took to the job immediately. A gregarious man in many ways, he has always been independent and self-contained and the solitude of his signal-box way out on the moor was pure joy after the hurly-burly of the bakery.

The first few years of their marriage were spent living with relatives while they scoured the area for a house of their own. They lived off Derek's wage and Margaret had her earnings paid directly into the Railway Bank. The house in Waterside came as part of a job lot – three cottages for £300. With Margaret's savings and a small loan from her father they had just enough to buy them. Numbers 10 and 11 Waterside they let immediately and they moved into Number 9. It consisted of a small sitting room and a kitchen downstairs with two bedrooms above. In the yard an ash-midden provided the only sanitation. This was little more than a shed around a hole in the ground, which a man came to rake out once a week. There was running water in the kitchen but no electricity. The rooms were lit by paraffin lamps and candles and heated by coal fires too small to ward off the dampness that rose from the river and crept, inexorably, up the walls.

This was hardly the ideal environment for childbirth

and, besides, it was something of a tradition in those parts for first-born children to be delivered, not in their own home, but in that of their paternal grandparents. So it was at Nanan Garrett's house that my mother was staying when I was finally born, characteristically late (and only then after the administration of copious quantities of castor oil) on 10 April 1955.

By this time my parents had already started the long and exhausting process of turning their ramshackle little cottage into a home. The work was slow and very hard. For every repair and improvement Dad had to learn new skills and acquire materials. The skills came from library books and from watching the workmen who were putting up the estate of new houses that he passed on his way home from his signal-box. He would hang around there for hours in all weathers, watching the builders, making notes and, if he was lucky and they were in a good mood, asking them searching questions about techniques and materials. It was a process that was to take years and it dominated my early childhood.

The local council saw the house as an affront to modern standards of healthy living and were determined to tear it down. Our family bogeyman was the buildings inspector who seemed to regard the eviction of the Garrett household and the demolition of 9 Waterside as a personal crusade. He would bear down on the house brandishing sheaves of regulations and, with an expression that combined distaste and triumph in equal measure, declare that unless such and such was improved, he would condemn the house. That word, condemn, would strike terror in my young heart, carrying with it resonances of torture and death. Somehow, my father would always manage to plead a stay of execution and he and Mum would work feverishly to remedy the fault.

For years, the house was in a state of almost permanent chaos. Rubble lay everywhere. The staircase became a pile of bricks and, for a time, when my father was looking out for some unwanted floorboards to replace the rotten ones upstairs, I had to be put into my cot through a hole in the sitting-room ceiling which was then boarded up until morning. Later on, when my parents' bedroom floor was a mass of holes, they had to lash themselves to the bed at night, like sailors in a storm, in case one of them was to fall out of bed and tumble straight down to the kitchen. One night I was woken by the sound of breaking glass. Mum and Dad had been tucked up and tied down when they realised that the light was still on. After a bitter argument about whose fault this was and whose turn it was to struggle out and switch it off, Dad simply picked up half a brick from beside the bed (there were always plenty of those lying around) and lobbed it at the lightbulb.

I went through a phase when I suffered terrible night-mares. It got so bad that Mum took me to the doctor. He asked if I was insecure for any reason and Mum replied that, on the contrary, I was part of a warm and loving family. 'Is there anything about her physical environment that's unreliable?' Mum didn't know whether to laugh or cry.

By the time I was seven, the house was more or less habitable. Mum and Dad had bought a small piece of land behind the house to give us a garden and with the help of friends and neighbours excavated a cess-pit. Drains were laid and a flush toilet installed in the yard. Inside, we had electricity and hot water, a watertight roof and window frames that fitted. Wood panelling on the downstairs walls prevented (or at least hid) the spread of rising damp. The Man from the Council had one last card up his sleeve. He arrived, unannounced as usual, on a Friday afternoon, brandishing a tape measure and yet another ream of small print from the building regulations. He solemnly circumnavigated our sitting room, measuring and scribbling, stopping only to shake his head and inhale noisily through his sharp little teeth. He could barely conceal his triumph as he pronounced that our ceilings were three whole inches too low. He began to fill out the forms that would send the bulldozers in and us out. My father has an engaging manner at the best of times and now he used his charm as a weapon. My mother and I held our breath as we watched him politely, genially, respectfully negotiate a reprieve until Monday when we would have the problem fixed. The inspector left, satisfied that he was dealing with a lunatic but a harmless one. Let him play it his way, for on Monday this long game of cat and mouse would finally be over and victory would be his. Even crazy Derek Garrett couldn't raise a ceiling three inches, let alone in just two days.

He couldn't, of course; but he could lower the floor. Late into that night and all through the next forty-eight hours my parents dug and I dug with them. Dad tried to make it into a game – we were miners and we were digging for gold – but I understood what was at stake and I saw the strain of exhaustion and worry in their faces as three inches of solid clay were grubbed away and hauled into the garden. Monday dawned and our tormentor returned. As he headed for the sitting room Dad called out, just a second too late, 'Mind your step!' He picked himself up, dusted himself down and sloped off, never to return.

The battle with the council was over, but for Mum and Dad the work on the house continued unabated. My sister Jill had been born in 1957 followed by Kay in 1959, both at home, and the house, for all its hard-won habitability, was far too small. Number 10 next door was empty so the solution was simple. Down came the adjoining wall and the building work started all over again.

The house was never the same from one day to the next. I would wake up in the morning and something else would have changed. Encouraged by my parents' inventiveness and sense of fun, every new building scheme inspired another game. During the weeks when a heap of rubble lay where the staircase should have been, we became mountaineers and scaled our own Mount Everest, then bounced down it on tin-tray sledges. When the floors were a sea of slow-drying cement, we were pirates walking the planks that criss-crossed the house.

Most of our games took us outdoors and Waterside was an absolute paradise for a child. Nature had reclaimed the shallow ox-bow lake and where coal and steel had once been ferried, now swans and reed warblers and water voles lived. Spring brought an explosion of life to the countryside and my father, who had a passion for natural history, would take me for long walks along the hedgerows and around the lake, pointing out all the different plants and birds, teaching me their names and helping me spot mushrooms and moles, caterpillars and wild crocuses. In the summer we ran and played from morning till night through the fields and along the lanes and around the deserted docks. I was avid for adventure and a stranger to fear. *Swallows and Amazons* was my favourite book and I longed for a boat to sail on 'our' lake. Following my parents' dictum of 'if you haven't got it, make it' I constructed a raft by lashing old planks to some empty oil drums that I found down by the quay and set off across the area of the lake known as Nelson's Pond with my two sisters as rather reluctant crew. Before we were half-way across, the rusty old drums had taken on gallons of water and we began to sink lower and lower. Kay had not yet learned to swim and was saved from drowning by the timely appearance of my mother and Uncle Colin, who plunged into the pond and hauled her out. Mum was livid with me but I was unrepentant. Although the game hadn't gone quite as planned, I had already imagined my heroic rescue of Kay as an interesting twist in the adventure. After all, as I explained matter-of-factly, I had passed my Bronze Life-Saving badge.

Most summers the family would go on holiday to the little seaside village of Skipsea where my Great Uncle Henry lent us his tiny white-wood chalet perched high up on the cliffs. It had a cosy sitting room with a stove on which we burnt driftwood, and two bedrooms, one for Mum and Dad and one for Jill, Kay and me, all three of us snuggling up together in a huge, soft feather bed. There was no running water, just a rusty old standpipe half-way up the lane. The toilet was a dark shed with a bucket which, at the end of the week and under the cover of darkness, Dad had to empty into the sea at low tide. A glazed veranda ran the length of the house and we would spend hours there, gazing out across the sea towards the distant horizon, watching the gulls swoop and soar over the waves. Every day we would go to the beach, filling our lungs with the clean, salty air. We clambered down the steps that Dad had cut into the soft clay of the cliffs then swam in the icy water, built sandcastles, and played in the half-buried pill-boxes, left deserted since the war. We went hunting for lugworms for our parents to use as bait as they took it in turns to catch fish for dinner. The fish always tasted wonderful, cooked on a little Calor gas stove in the open air. We even went to Skipsea in the winter. On New Year's Day 1963, when there was thick snow everywhere, we built a huge bonfire on the beach out of driftwood. It attracted the attention of the local coast guards who sent a rescue helicopter to investigate. Smoke billowed everywhere as they hovered over the blaze, shouting 'Are you all right down there?' through a megaphone. They seemed rather disappointed when we shouted back, 'Yes thanks, just having a picnic!'

Autumn was my favourite time of year. The fog would rise up from the dank-smelling river and mingle with the smoke from garden bonfires, bringing despair to house-wives struggling to dry washing but mystery and delight to me. There was an old yellow phosphorous street light in front of the house and we were allowed to play out under its beam in the evenings. We played tin can alley and hopscotch and double ball, and all the other children in the street joined in.

Just as the summers of childhood are remembered as long and hot and perpetually sunny, so the winters of my youth were all hard and bright and blanketed in snow. Every year the lake would freeze and we would slide up and down it wishing we could afford skates. Just after Christmas, when I was nine, my sisters and I went for a walk by the lake and found, to our horror, a pair of swans frozen into the ice. There was something grotesque about the sight of this beautiful pair of birds, who nested here every year, lying still and lifeless in the crystal-clear sunshine. Worse still, one of them had been attacked by a fox and the ice was smeared with crimson streaks of blood. The other swan was nearer the shore and, by holding Jill's hand and reaching out, I could just touch it and feel that it was still warm. We were stung into action by the possibility that it might still be alive.

I ordered Jill and Kay back to the house for a wheelbarrow and started hacking at the ice with a stick, desperately trying to free the swan. By the time they returned, I had made a big enough hole to enable us, just, to drag it to the bank. It was huge and we were very small; it must have weighed three or four stone, and it took all our puny effort and strength to lift the huge bird on to the wheelbarrow. Then, cold and wet and trying hard not to let the swan's head drag along the ground, we took it home to our parents who were astonished at the sight of their three girls pushing a wheelbarrow containing an enormous swan into the living room and shouting, 'Mummy, Daddy, build up the fire. We have to save the swan!' It was an awkward moment for them. They saw immediately that the swan was dead but they didn't want to hurt our feelings so they wrapped it in blankets and rubbed its feet and tried very hard to bring it back to life until eventually, very gently, they explained that it was too late. We buried the swan in the garden (though Mum confesses guiltily to a fleeting curiosity about how it would have tasted as New Year's dinner), which was an effort for Dad as the ground was frozen solid. Animal funerals were a family ritual but this one was particularly grand. We sang Christmas carols and recited interminable maudlin prayers and gave it a good Yorkshire send-off.

Animals seemed to play a large part in my life in those days, though most of them weren't pets or at least weren't supposed to be. My father bred prize-winning rabbits in a shed at the bottom of the garden. They were beautiful, soft, gentle creatures which I loved to help groom for the local shows. (There is something about Yorkshiremen that drives them to compete at everything. Rabbits, vegetables, brass bands – everything had its own local championship league.) I was allowed to have one rabbit as a pet of my own and it was my pride and joy. He had a long and happy life and I had just started at the grammar school when he died, peacefully, in his sleep. I was too upset to go to school the morning that I found him cold and lifeless in his hutch so I stayed at home, sobbing my heart out and making elaborate arrangements for his funeral. The next day I had to bring home a little slip on which my mother was required to write the reason for my absence. I was alarmed at how she would deal with this. I was certain that the loss of a pet didn't constitute an adequate excuse for absence from Thorne Grammar School, but I knew she couldn't lie for me. She handled the dilemma superbly, though. The next day I handed in my little slip which, under 'Reason for Absence', read simply 'Family Bereavement'.

There were goats at the bottom of the garden too, Nubian goats kept for their milk. Even the Garrett goats were musical for my father's saxophone was deemed too noisy for the house and he was banished to the goat shed whenever he played it. Like many of our neighbours we kept chickens, which we fed on leftovers. They particularly enjoyed the residue from my father's home-made wine. This potent brew resulted in spectacularly large eggs but also in spectacularly wobbly chickens which would stagger about the garden, bumping into trees and falling beak first off their perches. We also had pigs, which we fattened up on scraps and then passed on to a local butcher. He kept some of the meat – we would get the rest and some much-needed cash. Once, when Dad had been sent to take a pig for slaughter he met some gypsies who were camped by the side of the road, trying to sell their old donkey. His impetuous nature got the better of him and he swapped the pig for the donkey. Mum went berserk when he got home, but the donkey stayed.

Mum was as fond of animals as the rest of us, and she was particularly devoted to horses. For many years, she had an arrangement with the owner of a local travelling fair. We would over-winter his horses in our field, feeding them and taking care of them, in return for which we were able to ride them for a few months. My mother and sisters were always keener on horses than I was, but I loved to ride these gentle, patient old creatures. We only had one saddle, so we shared it between the four of us but we all learnt to ride bare-back so that we didn't have to miss out when it wasn't our turn for it.

One animal that was purely a family pet was a chipmunk called, unimaginatively, Chippy and he was a most delightful little creature. We taught him all manner of tricks and he spent most evenings on the arm of the sofa drinking beer from my father's glass before weaving back to his cage. One terrible day Dad came home and, not realising Chippy was loose, accidentally stepped on him, and killed him instantly. We were sent from the room and had to stay out of the way for a long time because Dad was crying, a sight that we girls were never allowed to witness. A fiercely proud man, my father has always felt there to be something shameful in showing his feelings, though he is subject to the most powerful emotions. This is a paradox which, while not peculiar to Yorkshiremen, is certainly part of what makes them a special breed. I have often wondered if it accounts for the intense musicality of the region, whether only in music can they find an acceptable outlet for emotions they feel they must otherwise repress.

A narrow lane leads north out of Waterside. Hedged shoulder-high with hawthorn and hops, it emerges after half a mile in the old market town of Thorne. St Nicholas's Church in the middle of town was built in the twelfth century on a little hill to protect it from the surrounding marshes, and it oversees Thorne life still. The market square, dominated by the Town Hall and the White Hart Hotel, was and still is the heart of the place. There were two railway stations in town, Thorne North and Thorne South, which even in those pre-Beeching days was a bit excessive. But Thorne was, above all, a railway town. The old Flying Scotsman used a long, straight stretch of line just outside the town for its speed trials and one of my earliest, most vivid memories is of that majestic engine. One bright winter's day, when I was little more than a baby, my father carried me on his shoulders to a bridge over the line. I heard a distant rumble as Dad pointed and whispered, 'Look over there! It's coming. It's coming.' The rumble became a roar and I saw it – a huge, shiny black beast hurtling across the moor, belching out fire and smoke. I clung, terrified, to my father's neck and buried my face in his thick, soft hair as the dragon flew towards us. I could feel its hot breath coming closer and closer but my screams went unheard as it passed beneath the bridge, enveloping us in a vast, dark cloud of acrid steam, and charged on and on over the horizon. I knew then that my father was a hero. He had saved me from the monster and would keep me safe for ever.

Not far from Thorne North Station, lived Grandad and Nanny Wall. Nanny looked just like a granny should – a round, rosy-cheeked lady in a soft flowery dress and slippers with little pink pom-poms. I have powerful, clear memories of their little house. It was old-fashioned, even for those days, but to Nanny it was heaven. As a girl she had never known a real home, only an endless series of dingy boarding houses. The joy of being settled in one clean, warm place never faded for her. She had painful memories of fleas picked up in cheap, dirty lodgings and the shame that went with them. She was obsessive about cleanliness and the smell of carbolic soap hung in the air, mingling with the pungent tang of Grandad's pipe tobacco and the warm, sweet scent of apples baking in the kitchen range. They were always Cox's apples, from the great old tree in the garden.

Because of the difference in their ages, Grandad always assumed he would die first. When Nanny died of lung cancer, at the age of sixty-five, he was inconsolable. He became convinced that the smoke from his pipe had caused her illness and was tormented by guilt. He withdrew into himself and closed the door on the world. He stopped reading the newspapers and chopped down the tree because he couldn't bear the intrusion of the local boys who came to rag the apples. The only comfort he now allowed himself was music. He would sit for hours late into the night in the dark, empty house, and listen to foreign classical music stations on his old radio cassette player. He had a vast collection of home-recorded tapes and sometimes I would sit with him and listen to them. I remember going to see him once and finding him in tears: 'It's all right, love, I've just had me ration for the day.' I knew he meant he'd been listening to Tchaikovsky. He could only manage to listen for ten minutes at a time before the music overwhelmed him.

Just around the corner lived my other grandparents, the Garretts. Grandad Garrett – Art to his wife and friends – was a great entertainer. He was a natural musician – he had no professional training but he could play practically any instrument you put in front of him and delighted in learning new ones. He formed a band called Arthur Garrett and the Blackout Boys which had considerable success in the local dance halls.

Next door to Grandad and Nanan lived my Great-Grandfather Appleton. He was no longer the fearsome creature of his youth. A cave-in at the colliery had caused a pit-prop to fall on his head, landing him in hospital in a coma. He was not expected to live but, miraculously, regained consciousness six weeks later and made a complete physical recovery. His personality, on the other hand, had been completely transformed. The great-grandfather I remember was a gentle, kindly old man, like a giant teddy-bear. I would sit on his knee and he would give me a threepenny bit and talk to me about the trophies on the mantelpiece that he had won in tug-of-war contests. I used to love to watch him wash at the kitchen sink. Only a man who has spent a lifetime in the blackness of the pits really knows how to wash like that. Naked to the waist, with his vest, shirt and braces dangling, he would lather and scrub and rinse, carefully and deliberately, every inch of his massive body, ending always with his enormous, cavernous ears.

At the age of five, I started at the local school, Thorne Fieldside, walking a mile there and a mile back, clinging on to the pram which my mum was pushing very briskly. It was a warm, happy little school, swathed in a delicious, sweet aroma of malt and hops which issued from Darley's Brewery at the end of the road. I did well at all my lessons but my favourite subject was Nature. There was a nature table by the classroom door on which we were encouraged to display interesting items we had found. I was an enthusiastic contributor to this collection and always tried to outdo the other children. Fauna rather than flora was my speciality and while the other children offered conkers and pussy willow, I would proudly deposit the smelly flea-ridden corpses of hedgehogs and voles that I had picked up as I rambled through the fields. My best friend for the whole of my time at Fieldside was Kathryn Waller. Her father ran the Premier Drum Company in Leicester and they lived on the other side of Thorne, in a large detached house set in beautiful grounds. She was a quiet, serious little girl with freckles and tight pigtails and we were inseparable, though I do remember being jealous of her once. The school Christmas play one year was *Sleeping Beauty*. I was desperate to play Beauty but that part went to Kath while I had to make do with the Wicked Witch. Dad softened the blow by building me my own proper spinning wheel from old bits of metal and I made her the wickedest witch Thorne had ever seen. Although we lost touch in our teens, Kath went on to achieve a celebrity of her own, becoming Kath Botham, the wife of Ian.

Money was always a worry, although we were never aware of being poor. We were as self-sufficient as possible, with the menagerie in the garden providing meat, milk and eggs. We grew most of our own vegetables which Mum laboriously pickled and boiled, and we baked our own bread. Nothing was ever wasted. Household scraps became food for the pigs and the chickens and Dad made gallons of home-made wine out of any edible surplus from the larder or the garden. His rice and orange wine was particularly interesting and became something of a Waterside legend. Mum was a fine needlewoman and made all our clothes on her ancient Victorian sewing machine. These clothes always seemed so much smarter and of better quality than the shop-bought garments my friends had to wear.

Going to school and meeting people from different backgrounds never made me resentful of our humble and eccentric home-life. On the contrary, the only thing that made us different from other families, as far as I was concerned, was that we had the cleverest father and mother in the world. No one else's mum had decorated and furnished their home the way my mother did: creating brightness and colour with almost no money – only a wealth of imagination and ingenuity. No one else's dad could plumb in bathrooms and lay floorboards and install new windows. We may have had an outside loo, but my father had built it with his own hands. He was a hero, a superman who could do anything he set his mind to. My innocence of how other people might view our situation is illustrated by one incident I remember as if it were yesterday.

Kath had been playing at our house, as she often did, and when her mother came to collect her at the end of the day, I gave her a guided tour of the house, picking our way round the litter of wood and bricks and tools, proudly showing off all my father's achievements. Dad arrived home from work as they were leaving and he flew into a rage, furious that I had allowed someone like Mrs Waller to see how we lived. I had brought shame on him and our family. My grandmother who was visiting that day and who never normally interfered between father and daughter spoke up for me and angrily reminded her son-in-law how grateful he should be to have a child who admired and respected him so much.

Throughout all these years of domestic chaos, there was always somewhere to put the old upright piano that was, more than anything, the focus of our family. Some of my earliest memories are of my father sitting me on top of the piano and making up songs for me. My particular favourite, which I insisted on him playing over and over again, was 'In the Deepest Jungle in Africa'. Dad and I would compete over who could sing the loudest and the highest. Music to us was like food and air – an essential part of our lives and one that we took absolutely for granted. Often my mother would play the piano; Bach two and three part inventions, Chopin, Debussy (the *Arabesque* was a favourite), John Ireland. Very occasionally Grandad Wall would play Liszt and Rachmaninov. For a few minutes, his tiny, half-crippled hands, which could barely span an octave, would dart and glide across the keys and we would listen in awed silence, but soon he would become frustrated with his hands which would no longer do what he wanted them to. When it was my father's turn, everyone gathered round as he hurled himself at the keys and, throwing back his head, let rip in his extraordinary tenor voice. The whole family would sing and play together. And we sang and played *everything*. Folk songs, Gilbert and Sullivan, operatic arias, old music hall songs – you name it, we did it. One of my father's favourites was a song we called 'None Shall Sleep Tonight', which I later came to know as 'Nessun Dorma'. As my mum said, nobody could sleep once he got started!

Friends and relations came often to the house, bringing whatever instrument they were having fun with at the time and the music would continue late into the night, fuelled by ample supplies of whatever variety of home-made wine was currently in season. As well as the mass sing-songs that regularly raised the roof, it was the done thing for everyone to perform their own 'turn', their solo party piece. Sometimes it was a song, sometimes a piano solo (I remember my cousin Janet being an especially fine player) or even a little dance or recitation. I was keener than anybody on these occasions. I would invariably sing the loudest and couldn't wait for it to be my turn for a solo. I sought attention as a flower seeks the sun.

I don't believe I was a born singer, in fact I don't believe anyone is, any more than a piece of wood is born to be a violin. But I was born to perform, to communicate, and to strut my stuff. Of course you need talent, and a feeling for music and the discipline to train, but what makes a voice special is a person behind it who is more than the mere operator of vocal apparatus. Success on any stage requires you not just to want to perform, or to be able to perform, but to need to perform. My family are particularly fond of reminding me of how, as a child, I spent hours standing on the window ledge while my long-suffering sisters shone torches up at me as I stepped dramatically through the drawn curtains to curtsey and acknowledge the applause of an imaginary audience.

My sisters, faced with my pathological attention seeking, found their own ways of being individual. Jill's party piece was a show-stopping rendition of Donovan's 'Intergalactic Laxative', accompanied by a one-chord guitar strum. She also specialised in Stanley Holloway monologues, like 'The Battle of Hastings'. Kay, though much shyer, would join in too, especially if we were singing rounds with all my cousins.

By now, my mother's sisters, Joan and Sybil, had moved to Waterside with their husbands Mo and John, so they often joined us, as did my father's brother, Uncle Fayne. Uncle Colin was also a frequent and, for me, especially welcome visitor. My mother's younger brother was only ten years older than me and I idolised him like a pop star. He even looked like a cross between Billy Fury and Elvis Presley. Bank Holiday Mondays would invariably mean a visit from Uncle Alan and Auntie Audrey. Audrey was the celebrity of the family. As Audrey Graham, she had won *Opportunity Knocks* for a record number of consecutive times and became a great favourite of Hughie Green who gave her a spot on *Double Your Money* called 'Audrey Sings'. The general public would write in and request a song and she would sing it. It would be light, lyric repertoire, operetta, songs from the musicals, in fact very much like the kind of material I do in gala concerts now. They would descend on us unannounced, sending Mum into a lather of anxiety about food but they were always welcome because their presence guaranteed a day-long sing-song.

Audrey was a very special singer and watching her perform fascinated me. Her face, indeed her whole being, took on an extraordinary radiance. She was clearly transported, with a look of absolute spiritual rapture which captivated me and which I have come subsequently to understand and share. Even then I could see that music meant more to her than personal pleasure and the entertainment of an audience. She showed me that the true essence of performance is channelling the emotional power of music from its divine source. (I couldn't begin to describe what that source might be, or impose my sense of it on anyone else but I am absolutely convinced that it is beyond our understanding and that divine is the only word for it.)

As well as the near-constant presence of Wall and Garrett relations, there were regular visits from people I called aunts and uncles but who weren't family at all – neighbours and friends who would also drop in to sing and play or just to drink and listen.

All this music-making wasn't some sort of family eccentricity. I don't come just from a musical family, but from a musical community. The musical heritage of Yorkshire is deep and wide. This was a land of smoke and fire, coal, steel and sweat. The community that underpinned my upbringing was born from the pits and the steelworks and the railways. And woven into the fabric of this harsh existence was music. When the men and women weren't working they were playing in the colliery brass band or singing in the local choir. And when they finished that they went to the pub or the working men's club and they sang and they played some more. This was popular music in its truest sense; Handel and Hammerstein, Bach and Bacharach, Sullivan and Strauss, Gershwin, Mozart, Sousa, Mahler and everything in between was the music of Yorkshire people.

Chapter 2

Wouldn't it be Loverly

The golden, careless days of childhood never can last for ever and as I grew towards adolescence changes began to take place, subtle shifts in the foundations of my life that left me bewildered and unsettled and longing for the certainties that could never be recaptured.

My father is a natural teacher. He is also a natural learner, a voracious reader, devouring facts from every source. His abilities had been overlooked at school where his inventiveness and impetuosity had been labelled indiscipline and where he was always in trouble. As an adult, he was able to learn in his own way and his experience with the renovation of our house showed him that he could master theoretical concepts as well as technical skills if he put his mind to it. When his daughters were born he recognised this same appetite for information in our eager enquiring minds. He was fascinated by every stage of our development and excited by the part he was able to play in teaching us.

Dad began to realise that his capacity for learning was greater than he, or anyone else, had appreciated. His enthusiasm for teaching his children had led him to expand his own knowledge, the better to answer our questions. If we asked him something and he didn't know the answer he would go to the library and find the right book. He would know the answer the next day. He couldn't stop teaching us. He turned a simple, home-made toy of two tin cans joined with string into a demonstration of the principles of telecommunications. Once we helped him lay a path around our garden and he turned the process into a lesson on the Burma Road.

Little by little he grew to believe that a real, formal education was within his grasp. What is more, if he could learn, then maybe he could teach. No one in his family had ever been to college; no one had ever had a career, let alone a profession. Yet no one in his family had ever owned their own home before and he had managed that, and not through good fortune either but by hard graft and single-minded determination. He had had the vision and the audacity to create a beautiful home from a ramshackle pair of old cottages; now he was ready for a new challenge. Dad approached his own self-education in the same resourceful way as he had tackled the house. He bought an old second-hand reel-to-reel tape recorder then borrowed armfuls of books from the library which he read into the machine. Day after day he cycled off to work with that huge machine strapped to his back. Alone in his signal-box out on the moor he would play his tapes over and over again until he knew the work backwards. Within a year he had taken and passed five O Levels. Now there was no stopping him. He obtained a place at Swinton Day Training College and resigned from the railways to become, at the age of thirty-three, a full-time student. He swapped a good wage for a grant. Money, which had always been tight, now became a serious problem. Mum went out to work – as school secretary at Thorne Fieldside which was handy – and we all had to tighten our belts.

But the financial strains were the least of my worries. For the first time, I was aware that my father was frightened. This man who had always told me, and shown me, that anything was possible, was afraid that he had jeopardised his family for the sake of his own desire for education. Although the pressure on him to succeed was intense, once he had overcome his initial fears, he revelled in his new life as a student both at college and at home, happily poring over his books hour after hour, well into the night. To me, though, he had become oddly unfamiliar and I felt I had lost him somehow.

I wasn't the only one to notice the change. Relatives and old friends became distant and we saw them less often. All our family had been working people for generations. The railways and the factories were their world and they were proud of their working-class heritage. In their eyes my father had deserted his roots in his desire to, as they scathingly put it, 'better himself'. No one said this to his face but barriers began to appear that were hurtful, most especially to my mother who felt torn, for the first time, between her husband and her family. However, before long, Mum decided that she too would train to be a teacher. She had left school well qualified and teaching was then relatively well paid. Unlike my father, however, teaching didn't come naturally to her and she found student life a huge strain. On one level she was excited by the intellectual challenge that college afforded but she was also very nervous. She tried valiantly to conceal her anxiety from us, but she betrayed her feelings in a number of small ways. I remember her smoking heavily for the first time and her usual calm temper began to fray. Secretly, I was very worried for her.

As I grew up and life at home became more strained, I turned towards school for the security and stimulation I needed. I had passed the Eleven Plus exam as expected and, kitted out in my new school uniform (my first ever shop-bought clothes) of navy gymslip, white blouse and school tie with a green stripe to denote Brooke House, I entered Thorne Grammar School. Founded in 1930, it had been opened with much ceremony by Princess Mary, daughter of King George V and Queen Mary, and mother of the man who became one of the most powerful influences on my career – the present Earl of Harewood.

The school provided the kind of education that the grammar school system excelled at and which has all but disappeared now. I felt immediately at home there, not least because music pervaded the whole school. We had several orchestras and choirs, music competitions and major productions of musical theatre. There were some wonderful singers there. I particularly remember a girl called Susan Tasker who had a top E I would have killed for (still would, come to that). My first experience of singing in other

34

languages came from sessions of French and German folk singing that the language staff would hold in the lunch hour. At least twice a year there would be a full-scale concert or show in which everyone was encouraged to participate. My first show was Benjamin Britten's *Noyes Fludde* in which I played one of the Gossips – a small role, but I was happy just to be part of the action. By the age of fourteen I had risen from the chorus to a singing part in *Summer Song*, a musical based on Dvorak's 'New World' Symphony. I played Milli, the frustrated wife of a travelling salesman who complains:

> *Birds and bees and old jack rabbits know just how to get*
>   *their stuff*
> *But for a girl with loving habits, once a year is not*
>   *enough.*

I hadn't a clue what I was singing about, but it always got a huge laugh and that was enough for me.

Although I felt I had lost one way of life – my father's undivided attention, my place in the wider family – I felt I was gaining a glimpse of another, much more sophisticated existence. By going to college, Dad showed me that with hard work and ambition anything is possible. It was – and always has been – the example that has sustained me throughout my career. The house was by now completely renovated and my mother, who has a marvellous eye for design, had decorated it in an excitingly bold and modern style. We had red furniture, yellow walls, and green and yellow curtains at a time when the rest of Yorkshire thought magnolia was adventurous. It had become the perfect family home – warm and bright and still full of music and people. My parents had acquired a whole new circle of friends, some of them much younger but some of them mature students like themselves. Family sing-songs around the piano gave way to wonderful parties when the house filled with strange and exotic-looking people, though the endless quantities of home-made wine continued to flow.

I was never allowed to attend these parties but I would sit at the top of the stairs, listening to the music being made and straining to make sense of the snatches of conversation drifting up towards me. Anyone wanting to use the loo – now installed upstairs (what luxury!) – had to pass me on the way and I always tried to engage them with feeble attempts at sophisticated conversation. It was on one such occasion that I experienced my first 'proper' kiss. I was stationed on the landing as usual when a rather serious young man (to my shame I forget his name) approached. He listened politely as I prattled on until, out of boredom, pity or desperation for the loo, he shut me up by planting his mouth firmly and moistly on mine. He left me standing there in my pale yellow, brushed nylon nightie, my recently grown and precociously ample bosom heaving with pubescent passion.

The changes in my family life that developed from our parents' quest for education were private and subtle. The events of the next twelve months were anything but. The ugliness of a world far beyond Waterside was about to intrude on my secure surroundings and strip me of the warm, comforting innocence of youth.

A family moved into the close-knit, co-operative community of Waterside whose values and attitudes were very different from those of my family and our neighbours. Their manner towards everyone became more surly and aggressive as time went on but, for reasons we never properly understood, they vented the worst of their hatred and rage on us. We were subjected to constant verbal abuse and barely veiled threats day in, day out. My parents did everything they could to protect their daughters from the worst effects of this insidious intimidation, but we were none the less aware of a brooding tension at home and in the street. Dad had been a battler all his life. He was not a man who gave in willingly to bullies but, like any husband and father, his overriding instinct at this time was to protect his family, to keep them safe and remove them from any source of harm or danger. So remove us he did, away from the house he and my mother had turned, through sheer hard graft, from a hovel to a home. Our sense of security had been shattered, cruelly and pointlessly. In the face of this, the time, effort and love they had poured into the house over so many years counted as nothing.

The house was sold to the first bidder and we moved to Red House Farm, a great echoing barn of a place a long way from our old friends and family and miles from the nearest town. It was also, like our old house had once been, in need of a great deal of repair. We were too demoralised to find any joy in the work this time. I was a teenager and sulky resentment came easily to me. None of us had wanted to move, but a move towards town would at least have saved me the long journeys walking and cycling to school and to see friends. Instead we had moved even further away from civilisation. I felt I was being buried alive. Jill and Kay, being younger and more enthusiastic about country life, coped much better with the move than I did, especially when they were allowed ponies of their own. They, like my father, enjoyed the independence and space we had acquired. But I was having none of it. I had outgrown the delights of nature and ponies had never really excited me. I longed for the town, the bright lights, the company of other girls and boys (especially boys). The nearest village was Hatfield Woodhouse, a mile and a half away. There were two buses a day and they didn't always stop. Mum was also miserable. She was in her first year as a teacher and finding the going harder than ever but there was no going back, not now with a mortgage to pay. She had begun the menopause and her mood swings were terrifying for her. Worse still, her mother, Nanny Wall, was dying of lung cancer; my mother, her sisters and Uncle Colin had to share the task of caring for her.

I began to escape in the evenings to join my friends in the hot-spots of Doncaster, hitching lifts with lorry drivers (my blood runs cold now at the danger I exposed myself to). I found a Saturday job helping on a fruit and veg stall at Thorne market, earning £1 a week which I saved up to spend on clothes – my new passion. This source of income came to an abrupt end one bitter November afternoon when, after standing for hours on the icy cobbles with only Wellingtons on my feet, I collapsed from the cold and had to be driven home by the greengrocer in his van, packed in with the potatoes.

I soon found another, only slightly warmer, job at the market garden, which was Red House Farm's nearest neighbour. Every Saturday (and Sundays too if I could manage it) I would hike across the fields and spend the day planting lettuces or grading and packing tomatoes. Each size of tomato was given a letter from C down to F. Only the Ds and Es were thought to be of any use and I stood for hours at a bench picking them out and putting them in punnets. The Cs and Fs – which we now pay a fortune for as beef tomatoes and cherry tomatoes – were simply discarded!

At the age of fourteen I went to my very first grown-up dinner and dance with my very first boyfriend, Malcolm Turton. I had my hair done at the hairdressers for the first time. I can remember even now what it looked like – a bird's nest on top and rock-hard ringlets hanging down. I had borrowed a voluminous long dress in pink chiffon, which I thought was the height of fashion (actually, I think it was). I had an absolute ball at the dinner and stayed the night afterwards with my friend Susan Shearman. The next day we went to Bridlington where I tried very hard to swim in the sea without getting my ringlets wet. I failed and ended up looking like a droopy spaniel. I came home to find my mother sobbing in the kitchen. Nanny Wall, after a four-year struggle with lung cancer (though we children were always told it was 'pleurisy'), had passed away that morning. She had died at home, as people did in those days, nursed by her family. I had to go to school the day of her funeral – I wasn't allowed to attend because my mother thought it would upset Grandad too much – but I stationed myself in the biology lab during lunch break so that I could watch her cortège going past. I waved her goodbye from the window and as I did so, Mum looked up towards the school, saw me and waved back. She somehow knew I would be there and was moved at my need to bid my grandmother a last farewell.

Malcolm Turton had been my first boyfriend, but my first love was Scott Parkinson, the tall, dark and heart-stoppingly handsome son of an RAF officer from the radar station near our house. Scott was at the grammar school too and took part in school shows both singing and working backstage, shifting scenery, which gave us plenty of opportunities for passionate moments in the wings. Scott introduced me to the delights of heavy rock music, to Led Zeppelin, Black Sabbath and Carlos Santana. We would listen to his records for hour after head-banging hour – it was very different to the music I had been used to but I loved its passionate intensity and the raw emotions it expressed. Scott's other great interest in life was fishing and I would rise devotedly at 4 a.m. (it must have been the Real Thing!) to go with him, trudging along the muddy river bank and sitting all day in silence with nothing to do but gaze mistily into his huge, dark eyes.

Red House Farm became more bearable as repairs were made and Mum worked her special magic on the décor. We took in a lodger, a young student teacher who was working at my father's school in Hatfield Woodhouse. Vicki Jones was only just twenty and she became like an older sister to me, sharing my room, helping me with homework and listening patiently to my dreamy teenage ramblings.

Friends and family began to visit us again, like Auntie Eileen and Uncle Harvey who weren't really my aunt and uncle at all. Harvey had been my father's best friend when they worked on the railways together and the families had remained very close. Uncle Harvey was a great eccentric and a passionate lover of classical music. He was tall, gangly and stick-thin, completely bald and positively cadaverously featured, but with a wild and wicked sense of humour. We would spend many evenings at their house and sometimes we would stay the night, sleeping on mattresses on the floor, which was a real treat, to be woken in the morning by the *1812 Overture* blasting from the record player, conducted by Uncle Harvey from the kitchen table. Eileen was a marvellous woman, a larger-than-life character for whom every event, however small, was a source of intense drama. Everything she undertook was approached with the same enormous passion and gusto. In contrast to her husband, she was short and quite round, with milk-white skin and prematurely white, tightly permed hair. She had a story to suit every occasion and would cross her arms dramatically under her ample bosom before launching into her vivid narrative, liberally sprinkled with innuendo and references to 'goings on'.

In the summer of 1970, when I was fifteen, Harvey and Eileen took me to London for a week. We stayed in the Bonnington Hotel near Russell Square and every day we explored the West End, looking in shop windows, mingling with the crowds, taking in all the sights and smells and sounds, revelling in the sheer, vibrant energy of this place. Every night we saw a different show – ballets, musicals, Diana Rigg and Keith Michell in *Abelard and Eloise* – and I was captivated by the richness and variety of the London theatre. On the last night we went to the London Coliseum

41

to see *Madam Butterfly*. I had never seen or heard an entire opera, and at last I understood what was going on when Cio-Cio San sings 'One Fine Day' (*Un bel di*). I always thought it was just a song about a girl missing her boyfriend. Now I fully understood the drama behind the song, the pain and the passion of the situation. Sitting there, in the upper circle, I had a profound sense that I knew where I was going to go. This place, this building was going to be my home. It wasn't a dream, or an ambition, it was a genuine sense of recognition. I came home knowing that my course was charted. I would never again be content just to sing for fun. I had to learn how to do it properly.

Lesley Wood, my music teacher at school, thought I had talent, so she tracked down Vivien Pike, who took a group-singing class every Saturday afternoon at a school in Wath. The journey took hours and the fares ate up most of my pocket money, but that lesson was the highspot of my week. My parents were happy enough for me to spend my time and money this way, but they had no inkling of my true intentions. I felt as if I was leading a double life.

Outwardly I pursued my academic career, getting good O level results and entering the sixth form to study for A levels in Chemistry, Biology, Geography and General Studies. I had always been good at science and the love of nature instilled in me by my father was still there. In my heart I think I already knew that nothing other than a career in music would satisfy me. My conviction was strengthened by that year's school show, which was to be *My Fair Lady*. I had always loved this musical and was desperate to play Eliza

42

Doolittle. For my audition, I sang 'Born Free', the theme tune to the movie which had just been released. An odd choice, perhaps, but I was drawn to it, I realise now, by the sentiments it expressed and the relevance I saw it had to my own situation. Yorkshire just wasn't enough for me any more. My desire for a career in music was inextricably bound to a desire to move away, to seek a wider stage for my life as well as my singing. Hearth and home had become my cage, my prison even, and I yearned for freedom and independence.

The audition was a triumph. I truly believe that at the heart of performance lies a complex connection between the artist and the material. Only when a powerful emotional bond exists between the singer and the song is it possible for that emotion to be communicated to and move the audience. On this occasion, the magic certainly worked and I won the part, hands down.

I worked on Eliza in every spare moment, as if I had been born to play her. I understood not just her desire to reinvent herself but also the pain that that departure brings with it. I persuaded myself that I had managed the cockney accent rather well. Accents aren't exactly my forte, as I was to find out later in my career, so goodness knows what it really sounded like! The rest of the cast were marvellous, with Charlie Smith whom I had known since infant school as Higgins, Chris Lewis as Pickering and George Lockett as Doolittle. Mike Clarke, my French teacher, produced the show and the musical director was Lesley Wood.

Everyone in the school worked together to help make it a success. The art department painted the sets, pupils brought in furniture and props and one of the music staff even lent me her wedding dress for the ball scene. By the end of the Easter term we were ready. We played four shows, on four consecutive nights, all to packed, enthusiastic houses and I revelled in every second of it. Nothing had ever felt so right. I had never been so alive. I wanted to be Eliza for ever.

One day at the end of a Biology lesson, as I was rushing to leave to get ready for a performance my teacher, Mr Croft, made a caustic, throw-away, remark which stuck in my mind. 'Of course, Lesley, once you get to university, you won't have time for all this music.'

In all my inner wranglings with my conscience, this was something that had never occurred to me. If I continued along the path that had been set for me, not only would I not be a full-time singer, but I wouldn't have time to be a part-time one. It was unimaginable, a life without music. There was no longer a real choice.

By the last night my voice had all but gone but I didn't care. If I had had any doubts about my ambitions then Eliza had swept them away. Yet still I hesitated, unable to see how my dreams could ever be fulfilled.

The evening after the final performance, I was lying in the bath, weeping bitterly at my dilemma. To make a career out of singing would seem outrageously frivolous to my parents. They had struggled so hard and sacrificed so much for their own education, that for me to cast mine aside in favour of a hobby seemed obscenely thoughtless and ungrateful.

My mother heard me crying and came into the bath-room.

'What is it, love?' she asked gently.

'I have to do the music, Mum. I just have to be on a stage.'

'If it's what you want to do, then you must,' she replied. 'You'll always regret it if you don't try.'

'But what about Dad?' I wailed. 'He'll go berserk.'

'Don't worry about your dad. He'll come round in the end if you give him time.'

He did, of course, on condition that I chose a music course that would give me a teaching qualification to fall back on. Mum and Dad were very anxious about my decision. They didn't see my voice as being anything out of the ordinary. Certainly I could sing but then so could everyone else in our family. They had both struggled to educate themselves, and here was I turning my back on a career in science that my father, in particular, had so hoped I would follow. But it was my father's example that burned so bright now. He had desperately wanted to become a teacher and had set about fulfilling his dream with inspirational single-mindedness. All I wanted was the chance to be like him – to follow my own star wherever it led me. I hoped in time to make him as proud of me as I was of him. In the meantime, my father resigned himself to my decision and my parents kept their worries to themselves.

The next day I went to see the headmistress, Miss Felton.

'I'm really sorry, Miss Felton,' I said, 'but I've got this all wrong. I don't want to go to university. I don't want to be a scientist or a teacher . . . I just can't. I have to be a singer.'

She looked at me, smiled and said, 'I know. I've been waiting for you to come and tell me yourself.'

That rather took the wind out of my sails – I had been expecting a battle. She spread the school timetable out on her desk there and then and began to rearrange my classes. She arranged for me to drop Chemistry and take Music A level instead, while insisting I kept the other subjects going.

My desire to become a professional musician was given a massive boost during the summer holiday that followed the triumph of *My Fair Lady* and the drama of my sudden change of course. Encouraged by Mrs Pike I went to Downe House School for the annual music summer school. I was seventeen, and this was going to be my first time away from home with no family or friends to keep an eye on me. Determined to make the right impression, I had saved and saved to buy two pairs of outrageous bell-bottomed trousers covered in embroidery and beads. My mother disapproved of the fashion for cropped T-shirts, so I took a pair of scissors to some of my old tops, to expose as much midriff as I possibly could, and set off on my great adventure.

Situated in the beautiful Berkshire countryside, Downe House is a girls' boarding school with rambling but elegant buildings amid acres of lush, green lawns. Like many young girls, I had always dreamed of going to boarding school. Now, at last, I was at one, complete with dormitories and communal washbasins and a refectory with long oak tables, and I adored it. I shared a dormitory with four other girls, including a much older girl who sang in the chorus at Covent Garden. I was terribly impressed by her because she represented everything I longed to be. She was sophisticated, elegant, beautifully dressed, and a real-life professional opera singer. She was also, and this impressed me more than anything else, having a full-blown affair with one of the teachers at the summer school. She rarely spent the whole night in the dorm. Sometimes she would be away until breakfast, sometimes she would creep into bed in the early hours and I would wake up and whisper excitedly: 'Stacey, where have you been?'

'Darling, you know perfectly well where I have been,' she would drawl tantalisingly as I hugged myself with vicarious delight at how thrilling grown-up adventures were.

Everywhere you went there was music from dawn till dusk and beyond. Aside from the organised classes, there would be impromptu recitals – guitar trios in the corridors, madrigal groups under the trees outside – I thought I had died and gone to heaven. I went to classes with the celebrated baritone John Carol Case and choir sessions during which I heard and learnt *Carmina Burana* for the very first time. *Carmina Burana* made a huge impression on me. I had never experienced, let alone sung, music that was so rich and complicated – and with words that were so bawdy! The atmosphere pulsated with youth and creativity and passion. It was hardly surprising that romance broke out around the school like a rash. Guitarists and singers have always made natural playfellows and Andy Osborne, a long-haired, long-faced Londoner, particularly caught my eye. He and I spent every spare moment together, playing and singing Dowland and Campion and working our way through the *Joan Baez Songbook*.

My visit to Downe House turned my desire for a musical career into a passionate craving. The next priority was to choose a college, and fast. I think my teachers and family had expected Manchester to be the natural choice – it was, after all, our 'local' school. It is a very fine institution indeed, but to me it was far too close to home. I wanted to spread my wings, not pop across the Pennines. I ruled out Edinburgh on the shameful basis that although I wanted to leave home I didn't actually want to go *abroad*. No, for me it had to be London or nothing. Ever since my first visit there with Uncle Harvey and Auntie Eileen I had seen London as my future home. It represented everything I associated with freedom and sophistication and excitement. I began making frequent sorties to the capital to see Andy, who lived with his parents in a flat above a shop in Hackney, and the more time I spent there the more convinced I became that it was where I belonged. I had to rule out the Guildhall School because their course was very academic and I doubted I could meet their entrance standards. Besides, it was really only performance that interested me. So that left the Royal College of Music and the Royal Academy of Music and I applied to both.

I had a lot of catching up to do if I was going to complete the syllabus for A level music in the one year I had left. I found the theory work a real struggle but I did my utmost to come to grips with it and rested my hopes on the fact that forty per cent of the marks would be awarded for the practical papers. With Vivien Pike's help, I had gained a Distinction in my Grade 8 for singing so I was confident that I could do well on the voice paper and I worked hard to improve my piano skills as I knew I would need to pick up marks there as well.

Despite my workload, I needed a job more than ever to fund my trips to London and so I took a job at the local RAF base, washing dishes in the mess. It was a mucky old job but I had a marvellous time because, being the only female on the base, I was invariably surrounded by hordes of young airmen who made a great fuss of me, and I received endless proposals of marriage (well, mostly marriage).

In the spring of 1973, aged eighteen, I went down to London and auditioned for the Royal Academy of Music. It was love at first sight. The building, close to Regent's Park, was imposing but inside everything was warm, light and airy. The teachers were white-haired and distinguished and the students were cheerful and animated. I sang 'The Sea Wrack' by Hamilton Harty and the examiners must have liked it because they told me there and then that I could have a place in September. Everything that had once seemed so difficult and unattainable now at last was within my reach. The doors were unlocking and I was passing through each one with ease. I wasn't just on the right track. I was on a moving pavement to paradise.

At this stage, I had only the vaguest idea of what form my musical career would take. *Madam Butterfly* was the only opera I had ever seen, although I knew dozens of operatic arias from singing around the piano. This was before the days of Opera North and although there was a local operatic society in Thorne, it confined itself to Gilbert and Sullivan and the great Broadway musicals. I had only once been to a real classical concert – the Halle Orchestra playing Sibelius's

Second Symphony in Scunthorpe. We didn't have a record player at home so, apart from *Madam Butterfly*, I had never even heard a whole opera. Opera for me was a fairytale. I aimed for it because, to my adolescent mind, the more out of reach something was the more desirable it became. Opera was grand and exotic and fantastically glamorous and, most of all, it belonged to another world, away from Yorkshire and home and family. Even before I set my heart on being a singer, I had always known that I would leave Yorkshire one day, even though most people I knew expected to stay there for ever.

Back home, Mrs Pike had formed her own girls choir in Sheffield. We used to tour round the various music festivals that flourished in the North East and sometimes I entered in the solo section. The Cleethorpes Festival is the highspot of the festival calendar and it attracted many eminent judges. That year, the overall adjudicator was Noel Cox, Warden of the Royal Academy, which I saw as a good omen. I remember I wore my lucky frock (actually my only frock), a suitably demure little puffed-sleeve number in blue and white crimplene. I was entered in the British Song class and, singing 'The Sea Wrack' again, I won. Winning the class meant that I qualified to be in the grand final, the competition for the famous Cleethorpes Cup. It was a bit like Crufts, I suppose, with the Best of Breed winners going forward to compete for Supreme Champion. I was thrilled just to be in the final, which probably gave me an edge because I wasn't nervous at all when the time came for me to sing. I sang my heart out and I won the cup. It was a huge silver thing, and I could barely lift it but I carried it home, bursting with pride. I think my father was prouder of me that day than he has ever been. I swear there were tears in his eyes as he picked me up and swung me round and round. I think he finally realised that I just might have been right all along. Maybe I *could* make a go of singing as a career. They were tears of relief as well as joy.

Such was his pleasure in my triumph that the next day, Sunday, he took me to the pub. He didn't really approve of his children in pubs and I had only just turned eighteen, so this was a great treat. The Cleethorpes Cup went with us and was appropriately admired by everyone in the bar, including a vast and noisy crowd of my airmen friends. We celebrated long into the night but, alas, things got completely out of hand. Out of sight of my father, the airmen prepared for me their own creation, a Blue Country, which consists of a pint of Guinness and a shot from every one of the optics along the bar. I was presented with this in the Cleethorpes Cup itself and I stood on a table and drank it in one go. And that is about all I remember of that night, other than waking up in the shed at four in the morning, snuggled up to Humphrey, my beloved one-eyed pig.

My first thought was, 'God, I'm going to feel terrible when I sober up.' My second was, 'Oh no, it's Monday.' Because this wasn't any ordinary Monday. At noon I had to attend an audition for the County Major Award, the grant I needed to go to college, my passport to the future. The appalling implications of my condition, the sheer scale of my stupidity swept through me and I was horribly sick. I gulped down gallons of water and was sick again.

Mrs Pike had offered to come to school that day, all the

way from Sheffield, to help warm up my voice before the audition. I managed to get there, but she could see I was terribly hungover and I could tell she was disgusted and furious. I tried to sing, but I sounded terrible and she dismissed me. 'You've ruined your chances – I hope you're proud of yourself' were her parting words as I stumbled queasily from the room. The college where the auditions were being held was three bus journeys away on the far side of Doncaster. I am a poor traveller at the best of times and I was sick as a dog at every bus stop along the way. Miraculously, I arrived on time and presented myself at the reception desk, green-faced, sweaty and trembling.

'Goodness me, dear, you don't look at all well,' said the kindly receptionist. I confessed that I had been ill on the journey there, which was at least partly true. 'Why don't you have a little lie down, pet? I'll move you to last on the list. See how you feel at 5 o'clock.' This saintly woman led me to a small rest-room at the other side of the building. I curled up on the bed and fell instantly into a deep, dreamless sleep. Five hours later I awoke wondrously refreshed, clear-headed and bursting with energy. The room where the auditions were held had a large window looking out over the countryside. I saw the south Yorkshire hills bathed in glorious late afternoon sunlight and I began to sing Purcell's 'Hark the Echoing Air'. Even as the last notes faded away I knew everything would be all right after all. The faces of the panel were wreathed in smiles and the chairman leaned towards me: 'Well done, my dear. You were worth waiting for.'

I was on my way.

Chapter 3

London at Last

I wasn't just planning to go to college, I was leaving home. My last Yorkshire summer was spent in a frantic and thrilling round of organisation and packing and leave-taking. Accommodation had been taken care of. My school friend, Charlie Smith, who was a very gifted pianist already at the Royal Academy, offered me a room in the house he shared with two other singers, Anne Mason and Mark Wildman. I was determined that London wasn't simply going to be where I stayed in term-time. As far as I was concerned, I was moving there for good. I packed everything I owned – books, records, ornaments, photographs, clothes, the lot. Looking back, I realise how hurtful this must have been for my mother, but at the time I was so desperate for a new beginning that I didn't even think of her feelings.

Certain mundane matters had to be attended to, however, like my severely impacted and agonisingly painful wisdom teeth. As soon as my final term at school came to an end (with a loud and, on my part, blubbery rendition of 'Lord Dismiss us with thy Blessing'), I went into hospital to have the wretched things removed.

As I came round after the operation I was blearily aware of a nurse speaking in hushed hospital tones to my parents: 'There is rather more swelling than we would expect, I'm afraid. But I'm sure it will go down in a day or so.'

The next thing I heard was a gasp of utter horror from my mother. She later described me as looking like a purple torpedo. My neck and chin had disappeared completely and from nose to shoulder I was a shiny swollen mess. It was actually weeks rather than days before my face reappeared, and I took to creeping around town with my head swathed in scarves, like the Elephant Man, until I was no longer likely to frighten passing children.

It was in this unprepossessing state that I made my last visit to school, to collect my A level results. I had scraped through Biology and General Studies and managed an 'E' in music thanks to the percentage of marks given to the practical papers. They weren't marks to be proud of, but it didn't matter any more.

The first Saturday in October 1973 was the kind of shiny, golden autumn day that makes you want to sing 'We Plough the Fields and Scatter' at the top of your voice as you kick your way through mountains of crackling leaves. Perhaps I should have felt sad to be leaving these mellow fields for the hard, grey streets of the big city. Instead, I felt light-headed with happiness and anticipation for my new beginning.

We squeezed into Dad's ancient, rusty old car and there

Grandad Wall the pianist (left), as a child, with his father William, mother Esther and four of their other children – Edward, May, Ivy and Olga.

Above Waterside early last century. Our cottage was number nine, in the middle of the row.

Left Great Grandad Frank Appleton with his wife Florence, my Great Uncle Arthur, Great Uncle Bill as a baby and, standing on the left, Nanan Garrett, in 1916.

Right Arthur Garrett, my grandfather, with the band originally called 'The Blackout Boys'.

Above Nanny Wall at about the age she met my Grandad – you can see why he was so smitten.

Right Grandad Wall with his certificate from the London School of Music.

Above My dad, aged about two in Thorne Park. With that stance he was obviously a tenor in the making.

Right My parents on holiday before I was born. Dad's nickname was 'Moppa' and you can see why.

Below left With my dad.

Below right With my mum.

Above left Me, aged 15 months, with characteristically open mouth, at St Ives.

Above right With my sister Jill, at Cleethorpes.

Right This picture of me with my sisters Jill and Kay always reminds me of the line from *La Bohème* 'A tela o a seta ricamo in casa e fuori' – 'I embroider flowers on linen or on silk'.

Even on the beach at Skipsea, sometimes my dad liked to carry on with his construction work (here building the steps up to the top of the cliff) . . .

. . . while my mother entertained us!

My first big frock!

I didn't last long as a girl guide – I never was very prepared.

With Auntie Eileen and Uncle Harvey in Trafalgar Square, summer 1970, a hundred yards as the pigeon flies from the London Coliseum, home of English National Opera.

'In Hertford, Hereford and Hampshire, hurricanes hardly happen': Eliza in the school production of *My Fair Lady*. Charlie Smith, who played Professor Higgins, had the important job of making the electric candle flicker in the right places during this number.

Aged 21, with my sisters Jill and Kay, in the photo we had taken for our parents Silver Wedding Anniversary.

was just enough room for Mum and me amongst the cardboard boxes and carrier bags as we set off towards the motorway. I was finally going to London! Actually I wasn't, at least not that day. The car managed about thirty miles before it expired in a cloud of steam and smoke. We had to be towed, ignominiously, back home. Friends rallied round, and one in particular came to the rescue and lent us her car. The next day we tried again. This time the journey was uneventful and I was successfully delivered to Hendon complete with all my worldly goods. It was dark when we finally arrived, but as soon as my luggage was unloaded, and at my insistence, Mum and Dad climbed straight back into the car and headed home again. Apparently Mum cried every mile of the journey back to Yorkshire.

Holders Hill Drive is a tidy, tree-lined road in the north London suburb of Hendon. It wasn't exactly the bright lights, but it was cheap and convenient for transport into town. I dusted and polished and hoovered my new home to within an inch of its life, arranged and rearranged books and ornaments and unpacked all my clothes. I trotted from wardrobe to mirror for hours, picking out outfit after outfit until I was satisfied I had put together just the right look of artistic sophistication and contemporary glamour that befitted a student of the Royal Academy of Music. I finally found what I was looking for and set off the next day in a long, checked, cotton skirt which I had acquired earlier in the summer from my favourite boutique, otherwise known as the Thorne branch of Oxfam, a cheesecloth blouse and a black velvet bomber jacket with fur sleeves. This last garment had been a present from one of the airmen at the RAF base. I happened to say I liked it one day and he had immediately whipped it off and handed it to me.

Even by the standards of the early seventies, I must have looked a complete dog's dinner as I strode purposefully down Marylebone High Street towards the imposing Victorian façade of the Academy. Up the broad sandstone steps I went, under the archway and through the huge swing doors. Inside, students milled around, laughing, joking and humming as they passed from room to room, instrument cases of every size and shape in their hands. The very walls of the place resonated with history. It was as if the music of generations had soaked into the bricks and was seeping into the air for me to breathe in. It looked, sounded and smelt just like a music college should. There were no classes on the first day, just an introduction to this extraordinary institution. I was shown round by Christine Taylor, a second-year student, who swept me along grand corridors, in and out of classrooms and practice rooms, up and down strange little winding staircases, showing me the magnificent library, the charming little opera theatre and such vital places as the canteen and the students' Union bar.

The next day it was down to some serious work and my first session with my new singing teacher. Charlie had played the piano for most of the singing teachers at the Academy, and he reckoned that the great Flora Nielsen would be the best for me. He told me that she had taught a young singer called Felicity Lott, who was beginning to make a name for herself: 'If Flora Nielsen can do for you what she's done for Flott, you're on your way.' Frankly, I would have gone to anyone, I just felt so lucky to be here at last. Miss Nielsen (as *everyone* called her) was a lady for whom the word formidable should have been invented. In her late seventies when I met her, she had a slight stoop but was still extremely tall and elegant. She had pinkish-grey hair worn in a tight chignon and dressed every day in a suit, a scarf tied neatly at her neck and her spectacles perched on the end of her nose. She was a much-revered mezzo-soprano who had been a very successful *lieder* singer in her day (the day that is when it was possible to have a career solely as a *lieder* singer). She had sung opera just once, when she had created the role of the Female Chorus in Britten's *The Rape of Lucretia* but her first love was *lieder* and French Song.

She looked me up and down slowly, gave a little snort and the lesson began. By the time it was over she had made a rather startling declaration. I had arrived at the Academy a soprano but Flora Nielsen now told me that I was a mezzo. There was no room for discussion let alone argument. I was a mezzo-soprano and that was that.

I left our first lesson perplexed and unsettled and I remained that way for some time, despite the many exciting aspects of student life. There was so much that was new and unexpected. I obviously had a lot of work to do, not just on my music but on myself, if I was going to fit into this world. Coming to London, leaving home, going to college at last was thrilling, but there was a dark side too. Amongst the gaiety and fun I very soon encountered values and attitudes that were as foreign to me as if I had landed here from Mars. At home, all forms and styles of music had been embraced with equal enthusiasm; here in London, and most particularly at the Academy, I met a kind of musical apartheid, which was shockingly alien to me. Classical music was the only music that mattered and within that narrow classification, an even more refined musical snobbishness existed. I discovered that the singing school was divided into very strict camps. The early music clique thought that the only music worthy of the word was composed before Mozart was born. The *lieder*/oratorio camp thought the early musicers were barmy and the opera buffs (who were second-years and above only) were regarded by both as overblown burlesque artists, far too showbizzy for their refined sensibilities. I didn't want to be a rebel; I wanted desperately to fit in and at the age of eighteen I was hardly in a position to change the way the musical establishment thought and worked.

I had come to London to escape country life but in those first few bewildering weeks I often found myself heading across the road to Regent's Park whose wide green peace calmed and comforted me. I didn't go home very often in my first year. Apart from anything else, I couldn't afford to make the long trip back to Yorkshire. And when I did, I was aware that my family didn't like me very much and, to be honest, I can't blame them. I was frantically trying to reinvent myself and home only served to remind me of values that I was desperately trying to lose. In the first term I went home just once. On the first of December, my mother's birthday, Dad rose at 4 a.m., drove all the way to

London, picked me up and drove all the way back, all so that I could be presented to Mum, along with breakfast in bed, as a birthday surprise.

Life at the Academy was an exhausting round of working and studying and practising. There were singing lessons three times a week, weekly piano lessons and music coaching sessions, and choir practice every Wednesday afternoon. There was theory work too, which I have to say I found much more difficult. Aural classes involved listening to and writing down melodies and chord progressions, identifying cadences and rhythms, tricky stuff which I managed to bluff my way through for years. Once a week I had to make my way to the fifth floor, a cobwebby rabbit-warren of cramped and musty attic rooms where the whiskeriest, most ancient professors taught the theory of harmony (some of us reckoned that they actually lived up there, forgotten by the administration). There were lectures too, mainly on the history of music, which were practically the only opportunity for all the students in the year to get together.

The Academy Library was a treasure house – a source of endless joy and fascination for me. Ranged on endless shelves were thousands of boxes containing the scores of more music than I had dreamt existed. Many illustrious former students had left their collections to the library and it was possible to go in search of a song by Elgar or Arnold Bax and find the music signed by the composer or even, in some cases, marked up by them. The Record Room was another of my favourite bolt-holes. Windowless and located in the basement, next to the boiler room, it was the warmest place in the building and I rarely got past the first movement of a symphony before drifting off to sleep with my head resting on the record player.

At lunch-times everyone would head for the canteen where the food was unimaginative but wholesome, edible, filling and, above all, cheap. The canteen was presided over by Florrie, a birdlike woman with astonishing luridly hennaed hair and a kind and motherly heart. She knew all our likes and dislikes and I could rely on her always to save me the crispiest, most overdone corner of any meat pie or apple crumble.

Apart from the occasional evening carousing happily in the Union bar, I went out little in my first year at the Academy. Partly this was because I was determined to work hard but mainly it was because I was permanently broke. I took a number of part-time jobs to make ends meet. For months I worked in a local newsagent, marking up the papers for the delivery boys. I had to get up at 4 every morning, which was a huge struggle, especially for me, as I have always been an owl rather than a lark.

And then, of course, there was Tom. Tom was a guitar teacher from the Downe House summer school, the same teacher that the glamorous Stacey had been sneaking out of the dorm for the first time I had been there. The summer before I came to London I had been back to the summer school. Stacey was not there that year, but Tom was. Tom was thirty-six when I met him, exactly twice my age. Not classically good-looking, he was astonishingly attractive. Tall, languid, with blue eyes and fine blond hair, which flopped fetchingly across his face, he was the very essence of the laid-back Californian intellectual. He was foreign and exotic and interesting and I had never met anyone like him in my life. He told me he was married, with three small children, but that he and his wife were 'estranged'. He was taking a one-year conducting course at the Academy and the passionate flirtation we enjoyed at Downe House blossomed into a full-blown, intensely physical affair. He came to town only once a week so we met infrequently and in secret.

My relationship with Flora Nielsen was not improving. Despite her efforts to maintain a professional detachment I felt she didn't understand me. 'You have a very fine voice, my dear. I just wish the rest of you could live up to it.' As a pupil/teacher relationship it was a complete disaster. I had finally broken free from the bonds of home and family and having arrived in London was determined to make the most of everything it had to offer. However hard I tried I was always late for her lessons. I was noisy, wild, exuberant, bursting with energy, and probably a pain in the neck. Discipline – most particularly self-discipline – was a religion to her and she expected similar respect and devotion from her students. At the time I could not understand such rigorous orthodoxy. I had never considered music to be rarified, to me it was part of everyday life and I saw it as something to be performed and shared.

I found her use of metaphor as baffling as I found her views on the merits of different musical styles. Singing is always going to be less straightforward to teach than, say, the guitar. A singer's 'instrument' is the body itself and it takes a very long time to develop the necessary consciousness of parts of your body that you can't even feel let alone see. So the teaching of singing depends heavily on the use of analogy.

'Miss Garrett,' she would say, 'you must feel the sound boring a hole in the roof of your mouth. Now, with me – bore, my dear, bore!'

And she would make a noise like an elephant with a clothes peg on its trunk and expect me to do the same. To be honest, I hadn't a clue what she was talking about half the time and, unlike her other students, I had the temerity to say so.

Miss Nielsen was not the only one who used unusual imagery to get her point across. I once attended a group class given by the eminent singer Ilse Wolf, where we were talking about the tricky problem of how to pronounce words and create consonants while maintaining the vowel sounds.

'You must imagine zat you are hanging out ze vashing, dahlink. Ze vashing line is your vowels, OK? Now you bring out ze vashing in ze vashing basket. You peg ze vashing on ze line. Ze vashing is ze vords and ze vashing vill be floating in ze breeze.' So far so incomprehensible. Warming to her theme, she went on: 'Ze consonants, zey are ze pegs vich hold ze vashing on ze line. And zere is your music!' It made an interesting picture, the thought of the great teacher pegging out her washing. My mind began to wander and I tried not to imagine just what kind of forbidding Teutonic undergarments might actually hang from Ilse Wolf's washing line. Then came the final flourish: 'Zen vun day, vun day my dear, you vill go into ze garden and you vill cast your vashing on ze ground and you mow ze lawn!' Now, twenty-five years later, I know what she meant. She was trying to explain that once you have perfected the correct technique you can put it to one side and concentrate on communicating the words. At the time I just sat mystified and open-mouthed.

Miss Nielsen's distinguished reputation as a singer and a teacher gave her great authority at the Academy – and not just over our vocal training. She was most particular about how we dressed, even on ordinary college days. I once rushed into her room breathless and late after spending the day at Ascot, dressed in pink bell-bottomed jeans, T-shirt and pink floppy hat. She was speechless for a while but soon recovered her composure and lectured me for the rest of the lesson on the importance of decorum. She had an ally in this area in the imposing shape of the dreaded Mrs Deller, whose job was to teach us Platform Deportment and who would stalk the corridors barking at those of us whose standards of grooming fell short of her own. She gave up barking at me after a year or so and would simply wring her hands and shake her head in ostentatious despair whenever she saw me.

I wasn't the only one of Miss Nielsen's pupils to stray from the sartorial straight and narrow. One friend, Carolyn Allen, a warm and wonderful human being with a marvellous contralto voice, was the worst offender. She had a wild, crazy dress sense which Flora Nielsen absolutely hated. At one stage she became so outraged by Carolyn's appearance that she ordered a complete make-over. Her naturally frizzy hair was shampooed and set and she was taken out of her leather jeans, skimpy T-shirt and cowboy boots and put into a knee-length, high-necked, black velvet tent. She ended up looking like a nineteen-year-old maiden aunt – a grotesque cross between Margaret Thatcher and Moira Anderson.

On the other hand, I developed an instant rapport with my piano teacher, Jean Anderson, and piano lessons became the highlight of my week. Despite my grandfather's best efforts, I am not a natural pianist and Jean knew it, but she didn't seem to mind. She was the most spirited and lively professor on the entire staff and she understood me better than anyone. Tiny, raven-haired and feisty, she attacked life with the same passionate, electrifying energy that she used when she played the piano and she played *wonderfully*. She became my unofficial tutor and confidante and is still, to this day, a great friend.

I wasn't the only person who struggled to fit into the rigid traditionalist structure of the Royal Academy. In my first year there were many non-conformists, some of them much more outrageous than I was. There was a flute student who was way ahead of her time. While I was shocking Mrs Deller and Flora Nielsen with my hippy gear, this girl was already an angst-ridden anarchist punk, who inspired enormous admiration and not a little fear amongst her contemporaries. Like many, she found the regime too narrow and repressive, so she left after three years. Her name was Annie Lennox. I struggled on; however hard things became, I never once doubted the rightness of my presence there. My youthful dream of being a singer was as bright and sharp as ever. I was where I was supposed to be, going where I was meant to be going. If the road was hard, too bad – there was no other.

After two terms the lease ran out on the house in Holders Hill Drive and my flatmates drifted away. I went to live at the other end of the road with a lovely landlady called Olive Orchard. She was very old and slightly demented and was a religious fanatic. She did beautiful embroidery and kept bees, but I was miserable in the bedsit. I was never on my own as a child and I hated it now. I did, however, find a less tiring and better paid job washing up in a Jewish Nursing Home called Waverley House (I am a class act at washing up). You would think washing up would be a simple job that even I could manage without difficulty, especially with my experience at the air base. But I hadn't really encountered Judaism before and I was hopelessly ignorant about the importance of separating the preparation of milk and meat. Every item of cutlery, china and cooking equipment was colour-coded – red for meat and blue for milk. I was constantly in bad odour with Matron who would descend on the kitchens to make spot checks and scream at me when I muddled things up.

One day, on my birthday, I came out of work and Tom was there, waiting on the pavement. I hadn't seen him for nearly a month and I was so excited because I thought he had made a special effort to see me on my birthday. Of course he hadn't remembered, he just happened to have an afternoon free and thought he'd come round for a bonk. 'Let's go out for dinner,' he said. 'Oh and by the way, could you lend me thirty quid?' I gave him my rent money to buy me dinner. He never paid me back.

I finally mastered the rules of the Waverley House kitchen although Passover proved a challenge as all the red and blue items had to be packed away and temporarily replaced with green and yellow ones. Even though I seemed to be the first colour-blind washer-upper they'd ever had, they were very understanding. I was sad when Matron told me that they needed someone to work full-time, as I had got to know some of the long-term patients and I enjoyed talking to them when I helped out at mealtimes. Reluctantly I returned to my graveyard shift at the newsagent.

Things went from bad to worse with my relation-ship with Flora Nielsen. We began to work on Handel's *Messiah*, which I knew backwards and was very comfortable with. Yet when I stood in front of Flora Nielsen and sang, 'And soodenly there was with the angel a mooltitude of the 'eavenly 'ost' in my best, broad Yorkshire accent, she threw up her hands in horror.

In the end, she became so exasperated with me that she persuaded a doctor to prescribe me Valium to 'calm me down'. Whatever it is within me that gives me my energy and exuberance and impetuosity, I am glad to say that it is impervious to Valium. Ten milligrams three times a day had absolutely no effect on me. When I asked for permission to leave her class at the end of Year One, we parted on good terms. We had both tried our best but she recognised defeat when she saw it. 'I think that would be best for both of us, my dear,' she said.

My spirits were higher than ever as my first year at college came to a close. During one of our infrequent meetings, Tom declared that he was going to divorce his wife, and asked me if I would move into a flat with him. I was ecstatic. From now on there would be no more clandestine meetings, no more living from one week to the next waiting for him to arrive, no more secrecy and shame. I would be his partner, for all the world to see; maybe his wife one day. I would sit at his feet, night after night, by a crackling fire while he played his guitar. It was agreed that I would go to the Downe House summer school again and that he would collect me from there and off we would go to our new life together. I gave notice to Olive that I was vacating the bedsit, packed up all my things and set off for Berkshire in a tizzy of excitement and happiness.

The routine at Downe House was the same as before, dozens of young people revelling in a week of music-making, fun and romance. But I walked through the seven days as if in a dream. I felt I didn't belong there any more. All I could think of was Friday when my knight in shining armour would ride up the road and carry me off to our new life together. Friday came, and after lunch I went down to the school gates with my suitcase to wait for Tom. The afternoon wore on and the other students took their leave, waving and calling farewells to their new friends and lovers; and still I waited, smug in the knowledge that my departure would be more thrilling and glamorous than they could possibly imagine. It was getting late, and they had all gone, every one of them. It was just me, and my suitcase, and my dreams, waiting.

As dusk fell, the kind old caretaker came out of his

gatehouse and gently touched my arm: 'He's not coming, love.'

Finally, I gave way to tears. Tears of anger, shame and
betrayal. What a fool I had been. The caretaker, taking
pity on me, drove me to Reading station and put me on
the London train.

Chapter 4

———••———

Spit on Your Hands

My old landlady, Olive, had re-let my room in Holders Hill Drive, so I was homeless as well as jilted. After a couple of nights on friends' floors, I found a poky little bedsit in Childs Hill where I cowered like a wounded animal, licking my wounds. One morning in the midst of my despair, I padded down the seedy staircase and found a letter on the mat addressed to me. Recognising my mother's handwriting, I picked it up. It felt heavy and strangely lumpy. As I ripped open the envelope, a shower of small stones fell to the floor around my feet. Inside was a single sheet of paper, which read:

> Dear Lesley,
>   I thought you might need some Yorkshire grit.
> Now spit on your hands and take a fresh hold.
>   Love,
>   Mum

For the first time in days, I roared with laughter. Mum was right, as usual. It was time to cut out the self-pity and get on with life.

Over the last nine months letters and phone calls from home had revealed a catalogue of troubles. Mishaps became dramas, dramas became crises with appalling frequency. I sensed that they were the symptoms of some underlying malaise, rather than the cause of it. There had been accidents, animals had died, grief hung heavy in the air. Red House had never felt like home in the way that Waterside had and now it seemed not just cold and isolated but ill-starred. Dad was strangely distant. He was a headmaster now, of a primary school in Sheffield, a truly amazing achievement, but the long hours, heavy responsibility and tiring journey seemed to have drained him of all the warmth and humour that had been such an integral part of his character. Mum had always been the one to bear the greatest burden of stress but she now seemed barely able to cope. Caring for Grandad Wall, who had had a serious stroke, was taking its toll, and her blood pressure was dangerously high. The teaching job that gave her so little pleasure had caused her to strain her voice, giving her nodules on her vocal cords. She had had to undergo surgery on her larynx to remove them but her voice was never the same. When I got home, I had to face an awful truth. The rock at the centre of my life, my family, was falling apart. It was falling apart because my parents' marriage, the relationship which gave the family its energy and strength and stability, was in deep, deep trouble. The suspicions that I had not dared express, even to myself, could no

longer be ignored. I confronted my father with my fears
but he brushed them aside. I found no comfort in his empty
reassurance. Naïvely and insensitively, I suggested to Mum
that she get some help with the housework as the house
was large and difficult to manage. My idea, sympathetically
meant but tactlessly expressed and hopelessly ill-timed, only
sent Mum into a furious rage.

If they needed to deny the truth of what was happening
then I would respect that. We reached an unspoken
agreement to speak of the subject no more. There was,
after all, still pleasure to be drawn from family life and we
made the most of what was left of the summer. Cricket
has always been the family sport (Grandad Garrett held
the record for the fastest century in the Doncaster area
– twenty-six minutes) and that year I relished more than
ever the hours spent lying half-asleep in the soft warm grass
watching Dad keep wicket for the village team. Sometimes
I helped Mum in the score-box – putting up the runs and
entering all the match statistics on the closely ruled sheets
that would later be bound into thick leather books and take
their place in the hallowed archives of the club.

I came back to London revived and eager for the new
term. I had not been in touch with Tom since he stood me
up at Downe House and he had made no attempt to contact
me, but I did at last find out, on the grapevine, why he had
failed to turn up. It was because his wife was having a baby!
I felt guilty, but also angry that I had been used. Now, above
all, I felt I wanted to move on. Before long, I was rescued
from the dreary bedsit by my dear friend Cathy Giles who
scooped me up and took me to live with her in the flat she

shared with a curly headed young conductor called Simon Rattle, just off the Archway Road. They were a glittering couple. Cathy was a magically gifted cellist – the greatest player since du Pre, many of us believed. Simon was already setting the Royal Academy alight with his idiosyncratic charm and extraordinary talent and the word 'genius', rarely spoken within that hotbed of musical excellence, was often whispered along with his name.

I had found a new singing teacher at the Academy, called Henry Cummings. Where Flora Nielsen had been the *lieder* queen, Henry was the king of oratorio. I became a soprano again, a dramatic soprano this time and he immediately set me to work on the Verdi *Requiem*. He wasn't as dismissive of opera as Flora Nielsen had been, though he disliked Mozart, which was a pity because that was actually exactly what I should have been singing. But I was so eager to please that I never questioned the material I was given to sing. Nor did I find it difficult. I enjoyed the challenge of this massive music; it was just my voice that rebelled and I suffered constant sore throats.

One evening in the Union bar at the Royal Academy, we were talking about ways to make money and one of the boys asked me an unusual question:

'How do you feel about taking your clothes off?'

I've heard some blunt chat-up lines, but this one got full marks for directness. Before I could come up with a suitably withering put-down, he explained that he had found a job as a model for a local life-drawing class. They were always in need of more models and the pay was good.

'Is it mostly women in the class?' I asked, modestly.

'There's a few men, but they're all ever so old.'

Thus reassured, it was with barely a qualm that the following week, off I trotted to the Hampstead Garden Suburb Institute and presented myself to Len, the teacher in charge.

'Ever done this before?' he asked kindly.

'No,' I replied feebly, as the first inklings of nervousness crept up on me.

'Ah,' he said. 'Why don't I make you a nice cup of tea?'

Len gently explained the procedure, reassuring me that his students were not in the least interested in my body in any prurient sense, only in the challenge of drawing me. I hadn't thought to bring a dressing-gown, which models normally wore to make the chilly trip from the store cupboard which served as a dressing-room to the dais at the end of the studio, so Len lent me an old smock. By the time I had got undressed and climbed into this scratchy, shapeless garment which smelled of chalk and turpentine and all things arty, the students had filed into the room. I walked nonchalantly to the dais, ignoring and ignored by the class, and, removing my smock with a nervous flourish, struck what I believed to be a suitably interesting pose. I squinted surreptitiously at my 'audience' who were engrossed in sharpening their pencils and chatting about the weather and the exorbitant price of canvas. Len had been right. No one took a blind bit of notice of me.

In my effort to please, I had posed in a particularly uncomfortable position and with a break only every twenty minutes, I ached all over by the end of the session. But I was gratified that Len and the students liked me and were keen to have me back. I was intrigued to discover from them that I have unusually perfect anatomical proportions. The distance from my shoulder to my great trochcanter, my great trochanter to my knee and my knee to my ankle are exactly equal, which is a highly prized attribute in the modelling world. My face, on the other hand, is very difficult to paint or sculpt. No one ever quite put their finger on why, but even the most talented of the students never managed to get close to a good likeness of my head.

I was a model for four years, and I was paid £5 a session plus a little bit extra from the contents of the 'model box' where the students were encouraged to place small tips. Before long, Len asked me to model for his sculpture class two mornings a week as well which brought me in around £20 a week, a huge sum for 1974. One year, I was asked to sit for the Easter course in sculpture. Sitting still for six hours a day, five days a week for two weeks was physically exhausting, but they paid me £60 a week and the work produced was of a fantastically high quality. I was modelled in terracotta, moulded in white clay, cast in bronze and carved in soapstone, and apparently I am still to be found festooned with ivy in various north London gardens.

I began going out again, to pubs and parties. I enjoyed cooking for parties almost as much as going to them and I nearly always turned up clutching a home-made chocolate cake in one hand and a bottle in the other. In the autumn term of 1974, Linda Rands, a fellow student, gave a party in her mansion flat in Maida Vale. Like most parties in those days it was taking place very much at ground level with guests lolling around on cushions and beanbags in a haze of strange-smelling tobacco. I managed to lose an ear-ring and as I crawled along the floor looking for it, I found Gerald. He was yet another married guitarist, but he was genuinely separated from his wife and awaiting a divorce. Kind and gentle and straightforward, he was just what I needed to restore my confidence in men and in myself. His failed marriage had left him with a vehement mistrust of commitment, but we developed an easy-going and comfortable relationship. If I had hopes of anything more permanent then I hid them, even from myself.

Gerald lived just round the corner from the Royal Academy in a rambling bohemian flat above Chimes Music Shop in Marylebone High Street, which he shared with a young actor called Nickolas Grace. His room was so small, he had to sit on the landing to practise and I used to sit for hours on the stairs at his feet, while the most glamorous actors and actresses wafted past. Nick and I had a rather prickly relationship then. One night over dinner when I had been holding forth about nothing at all and hogging the spotlight he had been used to enjoying alone, he enquired acidly, 'What exactly is it you're studying at the Royal Academy, Lesley? Entertaining the Troops?'

It was meant unkindly and I had the decency to blush, but actually he had put his finger on precisely what I did want to spend my life doing. I *am* an entertainer and proud of it. As a second-year student, I was now allowed to join John Streets's opera class. This was more like it. There were master classes and workshops where we prepared scenes from a wide variety of work. My first ever appearance in an opera at the Academy was in an extract from *Il Trovatore*. I was a gypsy urchin and gambolled around gaily, waving my skirt and showing rather more knicker than was strictly necessary. I hadn't taken part in a full-scale production since *My Fair Lady* and it was marvellous to be back as part of a team with all the theatrical trappings of rehearsals and make-up and costumes and *applause*.

The summer of 1975 was blisteringly hot and Gerald and I escaped from the dust and sweat of London to hitch-hike across Europe. I had never been abroad before and my newly acquired passport symbolised my grown-up status. We took the ferry to France and hitched lifts in lorries where I curled up and slept leaving Gerald to struggle with polite conversation in half a dozen different languages. Travelling through Italy I became obsessed with the idea of visiting Rome, so we broke our journey and, leaving the autostrada and the lorries, took a local bus into the city. I bounced up and down on the edge of my seat, impatient to see all the sights. Suddenly, an impressive and ancient domed building came into view. I stood up and squealed with delight, waving and pointing out of the window.

'Look, Gerald, look – it's the Vatican! Isn't it magnificent!'

The occupants of the bus burst into helpless laughter. '*O stupido inglese! Vaticano!* Ha, ha ha!'

Gerald curled up in a corner and tried to make himself invisible.

A kind lady in front of me who spoke some English

turned round: 'No. No *Vaticano. Il Ufficio Postale.* Ees Post Office.'

We arrived in Crete a week later. We slept in a cool, white-washed room in the unspoilt fishing village of Galini on the south coast and spent our days seeking out secluded coves where we swam in the clear, warm Adriatic waters, toasted ourselves on the beach and devoured endless trashy paperbacks. At night we ate in local tavernas, where I was determined to try all the new and exciting dishes on offer. After two weeks of this we were down to our last few drachmas so we had to abandon our plans to come home on the train and take the Magic Bus instead. The magic bus was a fantastically cheap and fantastically basic method of transport across Europe, much patronised by hard-up young students. It took you from Athens to Victoria in four days. There was just one overnight stop, in a little pension in Austria, where I slept under a duvet for the first time. It was like sinking into a giant marshmallow. All this for the princely sum of £15.

When we got back to London, Gerald and I moved in together. We shared a flat in Finchley with Nick Folwell, who was President of the Students' Union at the Royal Academy, and his girlfriend Joanne. In my mind we were now a proper couple and dreams of domestic bliss became harder to dismiss. Gerald had never promised me a permanent commitment, let alone anything as formal as marriage, and I understood the pain he had gone through when he separated from his wife. Yet our relationship seemed so strong, and I was so happy, that in my heart I believed we would always be together. I never suspected there was any other way of looking at our relationship, until just before the end when I discovered he was having an affair with a dancer, a long-legged beauty called Susan. I had always thought I would know instantly if he was being unfaithful; that our closeness and friendship and honesty with each other left no room for secrets or deception. I was wrong. When Gerald left me to join Susan in the unromantic surroundings of Felixstowe, I was devastated. Nick Folwell was the perfect friend to me at this time – as he still is to this day. He provided a shoulder to cry on, made me endless cups of tea and listened patiently for hours while I expounded my views on the iniquities of life in general and men in particular; he put me back together again. Gerald had never wanted to hurt me. He was much more mature than I was and valued our friendship too much to allow the end of our affair to part us for ever. In time I came to realise this too and I stopped hating him; we became friends again – close, trusting, life-long friends.

Being unattached again made me even more eager to immerse myself in work. Henry Cummings had been con- cerned for some time that my knowledge and experience of sacred music was weak and he suggested that I join a church choir. My friend Ellie Ransom, another singing student at the Royal Academy, helped me find a job with the choir where she was principal soprano, at the City Temple in Holborn. The organist and choirmaster there was Dr Kenneth Abbott, a kind-hearted, amiable man and a fine musician who also held the position of Professor of Music to the Royal Air Force. He taught me a great deal about church music and I found I looked forward to

Sundays more than I had expected. As well as singing in the choir, I became more and more involved in the church itself. I have always had a very keen sense of spirituality, particularly when I sing. Music is the most powerful vehicle for spirituality. All religions use it to inspire and to bind and to enhance the sacred experience. My family had not been church-goers, but I had gone through a period in my childhood when I had been drawn to the parish church in Thorne. I used to cycle there, alone, every Sunday. I had been attracted by the peace and stillness that I found there and also, I suspect, by the theatricality of the ritual.

I also managed to broaden my experience of religious music further when a friend at the Royal Academy asked me to stand in for her at the West London synagogue. Jewish music was entirely new to me and it completely bowled me over with its directness and blistering emotional power. I felt as if I was in the film *Exodus*. I found myself very comfortable with singing in Hebrew, which rather surprised me as languages have never been my strong point and I had been struggling with French and Italian in particular. The music at the Synagogue was such a contrast to the spare, intellectual music at the City Temple.

Despite Henry Cummings's disapproval, I continued to attend the opera class. I was in no doubt now that opera was what I wanted to do. As well as the workshops and master classes, we had weekly lessons in movement, given by a brilliant ex-dancer called Anna Sweeny. Part of her work with the class involved exercises to strengthen our lower bodies to allow the upper part greater freedom for singing. We also had sessions of improvisation, which I adored, though some of the other students found them shudderingly embarrassing. She recognised my intensely physical relationship with music and taught me how to harness it. I learnt how to inhabit a character, to play a role with my whole being, not just my voice and my brain. Flora Nielsen, Henry Cummings, even Ken, had been driven to distraction with my inability to keep still while singing. 'Keep your feet still, girl!' 'Put your hand on the piano *and leave it there!*' 'Stop fidgeting, Lesley.' My fellow students were less critical but they used to tease me about it. 'Lesley Garrett – If In Doubt, Run About' was what they called me. Now at last I was not just allowed but encouraged to use my body to communicate. Anna wrote a full-length mime based on Keats's poem *St Agnes Eve* which the opera class movement group prepared and performed. It was fantastically liberating to be on stage, interpreting music without opening my mouth once.

By the end of my second year I was allowed to graduate to a slightly more senior chorus part in Rimsky-Korsakov's *The Snow Maiden* (*Snegurochka*). Produced by a twenty-year-old Graham Vick, it was conducted by Mark Elder. All the girls in the opera class were desperately in love with him. On one occasion during a particularly hot and sweaty rehearsal he whipped off his sodden T-shirt like André Agassi, and the entire female chorus screamed with teenage passion. It was a complicated production, technically, with an offstage chorus and special effects. The offstage chorus was conducted by Michael Schoenwandt who had a TV monitor that enabled him to see Mark in the pit. My job was to operate the snow machine. At one point, the chorus had to start singing at precisely the moment that the snow stopped falling on King Frost. On the opening night, I listened carefully for my cue and at exactly the right moment flicked the switch to turn off the snow. Unfortunately it was the wrong switch. The audience clearly heard Michael shout, 'You stupid bitch – you've turned off the monitor.' King Frost was left standing in an increasingly deep drift and the chorus came in rather late. It was widely agreed that I should stick to singing after that and leave the stage management to someone who knew left from right.

As well as staging whole productions once a year, the opera class used to work on scenes from a wide variety of operas. Sometimes we were lucky enough to have staff producers from English National Opera (ENO) and Covent Garden to come and work with us. Christopher Renshaw from the Royal Opera House came to help with *Cosi fan Tutte* in which I was working on Dorabella. One afternoon he asked me, 'Have you ever been to Covent Garden, Lesley?'

'Never,' I replied, which was almost true. I had been to one or two dress rehearsals, but I had never been able to afford a seat for an actual performance, other than right up in the slips. Instead I preferred the Coliseum, where I was often able to deputise for my friend Jean Rigby, who had a job there selling programmes and ice-creams. Chris recognised that I could act as well as sing and that I relished words as well as music.

'You'll play Susanna one day,' he pronounced. 'But for now you must come and see Teresa Stratas playing her.

Come tonight and watch.' He didn't have to ask twice. There was no time to go home and change so I went as I was, in a pair of jeans and a faded yellow jumper. In the sixth row of the stalls, surrounded by gentlemen in dinner jackets and bejewelled ladies in satin gowns, I was totally out of place. And I didn't care. I was completely captivated. Teresa Stratas was just magnificent – more than an opera singer, to my mind she was the greatest exponent of music theatre of her day.

Mum often came to London to see me perform, Dad almost never. He hated big cities and, proud though he was of my success, he found watching me perform difficult. Grandad Wall was not especially fond of opera. In his later years, my grandfather became rather cantankerous and intolerant. 'Opera's grand,' he would say, 'except for t'singing.' He had only one suggestion for every group of people who inconvenienced him in any way: 'They ought to be put up against a wall and shot!' This was what should happen to postmen, archbishops, Roman Catholics, all union leaders, homosexuals, council busybodies, politicians of any shape, form or colour, and particularly coalmen who put his coal in the wrong place. He came to see me sing only once, as The Bride in Gilbert and Sullivan's *Trial By Jury*, in the winter of 1977. This was the Winter of Discontent and there were unpredictable power cuts every few days. The curtain was due up at 7.30 and at 7.20 the lights went out. We sat in the library extension, which was our makeshift dressing-room, trying to finish our make-up by candlelight. Everyone was impatient for the power cut to end and the performance to begin. I was particularly anxious, knowing that my grandfather was in the audience and wondering how he would behave. At 8.30, to our immense relief, the power came back and the show went on. It was not until the next day that I discovered what had been going on in the theatre for that blacked-out hour. I went to my regular music coaching session with Rex Stevens, a most proper and refined person, who had taught me a great deal about attention to detail and the importance of diction.

He congratulated me on my performance the night before and then, looking rather uncomfortable, asked, 'My dear, was there an elderly gentleman in the audience last night who had something to do with you? A friend, perhaps, a relative?'

'Yes!' I replied. 'Me grandad. Did you meet him?' Rex shuffled in his chair some more.

'Well, not exactly. When the lights went out, your grandfather stood up and, well, how shall I put it, regaled the audience in no uncertain terms and, I might say, at some considerable length, with exactly what he would do with the miners should he have the opportunity. We were left in no doubt as to his loyalties and his devotion to music, and to you.'

Mum had had to drag Grandad bodily from the hall to cool off, his tirade echoing down the corridors as the embarrassed audience sat stiff-backed and tight-lipped through the blackout.

Just after Christmas in 1977, Kenneth Abbott invited my friend Ellie and me to have lunch with his family after Sunday service. They lived in the Old Rectory in Aston Clinton, just opposite the famous Bell Inn. It was a beautiful house, built of warm red brick with wide bay windows, and filled with lovingly polished antiques and books and flowers. Lunch was a far more formal affair than I had been used to at home. The huge damask-covered table was laid with twinkling crystal and heavy silver. Ken was very much the old-fashioned head of the household who said grace before we sat down and carved the meat expertly.

Half-way through the meal, the dining-room door flew open and a young man tumbled headlong into the room. Tall, dark and extravagantly scruffy, he was dressed in a pair of crumpled denim jeans which looked as though they had been slept in since they were new and a vast, shapeless brown jumper the neckband of which had become almost completely detached from the body of the garment. This was Malcolm, the Abbotts' prodigal son, returned from the pub where his Sunday lunch-time was habitually spent. His dramatic and undignified entrance was treated with resigned indulgence by his parents. He flopped down in a chair next to me and proceeded to make me laugh non-stop for the next hour. I can't remember what he said that was so hilarious. I don't think he actually told me jokes. What I do remember is that he was the funniest man I have ever met.

Two days later, having extracted my phone number from his father without much difficulty, Malcolm rang me and asked me out for dinner. He took me to a restaurant in Beauchamp Place called Borscht and Cheers which was a popular and raucous haunt of London's youth in the 1970s. We talked and laughed non-stop for the entire evening. Malcolm's attitude to life was to find humour in everything. Nothing dented his perpetual optimism or dampened his determination to see only the best in everyone. It was impossible not to love him.

Malcolm taught music at a school in Berkhamsted and violin at the Tring Arts Education Trust. He lived, officially, in a room in a flat in Berkhamsted with a group of bachelor friends. The flat, and Malcolm's room in particular, was a symphony in squalor. Discarded socks lay in stiff heaps in every corner; coffee mugs littered every surface, dull green islands of mould floating ominously in their muddy brown contents; empty beer cans and half-eaten Indian take-aways oozed from under the bed. In practice, Malcolm lived mainly at home. He ate his meals there, took his washing there whenever he remembered and spent most of his weekends there with his parents.

In the spring of that year, Ellie and I went with the Abbott family – apart from Malcolm – on a tour of Denmark, which gave us much useful performance experience. We gave recitals in halls and churches all over the country, culminating in a magical concert in Roskilde Cathedral, burial place of generations of Danish kings. I enjoyed the trip, but I was looking forward to seeing Malcolm again, and Ruby and Ken seemed keen for me to spend as much time with Malcolm as possible. They were enthusiastic about the relationship that was developing between us, not least because they saw me as a steadying influence on their wayward son. He was starting to wear cleaner clothes with fewer holes in, he had remembered how to use a comb, and he was spending (slightly) less time in the pub.

The throat problems that had been grumbling on for months flared up when we returned from Denmark. Henry Cummings was still adamant that I was a big dramatic soprano and was introducing me to Verdi and Weber arias – large-scale music that I loved and found surprisingly easy to sing. But it was a fundamental misjudgement of the power and scope of my voice, which is not a dramatic soprano at all but a good, strong lyric voice. Both Henry and Ken Abbott were convinced that it was opera that was doing the damage but I resisted all their attempts to make me give it up. I was having regular consultations with the Royal Academy laryngologist, Mr Salmon, who was becoming increasingly worried about my sore and unhappy larynx. Drastic action was needed and I was ordered to take a term off singing. In any other circumstances this would have been a nightmare, but at that moment all I could think about was the extra time it would give me to be with Malcolm. I pottered round his flat, tidying and cleaning and making him nutritious meals, most of which were based on mince (I have an extensive repertoire of mince recipes).

By the end of term, my voice was no better. Mr Salmon decided I should be admitted to St Thomas's Hospital so that he could take a proper look under general anaesthetic, which was the only method available in those pre-endoscopic days. I came round from the ordeal to see Mr Salmon at my bedside with his finger to his lips, gesturing me not to speak. 'It's fine,' he said, 'nothing to worry about. Just rest it a while and your voice will be fine.' Huge relief flooded over me – I hadn't really admitted even to myself just how frightened I had been. As Mr Salmon left the room, Malcolm came in, half-hidden by half a dozen bright pink gladioli, and asked me to marry him. Forbidden to speak my reply, I nodded so hard I thought my head would come off. We became officially engaged at Christmas, with a ring made especially by John Brown from the Hampstead Garden Suburb Institute.

Our engagement made little practical difference to Malcolm's life. He was one of the lads and I was very happy to be with the lads. His world revolved around his job, which he loved, the pub, which he loved even more, and the squash court, which was a necessary laddish venue between the two. His family was also very important to him and I was glad to become part of it.

Despite being frantically attracted by the bright lights of London and the even brighter lights of the operatic stage, I was still very much the product of a warm secure family. The Abbotts weren't a substitute for my own parents – it was more like being blessed with a second set, very different from Mum and Dad but kind and loving, welcoming and encouraging just the same. They were very warm with each other and it was obvious to anyone who knew them that they were very much in love. They were married during the war and Ken had been sent overseas two weeks later, not to return for four years. Ruby's wedding present to him had been a gold watch, which he took with him as a reminder of his new wife. It was lost on the beach-head at Anzio but after the fighting died down he took a terrible risk and returned to look for it. He scoured every inch of the beach until he spotted a tiny glint of gold in the sand.

The watch was buried but undamaged. He was sure then that he would survive to see Ruby again.

My parents loved Malcolm but it was painful for them to see how comprehensively I had been absorbed into this new family. Their background could not have been more different from mine. My family had its roots in the pits and the railways and the shipyards of the north; Malcolm's ancestors had commanded regiments, owned estates, been pillars of Home Counties communities. My parents were self-educated professionals, who had made their own success through initiative and hard work. They were a shining example of the successful combination of working-class determination and post-Bevan opportunity. Ken and Ruby were survivors from a fast-disappearing age. As I was drawn into the family, I willingly absorbed their more traditional values and attitudes. I began to dress like a nice middle-class girl. My old singing teacher Flora Nielson had tried and failed to rid me of my frayed jeans and bright clingy T-shirts, now I was happily sporting twin sets and sensible shoes. Ken and Ruby were uncomfortable with the idea of their future daughter-in-law spending one day a week sitting naked in front of a room full of strangers (though I don't think Malcolm minded much) so I gave up my modelling job. I was sad to leave the Institute. The staff and students had become my friends and I had enjoyed the work, not least because of the peace that it afforded me. In the midst of my busy life it was lovely just to sit, my mind full of music, and let my inner thoughts roam free.

Although I missed the regular money that the modelling had brought in, I already had another source of outside income. Cathy Giles, who had so kindly taken me in when I was homeless years before, did me another huge favour. Her boyfriend, Paul Hart, had been a keyboard player and arranger for Johnny Dankworth but had now joined up with another musician, Joe Campbell to form Joe & Co, a company which wrote and produced signature tunes and advertising jingles, a highly lucrative business. Whenever they needed classical singers for their work, Cathy would send along her friends from the Academy and I managed to get in on the act. Recording for Joe & Co was always enormous fun as well as paying extremely well and I have made jingles for them on and off ever since. I was the Kenco Coffee girl for a while and, more recently, the voice of Ragu Pasta Sauce and Renault cars, but the first recording I ever made was a demo tape for a beer advert, singing 'Ho-ofmeister! Ho-ofmeister!' to the tune of the Hallelujah Chorus – heretical but hysterical.

In 1978 the great Gian-Carlo Menotti came to the Academy to produce his Pulitzer Prize-winning opera *The Consul*. This is a gritty, powerful, disturbing piece, written at the height of the Cold War. It tells of a group of people trying to obtain the necessary paperwork to leave their country for a better life elsewhere. Their efforts are thwarted by the dead hand of bureaucracy, embodied by the eponymous Consul and his Secretary, which was my role. No place names are ever mentioned, but it is pretty clear that he is talking about the USSR and the USA.

Menotti was a small, intense Italian American who led a reclusive life in a castle in Scotland. He had a wonderful dramatic sense – he was as interested in the technicalities of staging his work as he was in the music and the performances. The new theatre was still not quite ready so we put on *The Consul* in the Dukes Hall, which was really intended for concerts. There was a stage at one end of the hall but Menotti decided to reverse the layout and we performed in the large space where the seats should be while the audience sat on the stage. No one had ever tried anything like it at the Academy before and I doubt if anyone but the great man himself would have been allowed to try, but it worked extraordinarily well. The production got rave reviews from all the big London critics and they were particularly generous with praise for my performance. The show ran for three performances and on the last night I had my first experience of corpsing when Kevin Hughes, who played a character called Nikolas Magadoff, slapped his application form on my desk. It was signed, in large black letters, **Knickers Off Magadoff**. I lost the next five bars completely, while the audience wondered why the stone-hearted bureaucrat had been moved to such helpless mirth.

As the summer term ended in my fifth year at the Royal Academy, I got my first professional opera job. I had been having vocal coaching sessions with Tom Hammond, who was Chief Coach at the English National Opera. He recommended me for the part of Anne Page in a production of *The Merry Wives of Windsor* at Haddo House in Scotland. Haddo House was the ancient home of Lady Aberdeen, an energetic patron of the arts in Scotland and an opera enthusiast who staged annual productions using a mixture of professional and amateur musicians. I travelled up to Scotland by train. The railways are in my blood and making this long trip from one end of the country to the other seemed like a great adventure.

I was met at the station by Lady Aberdeen's chauffeur and driven to the house. I could feel my heart beating faster and the familiar gripe of nerves clutched at my insides as we swept up the great drive and I finally caught a glimpse of the elegant eighteenth century house. I had never even visited a stately home, let alone stayed in one. How was I supposed to behave? How was I supposed to address Lady Aberdeen if I met her? I felt a curious combination of disappointment and relief as we glided past the grand front portico and came to a halt at the back of the house. Young sopranos in minor roles were obviously ranked with tradesmen and servants, but that was fine by me. I was shown into a vast old stone-flagged kitchen where a grey-haired lady in a flowery apron, who I guessed was some kind of housekeeper, was tending a pan of delicious-smelling bacon and eggs. She turned and smiled.

'Hello, dear, I'm June Gordon. You must be Miss Garrett. Just let me finish this and I'll take you to your room.'

It was warm and comfortable in the kitchen and I began to relax a little. We chatted gaily for a while and then she picked up my suitcase and headed for the back stairs. 'Come on, my dear. I'll show you your room now.' We walked for miles along echoing corridors lined with ancient portraits of long-dead Aberdeen ancestors and lit with crystal chandeliers. My nerves were creeping back. 'Tell me about this Lady Aberdeen person. I've heard she can be a bit of an old battle-axe. When do I get to meet her?'

My guide stopped and turned towards me. 'I am she,' she declared, with a terrifying grammatical accuracy. 'You have already met her.'

I blushed from head to toe and stared firmly at my feet, desperate for the ground to swallow me up. There was a moment's silence followed by peals of laughter from my aristocratic host who assured me that she was not in the least offended. She was true to her word and was kindness itself to me for the three weeks of my stay. The opera was a huge success and I enjoyed my time there enormously, surprising myself at how much delight I found in the beauty and peace of the countryside. June (as I had now learnt to call her without shame) was a passionate gardener as well as a music lover and I used to go with her on her tours round the grounds, picking armfuls of flowers to decorate the house.

Malcolm and I were married on 12 August 1978 in Thorne Parish Church. The rain came down in sheets all day. It must have spoilt the fun of the grouse-shooters' big day but it didn't spoil mine. It was a splendid occasion, my very own operatic production full of drama and spectacle. The men were in full morning dress – well-worn and perfectly fitting on Malcolm's side because they all had their own; glossily new and incongruous for my family who had hired them from Moss Bros. I was dressed in a white mediaeval-style dress with a dainty veiled hat made by my sister, Jill. I had wanted to go the whole hog and walk down the aisle with the veil over my face but at the last minute, as we reached the church door, Dad had smiled and said, 'Don't cover your face, love.' My sisters, Jill and Kay, were both bridesmaids and Malcolm's three-year-old nephew was a pageboy. The poor little lad had been nervous and unhappy earlier in the day but Dad had won him round. He had knelt down beside him, reached into his jacket pocket then held out his hand to produce, as if by magic, a tiny day-old chick.

Ken composed an anthem for us, sung by my friends from the Academy and the City Temple who came and formed an impromptu choir. Ken played the organ himself and we filled the church with exquisite music. The marriage service itself was conducted by Canon Weaver – who had married my parents before me, and christened my sisters and me as babies – and Ken's RAF connections had secured us the Officers' Mess at the Finningly Air Base for our reception. Malcolm's best mate and Best Man, Pete, made an absolutely filthy speech and my father, who can always be relied upon to upstage me, brought the house down by rising from his seat to speak and removing his top hat to reveal his usual trade-mark bobble hat – not the usual grubby green one, but an elegant grey model, specially knitted for the occasion.

The best part of the whole day was in the evening when we repaired to my father's local pub, the Robin Hood and Little John, for a proper party. We sang and sang and raised the roof. Hywel Davis and Phillip Thomas, and the rest of the Welsh contingent from the Royal Academy, led us all in the most spectacular rendition of 'Bread of Heaven' that the pub had ever heard.

Chapter 5

Kiss my . . . I Come from Leeds

My first five years at the Royal Academy were not wasted years, but they were waiting years. My need to sing and my dream to sing opera never wavered but I felt I had been wandering aimlessly, taking many different paths. Sometimes I had gone in the right direction, sometimes I had come up against a dead end. My final year was utterly different. I simply took off and flew. Marriage had given me peace and security. I felt I had found the perfect partner. Now, at last, my voice too was to find its ideal match.

It was Anna Sweeny who first told me about Joy Mammen. Joy's parents were English but she had been born in Melbourne and grew up in Australia. As a young woman she had been tall, blonde and stunningly beautiful. At the age of eighteen she had sung for Frank Sinatra who asked her for a date, to which she cravenly (though probably sensibly) replied that she had to go home to her mum. She had taught at the Academy some years before when she was in her early thirties, prodigiously young for a singing teacher. She left to resume her own successful career, performing all over Europe and Australia (she even sang with Luciano Pavarotti) but now she was returning to the Academy and everyone was terribly excited about it.

Joy's methods of teaching sounded absolutely right for me. She was renowned for her holistic approach to singing, for her understanding of the importance of the whole body as the singer's instrument. Singing is a surprisingly athletic pursuit and you have to be very fit to do it well. The voice is suspended by an extraordinarily complex system of muscles, working in opposition to each other. There are muscles holding the voice up, muscles pulling the voice down, others moving it from side to side and front to back. To sing well, all these muscles have to be stretched and pliable and perfectly balanced. Best of all, Joy was a real-life opera singer, someone who would understand my need to perform. If my first five years of college had been a long struggle across the desert, then Joy was my glass of cool beer at the end of it, my very own Ice Cold in Alex.

I bounced into her room on the first day of term like Tigger, brimming over with energy and hope and ready to learn. She did what no teacher had ever managed – she made me understand the relationship between my body and my voice, and taught me how to incorporate my heart, soul and mind into it too. For the first time, everything made sense. It was as if I had been reading the book in Sanskrit for the last five years and now I had it in English. Apart from anything else, she could actually demonstrate what it was she wanted from me. Both Flora Nielsen and Henry Cummings were teachers in their seventies. Finally I had a singing teacher who was a soprano in her prime. I absorbed everything she said like a sponge and was able to put it into practice instantly. With my previous teachers it had often taken weeks to get something even half right. The sound I wanted to make had always been in my head, yet I had only been able to dream of creating it. I had always known that my voice was out there somewhere. Now Joy took my hand and helped me walk towards it, meet it and befriend it. Above all else, Joy taught me to *listen*. We developed an instant rapport and our lessons were filled with laughter and fun.

Malcolm and I were now settled into our new home in Tring, just a mile or so away from his parents. It was a tiny, two-up, two-down cottage almost identical to the one in Waterside where I grew up. The daily journey to college was a long and difficult one. Queen Victoria had been fond of Tring and used to stay at an hotel in the town. So as not to disturb her, the Railway Company had decided not to build the station in the sensible location in the centre of town but sited it some two miles outside. Malcolm tried giving me driving lessons but it was a complete disaster. I couldn't get the hang of steering the car at all and he couldn't understand why. It was years later that I discovered what my problem was. I had assumed that, because the VW Beetle's engine was in the back of the car, the steering wheel must be connected to the back wheels. No wonder I was swinging the car all over the place.

Although still a student, I was now doing more and

more professional work. In the Christmas holidays of my final year, I went to Belfast to sing the soprano solos in Handel's *Messiah* for the Ulster Orchestra. I was still at an age when travelling to far-away jobs was a big adventure and I was short of money as usual so, using my student railcard, I embarked on the lengthy overland route to Ireland. The night train to Stranraer harked back to a more gracious era of rail travel. The carriages were elegant wood-panelled affairs with glistening brass fittings and all the best Victorian trimmings, including a discreet cupboard containing a china chamber pot which bore the charming legend: 'Property of British Railways. Do not use for solid materials.' From Stranraer I caught the morning ferry for Belfast. It was a rough and slow crossing but it was worth every stomach-churning hour for the view which greeted me when we sailed up Belfast Lough as the sun set over the mountains of Mourne. I stood alone on deck, leaning out over the rusty railings, gazing in wonder at the fiery sky and the clear, beautiful evening light, drinking in lungfuls of the fresh, clean air. A kitchen-hand on the deck below threw a bucket of food out into the ocean and a huge flock of gulls swooped and wheeled around me. I felt deliriously alive.

I was met on the quay by Dermond Mulholland, the orchestra manager. 'Have you been to Belfast before? No? Well, I'll take you on the scenic route then.' This was my first visit to Ireland and I was stunned by the beauty and warmth of the country and its people, despite the terrible conflict that was taking place within their midst. He took me to the Bogside, down the Falls Road; he drove me down the Shankhill Road, through the barricades. I was never so afraid. But I was able to see the other side of Belfast too. I stayed in a lovely little hotel near the French Embassy, recommended by Maurice Miles who was conducting the oratorio. With his long, white, swept-back hair, camel coat and large black hat, Maurice looked every inch the conductor. He was Professor of Conducting at the Royal Academy, and taught Simon Rattle. He was charming and cultured and he gallantly escorted me around the city, showing me the stunning architecture, the art galleries and the graceful parks. I felt privileged to be there and to perform for such knowledgeable and appreciative audiences. All this and £200 – my first real professional fee.

The time came when decisions had to be taken about what path my career would follow when I left the Academy. I had been there nearly six years and I couldn't stay there for ever. I was already in demand as a soloist for oratorios and recitals and it would have been easy just to carry on down that road. This was certainly the career Malcolm and his family had in mind for me. But my sights were set on a very different future. The world of opera that I had encountered through John Streets's opera class at the Academy was a revelation. I was more certain than ever that opera was what I had to do. Joy understood my feelings and, with her encouragement, I applied for a place at the National Opera Studio. The National Opera Studio takes only twelve students each year from the entire country and places are much sought after. The studio was in its infancy as an organisation, having developed from the old Opera Centre to provide a one-year intensive post-graduate training course in opera. Competition for the places was intense, but I had to try.

The annual Kathleen Ferrier Memorial Competition was (and still is) *the* big competition for young British singers. Joy suggested that I enter, though I wasn't expected to do particularly well: there was a huge entry and I was still very young and inexperienced. Nevertheless I worked hard at my programme with Joy and Rex Stevens. I even bought a new frock, a long, red, high-necked creation that I had found in my favourite Oxfam shop. The competition was held at the Wigmore Hall, which is such a marvellous old building steeped in musical history and with a near-perfect acoustic. The preliminary rounds were at the beginning of the week, leading up to the grand final on Friday. The first round went well for me and I moved through to the next stage. By Wednesday evening there were a dozen of us left and the atmosphere became tense. Thursday evening was the semi-finals after which we all trooped into the hall to hear the names of the finalists. To my delight and surprise I had made it.

The final took all day and was open to the public. Joy had to teach all day at the Academy, and Malcolm was at work, but a large gang of friends came to encourage me, and Ken came up for the day to give me moral support. I was drawn to sing last, so I sat in the audience for the morning session and watched the first three contestants. These included a quite extraordinary counter-tenor who punctuated his performance with 'operatic' gestures involving a large, white silk hankie, and ostentatiously grabbed his crotch before every high note. I can't recall who sang in the

afternoon because by this time I was backstage, half sick
with nerves, until it was time to go on.

With a nod to Mark Tatlow, my accompanist, I began
with Mozart's 'Alleluia', which has a whopping great top
C at the end that I was glad to get past without trouble. I
followed this with 'Gretchen am Spinnrade' by Schubert,
which I managed to pace well enough to save my energy
for my next song, 'The New Ghost' by Vaughan Williams.
I had sung this many times before but though I say it myself,
never so well. For those few minutes, I was no longer in a
concert hall in front of hundreds of people, I was in that
cold, dark graveyard talking to the ghost. To sing well, you
have to connect with the song and sometimes you do more
than connect; you become transported. If you are lucky,
and I think I was that day, the audience is transported
with you. I finished my programme with 'Liese, Liese'
from *Der Freishutz* and left the stage, relieved to be taking
my place in the front row of the audience with the other
contestants.

After a tense fifteen minutes Dame Janet Baker, the
chairman of the judging panel, took the stage to announce
their decision. She congratulated us all on our performances and explained that, in view of the high standards
that year, two equal first prizes would be awarded, the
Kathleen Ferrier Scholarship and the Decca Prize, both
worth £1,000.

'The Kathleen Ferrier Scholarship this year goes to Mr
Alexander Garden.'

We all clapped as Sandy went up to collect his cheque.

'And the Decca Prize to Miss Lesley Garrett.'

A great roar went up from behind me as my supporters' club rose to their feet and cheered.

I went down to the Green Room in a daze, clutching my new-found wealth and hardly able to believe my luck. Dame Janet came over to speak to me and told me that two things had particularly impressed the judges: the clarity of my diction and my ability to capture character, especially in 'The New Ghost'. This would have been praise enough from anyone but to hear it from Dame Janet was wonderful. She has always been an inspiration to me, not just for her exquisite voice but for her commitment and dedication to the profession. I was longing to get back to the Academy and give Joy the good news, but everyone in the room wanted to shake my hand. One young man whom I did not recognise came up and introduced himself as a representative of the agents Ibbs & Tillett.

'Congratulations, Miss Garrett,' he said, handing me his card. 'It's obvious you have a great career ahead of you. We would be delighted if you would consider allowing us to represent you in future. Perhaps you could come and see us soon and discuss the details?'

Even in my excited state, I was stunned. Ibbs & Tillett had been in the business for generations and Amy Tillett was the doyenne of musical agents. In their early days they had been a literary agency as well and had once represented Charles Dickens. Now they were interested in me! It was all too much to take in. I extricated myself from the throng and, stopping only to change out of my long dress (I nearly forgot), I ran full pelt along Wigmore Street and up Marylebone High Street to the Royal Academy and flung open the door to Joy's room.

'We've done it, Joy, we've done it!' I panted, breath-lessly.

Joy hugged me to her ample bosom. 'Wonderful!' she cried. 'Now let's pop up and tell the Principal.'

So off we went, leaving a rather bewildered singing student to continue their lesson alone.

Sir Anthony Lewis was like a god at the Academy and his Olympus was an elegant, wood-panelled apartment on the topmost floor of the building, which he shared with his wife, the much-loved Lady Lewis. He looked like a cross between Elgar and Father Christmas and was loved and revered by staff and students more than both of them. As genial as he was wise, his favourite word was 'splendid' and that was, of course, how he described my victory, before and after he kissed me and half a dozen times more as he poured out the obligatory glasses of celebratory sherry. It was indeed a splendid achievement for the Academy. I was the first of its students to win the Kathleen Ferrier since Elizabeth Harwood in the 1960s.

Winning the Kathleen Ferrier Award made me believe I had the National Opera Studio in the bag. Joy quickly brought me down to earth. 'You've still got to pass the audition, Lesley. Don't count your chickens. Now let's get down to some work.'

The audition took place in the cavernous and daunting surroundings of the Old Vic. I watched from the wings as the first candidate took her place on the stage, a small, nervous figure, fidgeting with the music she had brought with her, so terrified was she that she might forget her words. No one had thought to tell her (or me, for that matter) that singing from your music was regarded as an unforgivable sin at the National Opera Studio. If you didn't know your pieces perfectly by heart you might as well not bother turning up. The poor girl didn't have a chance and my heart went out to her as she had to endure the humiliation of being told so. I would have suffered her fate had I sung first, as I had intended to have my music with me, just in case. Now I had no choice but to leave it behind backstage and manage without. Armed with the knowledge that, as someone had recently told me, the phrase 'kiss my arse, I come from Leeds' will, in an emergency, fit any line of music, I strode on and hoped for the best.

I spent the anxious few weeks of waiting to hear from the National Opera Studio preparing for my final appearance on stage at the Royal Academy in Michael Geliot's production of Chabrier's rarely performed comic opera, *L'Etoile*. The plot concerns a king and his intended bride, a princess from a neighbouring country who falls in love with a pedlar called Lazuli on her way to the wedding, and it contains all the usual improbable ingredients of misunderstandings and mistaken identities. I played Lazuli, my first ever trouser part, and made my entrance riding a bicycle on to the stage (this was before the device became so popular that it ended up a theatrical cliché). Peter Crooke was the king and we had great fun together in rehearsals, practising the moment when I had to appear to punch him in the face. We went over the scene again and again and I became adept at swinging my fist just past his chin and into my

hand to give the illusion that I had actually hit him. On
the first night, alas, I got carried away with the drama of
the moment, connected with his face and floored him. He
was a real trouper and picked himself up, reeling from the
blow, and carried on. The next day the poor chap had the
biggest black eye you have ever seen. All the major London
critics came to see the show and gave the production good
reviews, being especially kind about my performance (Alan
Blyth in the *Daily Telegraph* said that mine was 'a name
to watch'). On the last night, Martin Isepp, who ran
the National Opera Studio, was in the audience and he
came backstage afterwards. He took my hand, smiled and
whispered conspiratorially, 'You're in!'

I had one more obstacle to overcome and it was a tough
one. Ken Abbott had been trying, for some time, to steer
me away from opera and towards a career in recital and
oratorio work. Now that I had been offered a place at
the National Opera Studio he turned up the pressure
and advised me to reject it. He continued to maintain
that operatic repertoire was inherently damaging to my
voice, but I don't believe that was the only reason for
his objection, or even his main one. The truth was that
Ken did not really like opera. He claimed the music
was just not to his taste, but he had a puritan streak,
which found the passion, colour and all-round sexiness
of it slightly distasteful. He was, I believe, uncomfortable
with the idea of his daughter-in-law flaunting herself on
the stage of a theatre. He would rather see me, demure,
restrained, *respectable* in front of an orchestra in a concert
hall or, preferably, a church. I respected my father-in-law,

he had helped me enormously with my singing and I owed him a huge debt but I couldn't agree with him. I had no doubts that my heart belonged to opera. It was the form of music that gave me the greatest satisfaction. I enjoyed the challenge of learning new roles, getting under the skin of a character, working with other equally enthusiastic and creative people to put the production together. Best of all, I loved the final stage of stepping out in front of an audience and drawing them into the action as the drama unfolded.

My mother came to my rescue as she had done before and would do again. Despite the struggles we had with our relationship when I was a teenager, Mum has always understood me and my need to follow my own path, learning my lessons the hard way if need be. She, more than anyone, realised my need to find things out for myself, to listen to my heart, not my head. She and Dad arrived at short notice to stay with Ruby and Ken at the Old Rectory. After Sunday lunch, Mum went off with Ken to his study and they were gone for a long time. I discovered later that she had told him, as tactfully as possible, that if I wanted to go to the National Opera Studio he shouldn't try to stop me. She made him understand that I was a stage animal through and through and always had been. The strategy worked and my in-laws' objections faded away.

With my plans for the next year taken care of, I found time to study for and sit my LRAM. This was the teaching diploma, the 'something to fall back on' which I had promised my father I would get. I didn't think I would need it, but it meant so much to Dad that I took it and, to his relief, passed.

My final year at the Academy was the most successful as well as the most enjoyable. Apart from the stability and contentment I found in marriage, Joy had worked miracles on my voice. The Annual Prize Giving at the end of term was a grand, formal affair and I should have liked to have been there to have had the chance to say goodbye to the place that had given me so much, and opened so many doors. But I was absent and for the best possible reason – I had a job.

A man called Adam Pollock, who had seen me in *L'Etoile*, was running an organisation called Musica nel Chiostro (Music in the Cloisters), based in an exquisite ruin of a monastery high up on a hillside in Tuscany, close to the little village of Batignano. As a young man he had worked with Benjamin Britten but he had come into some money and was able to buy this beautiful old building and fulfil his dream of running his own opera festival in the country he loved the best. The operas were performed in many different parts of the monastery – in the walled garden, in the olive orchard or, as on this occasion, in the cloisters themselves. He offered me the role of Tibrino in Cesti's opera *Orontea*. I went out to Italy at the end of June and spent a magical month living and working with a wonderful cast which included Della Jones, John Rawnsley and his new wife Nuala Willis, Patricia O'Neill and an extraordinary counter-tenor called John Angelo Messana. He was an exotic creature, an Irish American from New York who had an air of mystery and menace about him. There were rumours of connections with unnamed sinister organisations which may or may not have been true but they did his image no harm and he made no attempt to deny them.

In a sense this was my first professional opera engagement, though we weren't, of course, paid a penny. A month in Tuscany in July, with a few hours work in the morning and the rest of the day on the beach, with as much pasta and Chianti as it's possible to consume, was enough reward for all of us. Malcolm came too, which made everything perfect. He willingly assumed the role of company clown and I was delighted to find that everyone else found him as funny and adorable as I did. It was the most marvellous, convivial time, despite the fact that the monastery had no mod cons at all. We slept in monks' cells on straw mattresses and if you were a main role you got a candle; the shower was a hosepipe hanging from an olive tree in the walled garden.

It was Graham Vick's production, conducted by Jane Glover and performed in modern dress, which was a boon as there was practically no money for costumes. For Tibrino, the pageboy, I was kitted out like Just William in cut-off trousers and a sleeveless pullover with my cap plonked backwards on my rumpled hair. I had sticking plasters on both knees, a catapult in my back pocket and one tooth blacked out. I also played Amor (Cupid) who appeared at the beginning and the end of the opera. My costume for that consisted of nothing but a pair of skin-tight silver cycling shorts and a towel draped strategically around my neck. At the very end of the piece, I had to make a declamatory gesture and on the night of the dress rehearsal, when the local villagers were given free tickets to provide us with an audience, my towel flew off. There was nearly a riot as the local black-clad matrons shook their fists at me and their bachelor sons tried to storm the stage. For the rest of the run the towel was glued firmly to my chest each evening.

It was hard to leave the warmth of Tuscany for the damp greyness of London in August, but I returned from Batignano relaxed and eager for the new challenges that awaited me. The National Opera Studio was based in Morley College on Waterloo Road, near Lambeth North tube station. It was a long way from Tring and my schedule in the first term was punishing. I continued to have lessons with Joy at the Royal Academy every Monday, Wednesday and Friday morning at 9 o'clock which meant leaving home at 7 a.m. to catch the train. Classes at the Studio started at 10.30 and we worked all day with hardly time to grab a sandwich at lunch-time. We were expected to learn five complete roles in the space of twelve months. On top of this there were music coaching sessions with Jane Robinson, who was to become a firm friend, movement classes with Anna Sweeny (hooray!) and language coaching, which I was in sore need of. Languages have always been difficult for me. I can imitate the accent and learn the vocabulary if I have to, but grammar eludes me. I became aware that, much as I enjoyed singing in English, the words of an aria are part of the music itself. When you sing in a translation you gain greater understanding for yourself and for the audience but you lose the original connection between the words and the music that the composer intended. With Henry I had sung mostly in

English. Although the workshops at the Academy were always sung in the original language, the full-length operas we put on there were all in English, so I had never had to learn an entire role in the original language. That year I learnt Pamina in *Die Zauberflote*, Adina in *L'Elisir d'Amore* by Donizetti, Despina in *Cosi fan Tutte*, and Susanna in *Le Nozze de Figaro*. Anne Trulove in Stravinsky's *The Rake's Progress* was the only English role.

I was working in the evenings too, for much of the first term. *Orontea* was transferring to the Riverside Studios in Hammersmith and I had to rehearse most days after classes. It was lovely to be back with the old team from Tuscany, and the production was as well received in London as it had been in Batignano. As soon as that run finished I began work on the role of Hermione in a new opera called the *King of Macedon*, composed by Roger Steptoe with libretto by Ursula Vaughan Williams. I was quite overwhelmed to meet Ursula, wife of the great Ralph Vaughan Williams, who later became a great friend and supporter. Roger was composer-in-residence at Charterhouse School and the opera was performed at the school with a mainly professional cast and orchestra, conducted by Bill Llewellyn, augmented by boys from the sixth form. Joyce Conwy Evans designed wonderful costumes and I splashed out £15 (my entire fee for the engagement) to buy her drawing of the wedding dress which I wore for my part. The relationship with Roger and Ursula continued when they composed a song-cycle called *The Looking Glass* which I premiered at the Purcell Rooms in London as part of the Hunt Trio, formed by my old piano teacher, Jean Anderson, and her son Gordon Hunt who is an amazingly talented oboe player. We made a recording of the work, in a little church in Guildford, and it was to be my very first record release. I don't suppose anybody ever bought it, except the three of us and my mum, but I still treasure that piece of shiny black plastic, even though I no longer have anything to play it on.

The second term at the National Opera Studio was mainly taken up with master classes and we had the opportunity to work with some legendary people who generously gave their time to us. Elisabeth Söderström came and talked to us about Strauss, bringing half the Covent Garden cast of *Rosenkavalier* with her to demonstrate; Tito Gobbi worked with us on *L'Elisir d'Amore*. Elizabeth Schwartzkopf taught us for a session but, alas, her English rather let her down and she spent the whole morning telling us how we must 'sing through our tusks'. Twelve students had sat at her feet wondering how it was possible to sing opera through their teeth (we decided in the end she had been talking about noses – perhaps she had meant to say 'trunks').

The National Opera Studio was the most wonderful shop-window for young opera singers, and thanks to it, offers of work began to arrive before my year was over. As well as working with Jane Robinson, I was still having voice coaching sessions with Tom Hammond from the Coliseum, and through him I was offered the tiny, two-line part of Alice, a young peasant girl in Rossini's *Count Ory*. I didn't care how small the part was, I was just ecstatic at the prospect of appearing on that stage. I was also contacted by Ibbs & Tillett who told me that the Wexford Festival were interested in using me, perhaps in Handel's *Orlando*. I went along to an audition with Adrian Slack who ran the Festival, although his main job was as a producer for Welsh National Opera, and sang Purcell's 'Hark the Echoing Air' which was the nearest thing I had to Handel and was my favourite audition piece. I had expected to be offered something small, if I was lucky, but instead they asked me to play Dorinda. It was the second soprano part in *Orlando* but it was nevertheless a significant role. I spent the last term of my time at the Opera Studio preparing the part and having coaching sessions with Brian Trowell, from Kings College London, who was the leading expert on baroque music in general and Handel in particular. I have never prepared a role so well before or since, and I learnt a huge amount about Baroque ornamentation and style from this shy, kind academic who has an enormous passion for his subject.

Rehearsals for *Count Ory* took up most of the summer and everyone at ENO was friendly and welcoming. Valerie Masterson, who played the countess, was especially kind and generous to me. There was a family atmosphere amongst the company and I felt instantly at home. With such a small role, there was not a huge amount of work for me to do but I was happy just to be at the Coliseum and I spent many hours exploring the rambling old building and chatting to the dozens of backstage characters who worked there. To walk out on stage at the London Coliseum on opening night was unimaginably moving for me. I had sat in the upper circle as a fifteen-year-old schoolgirl and dreamt of a career in opera. Ten years later I was on the stage. What did it matter if I only had a couple of lines to sing. My name was in the programme, my mum was in the audience, and I was on my way. For the last few performances, Valerie's place was taken by the great soprano Isobel Buchanan and I fell completely under her spell. She had been in Australia for a few years, worked her way up through the Australian opera system and had returned with the most glorious voice. Now she was sweeping all before her on the European circuit.

Australian opera was in its heyday and I began to entertain dreams of going there myself. One day I consulted Joy about it. Australia was, after all, her home. 'Hmm, good idea, Lesley. Why don't I have a word with Richard Bonynge? He and Joan are old friends of mine. Perhaps he could fit you into the chorus of the Australian National Opera.' I rushed home to tell Malcolm, but he could not understand my excitement, let alone share it. 'We live here,' was his reply.

Although I was disappointed at Malcolm's reaction I did not dwell on it. Maybe he would change his mind in time, there was no hurry. Besides, I was off to Ireland. Wexford is an extraordinary place at all times, but for its annual festival it transforms itself into an artistic playground like no other. The tiny theatre seats only 300 people and yet the festival produces international work of the highest possible quality and is regarded as an important platform for young singers and new works. Nor is there a friendlier place in the world than Wexford. There were more pubs per square mile than I have ever seen in my life and they were all filled with music. Guinness, steaming hot toddies (which I convinced myself were good for the voice) and *moules marinieres* were the staple diet.

I was lodged in a guesthouse at the top of a hill, right on the edge of town. My room was about six feet square and bitterly cold. When I complained about this to Mrs O'Connor, the landlady, she shook her head and launched into a rambling apology, claiming the boiler had broken down. After a few nights when I nearly froze to death in my sleep I went into town and bought a little electric fire. 'Will you turn that infernal thing off!' she screamed when she saw it in the corner of my room, guzzling her electricity. 'D'you think I'm made of money.' The boiler repaired itself, miraculously, overnight. She was mean about heating, but she was lavish with breakfast. Great steaming bowls of porridge and plates piled high with bacon, eggs, sausages and fried home-made soda bread were on the table every morning.

It was an extraordinary cast, full of well-established stars like Bernadette Greevy and Alison Hargen – and I felt very much the apprentice. The part of Orlando was taken by John Angelo Messana, my old friend from Batignano. It was wonderful to hear his phenomenal voice again – wild and at times barely controlled. But when he harnessed that sound it was electrifying. The first rehearsal was nerve-wracking. The entire cast had to sit round in a semi-circle and sing the whole opera from start to finish. I had never worked this way before. I'd always started rehearsals on my own or in small groups. Now here I sat, the youngest and most inexperienced member of a serious, grown-up professional cast, terrified of making a fool of myself. My first aria came a long way into the first act and the other cast had all sung before it was my turn. I stood up with my knees knocking, grateful that I had prepared so thoroughly, and began to sing. I finished my aria and there was silence. You could have heard a pin drop. Had I done something terribly wrong? Then everyone in the rehearsal room applauded. Their kindness in realising how nervous I was made a deep impression on me. Their applause helped calm my nerves, and I felt I was going to be all right. Dorinda the shepherdess was a wonderful character to play, full of life and energy, cheeky and irreverent, so I revelled in every second of being her for three hours each night.

I vividly remember how I felt as I sang on stage in my first professional role. Never before had I experienced the feeling that I was simply a channel between the composer – or some higher being – and the audience. I was the means by which the composer could bestow on people a gift they would treasure long after the performance, and which would have the power to change them. I know it sounds over the top, but that was really how I felt – and still do, particularly when I sing opera. It's hard to describe in words, but the closest I can come to it is to say that it feels like a kind of religious experience.

Before *Orlando* could open, the relaxed, festive atmosphere was shattered. Security at the theatre was provided by the local policeman, a much-loved character who appreciated his annual dose of opera as much as any of the patrons. One day there was a robbery at the bank and 'our' policeman gave chase and cornered the thieves in a quarry on the edge of town. There he was shot dead, leaving a widow and eight children. It was a dreadful shock to everyone in the town and to the whole Opera Company. Someone came up with the idea of a benefit concert to raise money for the family and we were all asked to do a turn. Everybody else chose to sing operatic arias or something sombre. It sounded to me as if it was going to be a pretty dull show and I didn't see why it had to be. It was a benefit concert, after all, not a memorial service. The more fun we could make it the more money we would raise, so I rang my sister and asked her to send me her book of Stanley Holloway monologues. Dressed in John Angelo's Orlando costume of full Roman armour, I gave them my version of 'The Battle of Hastings' and it went down a storm. Even the policeman's widow managed a smile. The theatre was packed to capacity and we made the extraordinary sum of £10,000. A generous American businessman who was in the audience doubled it.

The night before we opened, I had a strange and unnerving dream about my grandfather. It was so vivid and frightening that I rang home to check that all was well. 'Don't be daft, lass,' said my father. 'Everyone's fine.' Malcolm arrived, having driven over from England, and he too reassured me.

The first night was a triumph for us all. After my biggest number, I had to exit and do a quick costume change while John Angelo Messana sang his next aria. As I was about to rush back on to the stage in my new costume, the stage manager held me back. 'Wait, Lesley. John hasn't been able to sing yet. They're still applauding you.' It was a magic moment. The audiences loved the whole show and so did the critics. Bernard Levin came, as he did every year, and gave us a great review. He was particularly generous to me: 'a sensational debut' were his words.

By the last night I had a sore throat and the beginnings of flu, but I managed to get through the performance and the party afterwards. The next morning I was feeling terrible and the journey home was nightmarish. I was horribly sick on the sea crossing and the car barely got off the ferry in Fishguard before it broke down. After a long delay while an AA man mended our cracked distributor cap with nail varnish (mine not his!), we drove on and arrived in Tring at tea-time to find my mother on the doorstep.

'I've got some awful news, love. Your grandad died while you were away.'

While I was in Ireland, he had suffered a massive stroke. Nursed tenderly by my mother, he had lingered, barely conscious, for days, dying during my opening night. 'Why didn't anyone tell me?' I pleaded. But I knew perfectly well why. I could never have gone on working, knowing how ill Grandad was, and the whole family, including Malcolm, had conspired to keep the truth from me. In the end I had even missed the funeral, so I never had the chance to say goodbye. I was heartbroken.

'As the pedlar Lazuli, a male lover's role written for a girl,
Lesley Garrett displayed a gift for comic acting (sometimes carried to
excess) and deeply felt singing quite out of the ordinary. . . here is a name
to watch.' - Alan Blyth, *Daily Telegraph*, on the Royal Academy
production of Chabrier's *L'Etoile*.

Dido, in Purcell's *Dido and Aeneas*, Royal Academy – on the back of the photo I sent to Grandad Wall I wrote, 'Relieved and pleased to have got through the first aria'.

As Adina at the National Opera Studio with William Pool, in a scene from *L'Elisir d'Amore* produced by Tito Gobbi.

Pat O'Neil and I, with Gerald Macdonald at the piano, celebrating our Peter Stuyvesant Awards at The National Opera Studio.

Anne Page in *The Merry Wives of Windsor*, Haddo House, 1978, with John Winfield as Fenton.

As Dorinda in Handel's *Orlando*, Wexford, with John Angelo Messana, during a complicated piece of stage business involving me catching his helmet and putting it on while singing.

Right 'Singing in the rain' – publicity shot, Buxton Festival 1981.

Below Carolina in *The Secret Marriage*, Buxton, with Renato Cappechi.

Above Learning to walk the tightrope in the Larenty's garage: 'Your foot is like sausage', as Papa Larenty would say.

Right Putting my training into practice in *The Bartered Bride* for Welsh National Opera. My teachers, the Larentys, were amazed to see my costume because it was very like what they wore as performers in the early part of the last century.

Getting down to business with Petros Evangelides in Sir Peter Hall's production of *L'incoronazione di Poppea* at Glyndebourne.

Chapter 6

---◆---

Walking the Wire

With my triumph in Wexford receding into memory,
I settled into a very different role as a Hertfordshire
housewife. For the first time in my married life I had
no college or job to go to and I found myself lonely
and frustrated, missing the excitement and the stimulus
of being part of an artistic community, and impatient to
be working again. In the New Year, when offers of more
work began to arrive through Ibbs & Tillett, I was relieved
and excited. They were very good offers as well – good
roles, good companies – enough work for a whole year.
Malcolm was less enthusiastic because it would take me
away from home so much. It was a difficult choice for
me. I had never expected to be offered so much work
so quickly and had naïvely assumed that our lives would
adapt to the demands of my career in a gradual and natural
way. But after my experience in Wexford I knew beyond
any doubt that I would never be satisfied unless I could

make opera my life. The satisfaction that I had found in preparing a role, then performing that role in a way that made people laugh and cry and clap the way they had done in Wexford was so powerful that I could not envisage my life without it. Bernard Levin had said I had a great future. Not my mum, not my teacher – Bernard Levin had said it. So, one morning I took a deep breath, picked up the phone, called Ibbs & Tillett and said yes to the first of the offers, with the Welsh National Opera.

Wales is famous for being a deeply musical country, and Cardiff particularly is steeped in song. The combination of a big city with a thriving artistic community, an ancient musical heritage and an industrial landscape was everything I could have asked for. It felt exactly like south Yorkshire. From the moment I stepped off the train I felt instantly at home. All over the city there was a buzz, an artistic energy I had never experienced before.

The opera I had come here to do was a new piece by John Metcalfe called *The Journey*. It was an intense and serious work but the music was breathtaking. The small cast included Menai Davis, Yolande Jones, Tim Jerman and Henry Newman. My character, Nicola, was a sensual, passionate woman who goes on a journey to find herself. It was a fantastic challenge to create a character absolutely from scratch. In most operas, however hard you try with the director to bring freshness to a part, you cannot avoid being aware of the interpretations that hundreds of other singers have contributed down the years. Nicola was different – a completely new and exciting role, just waiting for me to breathe life into her. To work on an opera with the composer himself present was thrilling, but a terrific responsibility.

Anthony Hose conducted and John Eaton was the producer. Both were highly intelligent Oxbridge graduates, and one day when we all went for a walk I discovered that they were both the kind of men who could tell you the word for sycamore in five different languages but wouldn't know a sycamore from a sequoia. While I was the only one who knew what a sycamore actually looked like, I became very conscious of the huge gaps in my artistic education. For years I had had no time to read a book, other than the odd Catherine Cookson on train journeys, and no money to go to the theatre. Surrounded by earnest intellectuals talking about Beckett and Joyce and using words like metaphysical and angst, I was appalled by my own ignorance but I loved to listen, and when I plucked up courage to ask questions everyone was enormously kind.

I stayed with Adrian Slack and his wife in their huge, warm, Victorian flat in Penarth. Every single day I awoke in a fever of excitement and joy, barely able to believe that I was finally achieving my ambition. I was a member of a leading opera company, playing an important role. For the first time in my life I was earning enough to live on without grants, scholarships, bursaries or prizes.

I spent all my spare time with the company, mostly in the Chapter Centre, a converted school building which was the artistic heart of Cardiff, dedicated to making the arts accessible to all. There was a café, an art gallery, 'spaces' for dance and mime, pottery demonstrations, poetry readings.

It was, as they said in those days, a happening place, a place to hang out. I also took up sailing, on a fifteen-foot, one-sailed boat which John Eaton had bought with a couple of his friends. They kept the boat at Penarth in what is now a rather glitzy marina but in those days was a muddy, run-down old harbour. Cardiff Bay is not the easiest water for a novice sailor. The tide differential is enormous and the slightest error in timing could leave you adrift for hours or stuck in the mud. Out on the water, you are at the mercy of powerful cross-currents which froth and boil when they meet (the locals call this 'the rannies'). This would be tricky enough for a bunch of beginners, but the bay is also a major shipping lane, one of the busiest in Europe, and sailing there was like negotiating Hyde Park Corner in the rush hour on a fairy cycle.

One day, when a group of us were out on the boat, the wind suddenly dropped, leaving us becalmed in the middle of the bay. As we struggled to coax our rusty outboard motor into life, we noticed that a small, dark speck on the horizon was growing larger and larger. It was an oil tanker, *en route* from Bristol to Milford Haven. This great, black monster was the size of Wembley Stadium and just about as manoeuvrable and it was heading straight for us. We could do nothing but pray for a breath of wind and wave frantically at other craft for help. As it bore down on us the sky grew dark and a disembodied voice boomed:

'YOU ARE IN A SHIPPING LANE – MOVE OVER!'

'We know!' we all screamed back, though there was no chance of us being heard.

With minutes to spare before the boat was crushed to

matchwood, as we were seriously contemplating jumping for it and taking our chances with the bone-freezing waters of the Bristol Channel, a motor launch came alongside us, attached a line and managed to tow us out of the path of the leviathan and back to the safety of the harbour. Although it sounds almost comical now, it was terrifying at the time. I have not set foot on a sailing boat since, and never will.

Before we took *The Journey* on a tour of the West Country, Anthony Hose, who was also Managing Director of the Buxton Festival, asked me if I would like to spend the summer there, playing the part of Carolina in Cimarosa's *The Secret Marriage*. I had been intending to go back to Batignano for the summer but this was too good an offer to refuse. Adam Pollock would understand, I thought, and I am sure he would have done if only I had rung him there and then and explained the situation. Stupidly, though, I put off calling him and he found out through a third party that I had changed my mind and wasn't coming to Tuscany after all. He rang me, furious and hurt that I could treat him in such a cavalier fashion. I apologised as best I could, but there was really no excuse for such unprofessionally bad manners and I headed off north with his angry words ringing in my ears.

In contrast to the thriving modern city of Cardiff, Buxton is a small, elegant, Georgian spa town perched high in the Pennines, which transforms itself every summer into a musical Mecca. The Festival attracts artists of international stature and I was thrilled to have the opportunity to work with Renato Capecchi, a legendary Italian buffo bass who was playing my father.

He was already in his seventies when he took this role, in English for the first time, but he took it in his stride. He was an absolute perfectionist and we rehearsed our scenes together, hour after hour. Renato taught me a great deal, especially about comic timing and the importance of giving other singers space. In rehearsals he would always wag his finger at me: 'Darleeng, you are too close. Go away, go away, go away. I 'ave to 'ave a metre, meeneemum, or I cannot create!'

Wexford in the autumn was as mellow and marvellous as I remembered it, and the company was a welcoming mixture of old friends and new acquaintances, many of whom, like Harry Nicholl, were to become friends. But I was unable to repeat my professional success of the previous season. *Zaide* is one of Mozart's earliest operas and no one could call it his best. I was hopelessly miscast in the title role, but to be honest the real problem was that I was inadequately prepared. I had only had a few weeks to work on the role and although I had mastered the words and notes with the help of the conductor, Nicholas Cleobury, and my German coach, Hilde Beale, there had been no time to assimilate the part properly. I didn't give my best to the role and it showed. Within the space of one short year, Wexford had given me the best reviews and the worst reviews of my life.

I had travelled the length and breadth of the country and played very different roles in a wide range of operas, learning more and more about my craft as the months went by. One thing remained constant, however, and that was the pleasure and satisfaction I derived not just from performing in opera but from being involved in the whole process of production from rehearsals to final-night party. Beyond the confines of the theatre, I enjoyed spending time with other members of the companies with whom I worked. I was part of a transient community which made me feel comfortable and valued and alive. But as the year passed I became increasingly and painfully aware that my new life was doing more than taking me away from Tring for months on end. It was taking me away from Malcolm. On the rare occasions that I went home I felt out of place and restless. When Malcolm came to stay with me for weekends, he seemed equally uncomfortable and ill at ease. The two halves of my life were just not fitting together any more.

When I came home from Ireland I was depressed by the impossibility of bridging the gulf that existed between my husband's world and mine. The only person in whom I confided was my old love and dear friend, Gerald.

Despite my confusion I was exhilarated by the prospect of my next challenge. Welsh National Opera had been in touch with me again, with an interesting offer. They were planning to stage Smetana's *The Bartered Bride* and the producer, an eccentric Eastern European called Rudolf Noelte, wanted the part of Esmerelda to be played by a real tightrope walker. What lunatic soprano could they possibly find who might be prepared to learn to walk the wire for this small but charming role? It seems I was the obvious choice and I was all for it.

For many weeks I made the laborious journey from Tring to Twickenham every day to work with the Larentys, a real-life Italian circus family. Mama and Papa Larenty and their daughter Brenda had set up a tightrope, two feet off the ground, in the garage of their house and they schooled me just as they would any novice. Papa Larenty was particularly strict and would whack my feet with his elegant cane if I failed to stretch them to his satisfaction. 'Ees like sausage, pah!' he would complain as, hour after hour, I struggled to keep my balance and edge my way from one end of the wire to the other. I loved every minute of it. By the end of the year I could not only walk the wire with ease, I could bounce up and down on it – even walk through hoops. At our last session, Papa Larenty did me the great honour of saying that if I ever wanted to give up singing he would be happy to take me into the circus. After the training sessions in the garage we would go upstairs for tea and they would enthral me with stories about their extraordinary family. All around the walls, and in the albums they proudly showed me, were mementoes of a bygone age. There was even a link with the life of opera: an invitation from King George for them to appear at a Royal Command Performance before the Second World War at the London Coliseum.

My tightrope training continued intermittently, but I still had weeks to wait before it was time to go back to Wales to transfer my skills to a higher wire and start work on the musical side of the part. I kicked my heels in Tring, thinking of nothing but how much I was looking forward to being back in Cardiff. As Christmas came and went I became more and more uncomfortable with the double life I seemed to be leading. I was being dishonest with

myself and dishonest with my husband. I was still acting as
if we had a future together but in my heart no such future
existed. Outwardly, I played the part of the Home Counties
housewife. Inwardly, I ticked off the days until I would be
back in the warm embrace of the Welsh National Opera.

I have always lived my life trusting and responding to
my instincts. Act first and think afterwards pretty well
describes my approach. There was still a fortnight to go
until rehearsals were due to start, but I knew many of my
friends were already in Cardiff and I longed to join them
and be back as part of their community again. A year ago
I had wanted only two things in life – to be married to
Malcolm and to sing opera. Twelve months on I faced
the uncomfortable truth that I could not have both. I
decided to go to Cardiff early. As we drove to the station,
Malcolm asked me when I would be back. I hesitated. 'I
don't know if I am coming back,' I replied. Malcolm asked
me if I was leaving him. 'I think so,' was the best answer I
could give.

By the time I reached Euston, the enormity of the step
I had taken had sunk in. By the time I reached Gerald's flat
I had begun to cry. I had telephoned Gerald from Tring
station and asked if he could put me up for the night.
He had asked no questions then and he didn't ask them
now. He just let me cry until I had no tears left and I
was at last able to tell him what I had done and how
wretched I felt about doing it. I spent a restless night
on the sofa and a restless day mooching around the flat,
wracked with guilt and indecision. I sat for hours gazing
listlessly out of the window, watching snowflakes falling

gently but persistently on the street below. As it got dark, Gerald asked matter-of-factly, 'What do you want to do?' I took a deep breath. 'I just want to go to Cardiff.'

Paddington station was only a short walk from his flat and Gerald took me there straight away, slithering and stumbling through the snow. The weather was obviously even worse in the West Country because the departures board read CANCELLED against practically every train. There was one last train to Cardiff, and I boarded it with trepidation. We inched our way out of the station and set off at a snail's pace. The train grew cold, battered by the blizzard as the miles crawled slowly by, and hour upon hour passed. The buffet ran out of food and irritation gave way to despair amongst the passengers. Despair turned to resignation, resignation to stoic acceptance and then, as midnight came and went we became friends. We swapped names, told jokes, had sing-songs. We even played charades. Ten hours after it left London, the train limped into a deserted Cardiff station at 5 in the morning.

If my friends at the Welsh National Opera were surprised by my sudden arrival two weeks early for rehearsals they didn't show it. They were pleased to see me back and welcomed me into the company again. I now had to put my tightrope skills into practice on a wire six rather than two feet from the ground. Six feet is a lot higher than it sounds, especially when you are balanced precariously on a half-inch steel rope, with nothing between you and the stage; even more so when the tightrope is moved to the front of the stage and you are perilously close to the orchestra pit. My dear friend Harry Nicholl was playing

Vashek, and playing him so well that I sincerely believe that his is, to this day, the definitive interpretation of the role. We developed a strategy in the event of my falling off the wire (I did, twice) which involved him doing some elaborate acting, commiserating with me and vigorously rubbing my legs. *The Bartered Bride* opened in February to enthusiastic reviews and ran for the whole of March.

I was in an extraordinary, half demented, state of mind. I was exhilarated by the freedom of having broken away from my life in Tring. I was independent, professionally successful and financially secure. At the same time I was tortured by guilt for walking out on my marriage. I spent a lot of my spare time with John Metcalfe and his artist wife Gilly, who lived with their young children in a cottage in St Donats, and with John Eaton, to whom I became increasingly close. They led a wonderfully rich, bohemian life and I drew comfort from them and the artistic community within which they lived.

Then, through the spring, we took the production on tour. At the end of April we ended up in London, at the Dominion Theatre in Tottenham Court Road. We were well received, though one particular review, from William Mann, said: '. . . a wonderfully spirited performance by Lesley Garrett . . . and an unnamed wire-walker. The quick change was so slick you would never have known it wasn't Miss Garrett the whole time.' I was furious!

Sadly, too soon, it was time to leave Cardiff. My next job took me back to Yorkshire where I played Sophie in Massenet's *Werther* for the newly formed Opera North in Leeds. To save money, I lived with my parents seventy-five miles away, but this did nothing to cheer me up, as the atmosphere at Red House was now painfully strained. Jill had been married in 1979 and Kay in 1981 and the house, which had always felt too big and cold, was enveloped in a suffocating silence. My parents no longer seemed to function as a couple at all. Somewhere along the line, amongst all the years of caring for their children and for their ageing parents, maintaining a house and two careers, they had simply lost each other. Mum and Dad made every effort to avoid being in the house at the same time and when they failed they barely spoke. They were sympathetic to my distress over Malcolm but, though they loved me dearly, they could not hide their disappointment over my leaving him.

The fact that Red House felt even less like home than before highlighted the fact that I no longer had a home of my own. It was June and I had been adrift and rootless, literally living out of one suitcase since January. I felt I needed to get back to London, not least because my singing teacher, Joy Mammen, was there. I depended on her not just for regular singing lessons but as a wise friend and confidante. But I was tired of imposing on friends for a bed for the night whenever I came to London.

Through the summer and autumn I shuttled back and forth from London to Leeds where I was rehearsing for the part of Susanna in *The Marriage of Figaro*. The role of Susanna meant so much to me. This was the role that Christopher Renshaw had said I was born to play. It seemed such a long time ago. My Figaro was the gifted baritone Bill Shimmell. He was darkly handsome and sensitive, with a simply beautiful voice, and the attraction between us, both on and off the stage, was instant and irresistible. Bill gave me the strength to try to get a grip on my life.

I began looking for a flat of my own in London to buy. I traipsed round dozens of properties, most of them unsuitable, many of them unaffordable, some of them downright unpleasant until I found a one-bedroomed ground-floor flat in Brondesbury Road in Kilburn which seemed perfect. But before my offer on the flat could be considered, I found myself in hospital.

I had been suffering from a series of minor illnesses – headaches, urinary tract infections, stomach aches – all of which I put down to stress and managed to ignore. By the time *Figaro* went on tour, however, I knew I was in real trouble. The stomach pains were getting worse and there was a dull ache in my back that never went away. Worse still, my voice was starting to let me down. My throat was constantly sore and singing was increasingly difficult. Physically weak and emotionally drained, despite Bill's tenderness, I ploughed on as we took *Figaro* to Nottingham, Manchester and Halifax.

One dark wet Thursday in Hull, I was passed word that Lord Harewood would be in the audience that night. ENO had promised to keep an eye on me after *Count Ory*, but I had never expected that the managing director of the company would be talent-spotting himself. How could I possibly impress him in the pathetic state I was in? I took a drastic decision. Susanna isn't a big sing, but it is a long one. I had been pacing myself in the role to stretch my dwindling energy over the whole four acts. Tonight

I would give it my all from the very beginning and pray that I could find some extra strength to make it through to the end. The first two acts went well but by the interval I was on my knees, my throat was like sandpaper and I felt feverish and dizzy. For the rest of the opera I went through the motions, but I fluffed entrances and sang flat. At the end of the performance, my applause was lukewarm and rightly so. I sat in my dressing-room and wept. I had blown it. There was a knock at the door and the company manager came in with a message for me. Lord Harewood sent his apologies but he would not be able to come and say hello. He had another engagement that evening and had had to leave at the interval. My prayers had been answered and just a few days later I was offered the part of Clorinda in *La Cenerentola* at the London Coliseum the following spring.

The offer raised my spirits at last but my body was another matter. On the last night of the tour, the pain in my stomach became agonising. By some miracle I made it through to the final curtain and drove home to my parents. The next morning my father took me straight to the doctor. He examined me then asked, 'Is there someone here with you? Do you have transport?' 'My dad's here, why? What's the matter with me?' 'You need to be in hospital *now*. Either your father takes you or we call an ambulance.' We drove straight to Doncaster Royal Infirmary where I was poked and prodded and underwent a battery of tests. They knew immediately that I had a kidney infection and gave me massive doses of antibiotics. But there was something else going on and it wasn't appendicitis, as my GP had feared. Various doctors scratched their heads over

me for a day or so, organised further tests on my kidneys
and came up with the imprecise but devastating diagnosis
that there was a mass next to my appendix. A mass sounded
like very bad news indeed. It was obviously a euphemism
for something, but what? No one was prepared to commit
themselves. I would have to wait for the results of more
tests. I was discharged from hospital still very weak, and
terribly afraid of what might be the matter with me.

Back home, at Red House, I felt empty and spent
and lost. Mum and Dad cared for me, worried not just
about this illness but about the stress I was under and the
depression caused by my nomadic state. A week later I
went back to the hospital, expecting to hear the worst.

'Miss Garrett,' said the doctor, holding up one of the
X-rays they had taken, 'you seem to have a mass here.'
He pointed at a shadow lurking ominously amongst my
insides. 'It is what we call a pelvic kidney,' he continued.
'This little fellow here ought to be nine inches further
up, with the other one. Instead it is squashed up between
your uterus and your appendix. Worse still, it has obviously
been infected for years. It's wizened and small, but it is still
working – just. We can only treat the infection and hope
for the best.'

The word 'uterus' sounded warning bells. 'What about
children?' I asked. 'Will I be able to have children?'

'I'm no expert, of course . . .' He stared at a corner of
his desk which had become suddenly fascinating. '. . . but
shall we say that could be difficult.'

I thought I had already hit rock bottom, but nothing had
prepared me for this blow. Like any young woman with a

busy career I had no immediate desire for a baby. But to be told, out of the blue, that I might never be a mother was completely devastating. It was nearly Christmas and 1983 was looming. I had no home, no husband and now no prospect of children. What did I have left? There was a simple answer. I had my work.

I was due to start work at ENO at the end of January, and my ailing voice had had a good rest, so it was about time I started singing again. Alone in my room at Red House I opened my mouth to sing, but all I could produce was a hoarse croak. I tried again, but there was nothing there. Just as a wounded soldier feels no immediate pain, I did not panic – the shock was too great for that. The only thought in my head was to seek Joy's help and I took the next train to London. Joy obviously thought I was exaggerating when I told her that I could not sing. 'Let's see what you can do,' she said, smiling encouragingly. As soon as I opened my mouth it was clear to Joy that I was right – something terrible had happened. I could sing only two notes. I cried then and nothing Joy could say or do could stop me. Joy was upset too, but she wasn't going to let me dissolve into self-pity. She declared without hesitation that my voice would return – she would rebuild it. Whatever it took, however long it took, I would sing again and she would help me.

Chapter 7

———◆———

Dark Days

Joy's first step was to take me to Harley Street to see
a Mr Alexander, an eminent Viennese laryngologist who
knew everything there was to know about singers and their
problems. He looked down my throat and pronounced it
completely fit. 'There is no problem with this voice,' he
declared. 'Just suck one of these.' He handed me a box
of his famous creosote lozenges. They had no noticeable
effect, other than making me smell like a freshly painted
fence. I suspect Joy knew what he would say. But to
her this was a necessary starting point on my road to
recovery. If there was nothing physically wrong then it
must be possible somehow to reclaim my voice. I was less
optimistic. I had lost my ability to sing but I had also lost
all memory of what it felt like to sing. For me singing had
been like walking, running, blinking or breathing. It had
been entirely automatic and instinctive. What I had lost was
not just my muscular memory of singing but my emotional

memory of it too. Singing is ninety-nine per cent vision. You visualise music, almost like a colour, and sing towards it. It was as if I had been blinded.

Joy knew that before she could start working on my voice, I had to have somewhere to live. I contacted the estate agents I had used the previous year and discovered, to my great surprise and delight, that the flat in Brondesbury Road was still on the market and my previous offer was once again accepted. I saw it as an omen that maybe, just maybe, my luck was going to change and I used the last of my savings to put down a deposit.

Joy outlined her strategy to me. If I could sing two notes then I could learn to sing three. Three would become four, four become five and so on. We would build up my voice note by note. At the back of her mind, she still held out hope that my voice would return as dramatically as it left and so we also started to work on Clorinda with her doing all the singing while I tried to learn the role in my head.

I moved into the flat in January 1983 after nearly a year of homelessness. Everything I owned was contained in the battered suitcase that I had been carrying around the country for the last twelve months and I couldn't even unpack that because I didn't have a stick of furniture to my name. I spent the first night in my new home sleeping on a blow-up lilo. Between them, Gerald and Joy persuaded me that I had to reclaim some of my possessions that I had left in the cottage in Tring. I really didn't want to go back but I was penniless and had to accept there was no other choice. Gerald acted as go-between and explained the situation to Malcolm, who

put up no objection. It was very strange, letting myself
into the cottage one last time. Everything looked just as
I had left it and I felt like a burglar, walking from room
to room collecting clothes and books. I left my records, as
I had nothing on which to play them. Finally Gerald and I
loaded the sitting room sofa-bed and the cooker on to the
van he had borrowed. Malcolm had agreed to me having
them, but I hated having to do it. The house looked empty
and spoiled as I left it for the last time and quietly locked
the door.

As Joy had promised, I had progressed from two notes
to three, but three notes weren't going to get me very far
with *La Cenerentola* so I was forced to cancel, only a few
weeks before rehearsals were due to start. With no work
in prospect and a mortgage to pay, I threw myself on the
mercies of the Social Security and claimed sickness benefit
for the only time in my life, which covered my interest
payments and gave me a small amount to live on. It felt
like being a student again. My flat continued to be a source
of pleasure and comfort. I had time to kill for the first time
in years and I used it to turn the place into a home. I had
been brought up surrounded by non-stop DIY so I had no
trouble putting up shelves, making curtains from remnants
of fabric I bought in the market and hanging wallpaper. I
scoured local junk shops for treasures and bought bits of old
plywood furniture which I painted and made my own.

I had only been in the flat a few weeks when Mum rang
and told me she was coming to visit and bringing me a
flat-warming present. At last, I thought, some saucepans
or maybe even a toaster. She arrived and I stared greedily

at the large bag she was carrying. 'Have a look,' she said. I opened the bag and peered in. Two huge, round, blue eyes stared back at me. I reached in and found the eyes belonged to a tiny ginger kitten, barely six weeks old. Yet again, my mother had understood what I really needed. Kitchen utensils were all very well, but what this flat needed most, what I needed most, was someone to share it with. I christened my blue-eyed friend Frank and he became my constant companion. Wherever I went, he went. 'Have Litter Tray Will Travel' became our motto.

Friends, too, were kind and did their best to cheer me up. I had letters and phone calls from people I hadn't seen in years. Some offered me advice, most just wanted me to know they were thinking of me. Jane Robinson, who had been a friend, confidante and occasional music coach since National Opera Studio days took a firmer line with me than some. She thought I was wallowing in my own misery and wasn't afraid to say so. I heard my mother's words echoing in my ear. It was time to spit on my hands and take another fresh hold. Gerald encouraged me to learn to play squash and I became quite keen for a while. I am not really built for squash, though, and gave it up when I finally got tired of my racquet colliding with my 34 DD cup every time I reached for a ball to play a cross shot. One night I insisted that Joy come with me to the Coliseum to see *La Cenerentola*. It was a big mistake and I had to leave at the interval. What had upset me most was not the sight of the place, or the sound of the music, but the smell of the building, which hit me the minute I walked into the auditorium. It was a heavy smell, almost impossible to describe – of dust, greasepaint and drama. It was the smell of a world from which I felt I had been exiled, possibly for ever.

My greatest ally in these dark days was to be found, quite literally, next door. My flat was 93a and at 93b lived Joan Batten. She too lived alone and had recently been made redundant but was, like me, determined not to be defeated. We became firm friends and buoyed each other up. We might be clinging to the wreckage of our lives but together we were unsinkable. We spent hours together, talking, laughing, helping each other with the laborious process of making a new home on next to no money. At the end of the week when neither of us had a penny to our name and practically no food in the house, we used to raid our fridges and combine the sad remnants we found there – a bit of cheese, a limp stick of celery, maybe an apple – to produce a meal which we told ourselves was fit for kings.

One evening I went to have supper with Roger Steptoe, whom I had met when I appeared in his *King of Macedon* when I was a student, and his librettist and friend, Ursula Vaughan Williams. I told them all about my troubles and how I was working to try to rebuild my voice.

'My dear!' cried Ursula. 'You *must* get in touch with the Musicians' Benevolent Fund. This is *just* the kind of situation they like to help with.'

I had never considered asking a charity for help, but Ursula and Roger were so insistent that I took a deep breath and wrote them a letter. They sent me to see their doctor at his rooms in Wimpole Street. Dr Hudson listened patiently

as I told him my story. He said very little, he just let me
ramble on and then, when I was finally done, he declared
that my problems had to be tackled on three levels. Firstly,
we had to get my kidney sorted out. I was still in a lot of
pain and he wanted me to see a surgeon about having it
finally removed. Secondly, he sensed that I had lost my
emotional balance. For that, he recommended classes in
the Alexander Technique, which I had heard about and
was keen to try – it certainly sounded less daunting than
surgery. Lastly, he wanted me to have psychotherapy. He
was of the opinion that the reason I had lost my voice
was that I felt so guilty about leaving Malcolm that I was
punishing myself by taking away the reason I had left him.
There was no denying that what he said made sense but I
was very resistant to the idea of psychotherapy. The other
two suggestions were practical but the thought of sitting in
a room with a stranger talking about myself for hours on
end sounded self-indulgent and sat uncomfortably with my
practical, northern background. Dr Hudson was firm with
me. 'It's all three things or nothing. Take it as a package
or leave it.'

Although Dr Hudson had thought my kidney might
need to be removed, the surgeon I went to see disagreed.
After more tests he decided that, whatever the medical pros
and cons, I wasn't ready to give up my kidney quite yet and
sent me to a clinical nephrologist colleague of his, to see
if its function could be improved. Dr William Cattel at St
Bartholomew's Hospital was pioneering a new treatment
called long-term, low-dose antibiotic therapy and he agreed
to try it on me. I took one tiny dose every day, large

enough to keep infection at bay, but small enough to enable my own defence mechanism to re-establish itself. I was pain-free for the first time in years.

After suffering years of chronic laryngitis, the actor Frederick Matthias Alexander devised the technique which bears his name. In trying to discover the cause of his affliction, he developed a method of freeing the larynx by aligning the head, neck and spine to facilitate effective vocal production. The Alexander Institute in London was run by people who had worked with Alexander himself and it was here that Dr Hudson sent me. I had regular sessions with Inge Henderson and I began to regain my sense of physical and emotional equilibrium.

My psychotherapist, Sheila, practised in Knightsbridge and I went to see her, reluctantly and sceptically at first, twice a week. It proved to be the most useful of all my treatments. She was surprisingly down to earth and talked a great deal more sense than I had expected. With her help I was able to deal with the corrosive guilt I felt at the breakdown of my marriage, to confront it face to face, learn from it and try to come to terms with it. She told me one day that I had fallen off Life's bike and I needed to get back on it again. What is more, I had to learn to pedal the bike with the wheels both going in the same direction at the same speed. I enjoyed the analogy, but it was easier said than done.

Joy continued to give me singing lessons for nothing. I thought I had received enough charity for one lifetime so I insisted on repaying her and cleaned her house in return. We had lessons every day and her gentle, unhurried approach was paying off. Just as she had predicted, my voice was coming back, sometimes a semi-tone a week, sometimes less. When I reached an octave I began to believe Joy's promise – I would get back on the stage.

One morning in June I bumped into Adam Pollock. 'I hear you've been having a rotten time,' he said.

I was surprised that he even spoke to me after I had let him down badly two years before. But he seemed to have forgiven me because he greeted me very warmly. I started to tell him what had been happening to me.

'Sounds to me like you need a break somewhere warm,' he said. Too right, I thought. 'Why don't you come back to Batignano for the summer?'

'It's no good, Adam, don't you understand, I can't sing.'

'Come anyway,' he replied, 'you can help with the washing up.'

Now *that* was one thing I could do, so I scraped together enough money for a bucket-shop ticket to Rome and set off towards the sun.

It felt marvellous to be off on another adventure, free and independent, just me and my suitcase and a timetable. From Rome I caught a train to Grosseto and then a bus to Batignano and then I walked through the glorious Tuscan countryside until I arrived, dusty and tired, at the Monastery of Santa Croce. Adam welcomed me with open arms and immediately promoted me from Head of Washing Up to Assistant Cook. The Head Cook was an Australian actor friend of Adam's and the two of us set about catering for thirty people, three times a day. It was the most perfect therapy. Cooking is, above all else, a caring, nurturing activity and by nurturing others I was healing myself. Patricia Rozario, a friend from the National Opera Studio was there with her new-born baby and, to this day, I carry an image in my mind of me, at the head of a long refectory table, dandling the baby on my left hip and doling out pasta from a huge, steaming bowl with a large fork in my right hand.

Every morning at dawn I went down into the walled garden and collected herbs to brew a huge vat of iced herb tea for the cast to dip into during the day. Then Adam, the cook and I would go into town to the market to buy vegetables, or down to the quay to buy fish straight off the boats. During rehearsals, the kitchen became the focal point of the whole community and singers drifted in and out when they had nothing else to do and chatted while they helped chop the vegetables for lunch. Sometimes they would sing, too, and once, when the right number of the right voices happened to be in the room at the same time, they sang the finale of Act II of *The Marriage of Figaro*. In the warm, relaxed surroundings of that kitchen, I realised that I too could sing and I joined in, singing properly for the first time in six months. Adam, whose study was next to the kitchen, emerged in fits of laughter. He had been on the phone to Rome's most influential opera critic, struggling vainly to persuade him to come and see our production of *The Turn of the Screw*. He had been lukewarm about the idea until he heard the sound of singing in the background.

'Is that rehearsals going on?' he asked.

'Oh no,' replied Adam, 'that's just the kitchen staff.'

The critic came to see *The Turn of the Screw* after all and gave it a rave review.

I came home bronzed and happy. All I needed now was to get back to work, but there were still no offers coming my way and I faced spending the rest of the summer kicking my heels in London. Joy was spending a couple of weeks teaching on a singing course at Stowe School and she invited me, at the last minute, to go with her. 'What would I do there?' I protested. 'I don't know how to teach and I don't suppose they need a cook or a cleaner.' 'Just come anyway. You could always do some movement classes,' she suggested. The course was very popular and when we arrived every single bed in the place was taken, so I spent the fortnight sleeping on the sick-bay examination couch under a thin, scratchy blanket. I had never taught before but I had a whale of a time pretending to be my old movement coach, Anna Sweeny, teaching exercise and improvisation to a group of rather surprised but enthusiastic amateur singers.

I had only been home for a few days when I had a phone call from Brian McMaster at the Welsh National Opera. They were reviving *The Bartered Bride* and needed a tightrope-walking soprano again. Could I please come and do it as they had neither the time nor the money to train somebody else? I was not at all sure if I was ready for work yet, but I discussed it with Joy. As far as she was concerned there was absolutely nothing wrong with my voice any more. What I needed now was confidence and this was the perfect opportunity to get that back. It was not a big part, or a vocally difficult one and, as to the wire-walking, it would be a great boost – a chance to test and show off my newly regained balance. I went back to the Larentys and threw myself into the task of brushing up my old skill. It was hard at first, but one thing the last year had taught me was the value of patience. As I reported excitedly to Joy after the first week of training: 'Of course I fell off to begin with. But at least I know how to fall correctly.'

The Welsh National Opera was not the only company to remember me. Despite my letting them down when I became ill earlier in the year ENO had not forgotten me either. Just before I set off for Cardiff, they rang me up and invited me for an audition, not just for a part but for a proper job – a contract as Principal Soprano. It was like a dream come true. No more waiting for the phone to ring with offers of work heaven knows where. No more wondering where the next month's mortgage payment was coming from. This was the operatic equivalent of a day job, with a regular monthly salary coming in. And more than just a job, this was an opportunity to join a family. It meant being able to play a wide variety of roles, and understudy even more. It meant having access to wonderful coaching, working with the best conductors and producers. ENO had a reputation for giving opportunities to young singers but it did a great deal more than that. It developed them and took care of them.

The auditorium of the Coliseum was dark and echoing that autumn afternoon. I have never had much of a problem with stage fright and auditions were something I normally took in my stride. This time it was very, very different. The fearless self-assurance of youth was long gone. The fragile confidence I had regained was a more mature variety, founded on an awareness of life's pitfalls and the beginnings of a belief in my ability to overcome them. I knew I was incredibly lucky to have been offered a second chance with this company. If I blew it this time I would never be asked back.

I had done everything I could to prepare. My voice was in better shape than it had been for months and I had spent hours getting ready. I'd done my hair, painted my nails and put on my lucky audition frock and shiny black high heels. The stage was set for the evening performance. It was steeply raked and had a grooved floor. I could feel my knees shaking as I walked out into this space. I offered up a silent prayer, held my head up high and took a deep breath as I crossed to where the accompanist sat patiently at the piano. Suddenly, my heel caught in a crack, I tripped and fell head first towards the front edge of the stage, landing in a heap a few feet away from where Lord Harewood and his colleagues were. The deafening silence was broken by a nervous giggle, which grew into a peal of laughter. I realised, to my surprise, that it was me who was laughing. The panel joined in and after assuring them that I had broken no bones, I began the audition. My nerves had evaporated and I sang Lazuli's first aria from *L'Etoile* better than I have ever sung it before or since.

I could tell that they were happy with my singing, but the audition didn't end there. There were still doubts about my physical fitness and my stamina, so they asked if I would be prepared to take the small part of the pot-boy in their forthcoming production of *The Adventures of Mr Broucek* for which rehearsals were about to start. Of course I was only too happy to agree. I longed to be back on the stage at the Coliseum again and was excited at the prospect of working with the legendary Sir Charles Mackerras who was conducting the opera. *Mr Broucek* is an extravagant, fantastical piece, full of action and theatrical fireworks. My role involved little more than perching on fifteen-foot-high scaffolding at the back of the stage with a rope of sausages draped around my neck shouting 'sausages, sausages' at frequent and appropriate intervals. This proved more difficult than I had thought. All went well until the first stage rehearsal with the orchestra. I made my first entrance, sausages twirling, only to find that Sir Charles had stopped conducting.

'Your sausages are late, dear. On the stick, on the stick,' he barked.

'What's he on about?' I hissed to Philip Turner (a wonderful stage manager who has rescued me on many more occasions since) in the wings.

'Anticipate his beat a bit, love. Don't listen, just watch his stick.'

What I had to learn, and learn very quickly, was that if I sang with what I could hear the orchestra playing I would be woefully late with my 'sausage entry'. I knew I only had one more chance before the great man became really cross. The standards of musicianship he expects from his performers are quite rightly very high. I tried again: it felt wrong, but apparently sounded right, and was a very important lesson to learn, especially singing on the huge stage at the Coliseum. By the end of the run, Sir Charles

147

seemed happy with my sausage-selling abilities and Jeremy Caulton, ENO's Head of Opera Planning, called me into his office and offered me the principal's contract I had been longing for.

'I'm going to sing here for ever!' I declared, delirious with relief and joy. 'I'll never leave.'

During the run of *Mr Broucek*, Martin Isepp had come to see the production. Martin was a legend, an outstanding accompanist and vocal coach who was not only very involved in the National Opera Studio, but was also Head of Music at Glyndebourne. After the performance he came backstage to say how pleased he was to see me well again. 'How would you feel if there was some work for you at Glyndebourne?' I auditioned in London and was astonished when I was offered a role not just in the Touring Company, but also for the summer season itself. I accepted at once, and Ibbs & Tillett went to work negotiating my contracts with both the ENO and Glyndebourne.

At last everything seemed to be working in my favour. But once again, I was brought down to earth with a bump. Before they could even start negotiations on my contract, the firm of Ibbs & Tillett who had been my agents since my student days, reviewed their artists list. They were a big agency with hundreds of singers on their books, dozens of them sopranos. On the first of April many of us were dumped on the market. I had to find a new agent and quickly but I was confident that with my offer of an ENO contract in my pocket, I would have agencies falling over themselves to sign me up. I started ringing round and quickly found that I had been wrong. Far from queuing up for me, all the agencies had plenty of sopranos on their books already and didn't feel they could cope with another one. I tried hard not to panic, but the situation was becoming desperate. I had come so near, but without an agent there would be no one to negotiate my contract. I was rescued by Robert Slotover of Allied Artists who was not just willing, but delighted to take me on. Robert was urbane, charming and cosmopolitan. He loved all classical music, especially opera, but his great passion, somewhat surprisingly considering his musically traditional background, was for modern, contemporary work.

Soon after I signed up with Allied Artists, Robert asked me to do him a favour. His good friend Sir Hugh Fraser had recently died. Would I be prepared to sing at his memorial service in Westminster Cathedral? I was pleased to have the chance to say thank you for his kindness in taking me on and readily agreed. I sang 'I Know That My Redeemer Liveth' from Handel's *Messiah* and from my vantage point high up next to the organ loft I surveyed the vast congregation of the great and good in the pews below me. Almost the entire Cabinet was there as well as a large contingent from the world of literature and the arts. When I finished the aria, I climbed down the narrow wooden stairs and was met at the bottom by Cardinal Basil Hume who complimented me and thanked me for my singing. We only said a few words but he made a life-long impression on me. He was tall and imposing and his holiness shone like a light around him. As he took my hand I felt as if I too had been touched by the light: this man was closer to God than anyone I had ever met.

On the minibus which drove me from Lewes station to Glyndebourne, I found myself sitting next to a charmingly scruffy young man who introduced himself as Hector Christie, grandson of the founder. He gave me a potted history of the house and the festival for which I was extremely grateful as I had never been there before and was rather daunted by the place and its traditions. That year, 1984, was the fiftieth anniversary of the first opera season staged by John Christie in what was then his private opera house in the grounds of his family home nestling in a hollow of the Sussex Downs. The Christie family still lives in the house and is as involved as ever in the running of this most prestigious and eccentrically British operatic festival. Hector admitted that it had been a little strange growing up at Glyndebourne and told me how, as a small child, he had been playing at a friend's house when it began to rain. His friend's mother called them to come inside, to which Hector replied, 'Can't we go and play in your opera house?'

The production in which I was to sing, Monteverdi's *L'Incoronazione di Poppea* was produced by Peter Hall and conducted by Raymond Leppard and I was in awe of them both. The scheming and seductive Poppea herself was played by the luminescent Maria Ewing and I was Damigella, her saucy young servant. Anne-Marie Owens, another new girl, who was also joining the ENO, played Arnalta, Poppea's old nurse, and she and I (and Frank the cat, of course) shared a little cottage in the nearby village.

Poppea is a powerful tale of passion and murder, jealousy and intrigue; as so often happens in opera, sex and politics collide with dramatic results. There were unscripted dramas too, including one incident which could have put to an end my revived career, once and for all. There was a point in the production when Poppea takes a bath. The bath was revealed to the audience by sliding open a section of the stage floor, which was replaced and bolted firmly at the end of the scene. One night the bolts were not re-secured, and as I crossed the stage it gradually gave way and I sank slowly into the bath. By some miracle I managed to catch hold of the edge of the opening and I hauled myself up, still singing, back on to the safety of the stage, amid much mirth from the audience.

Despite the obvious delights of singing at Glyndebourne – the quality of the musicians, the exceptional coaching facilities, the chance to work with the greatest international artists, not to mention the staggeringly beautiful surroundings – it poses a technical challenge. The extended dinner interval provides the unique vision of hundreds of prosperous ladies and gentlemen picnicking in full evening dress while sitting on rugs spread out over the lawn. It is a charmingly eccentric sight and an integral part of the Glyndebourne experience, but it is less than ideal for the singers. To sing a long opera (and most operas are long) you have to pace yourself, like a runner paces a marathon or a bowler paces his innings. Simple things like what and when you eat have to be geared to the physical demands of the performance. By the end of the first half, your voice and body are very warm and the adrenaline is pumping through your veins. The last thing your body wants is to stop and lounge around a Green Room for an hour and a half before you can carry on. Everybody has their own way of coping with the enforced lay-off and sometimes we would sing a little just to keep our voices oiled.

One particularly hot afternoon, Anne-Marie and I decided it was time for a proper sing-song. We threw open all the windows, briefed the pianist and the cast and chorus gave a show-stopping rendition of 'Bless This House' in perfect four-part harmony. As we hit the final, climactic note (what Michael Ball calls the 'money note'), the usual clattering and clinking from the gardens was stilled and champagne glasses hovered beneath open mouths. The picnickers took our subversiveness in good part and gave us a hearty round of applause. There were even calls for an encore which I would have been happy to provide – I would have liked to do 'On Ilkley Moor Baht 'At' for them – but I was outvoted and we decided to quit while we were ahead.

Mum came down with Joy for the opening night. The situation at home was really bad at the time and I could see that she was only just holding herself together. She was ill as well, her blood pressure was through the roof and she had lost huge amounts of weight. And yet she was determined to make the most of the unique experience that Glyndebourne offers. She had treated herself to a new evening dress, had a new perm, and to see her there, tired and drawn and thin, but still managing to look glamorous, made me realise, certainly not for the first time, how very, very much I loved her.

Chapter 8

———◆———

Goin' Home

The London Coliseum is situated at the bottom of St Martin's Lane, just a hundred yards, as the pigeon flies, from Trafalgar Square. It was built in 1904 as a music hall and from the outside looks very much like one still, right down to the giant, illuminated silver ball perched high on the roof. Inside all is gilt and plush, mirrors and polished wood. At least, that is what the patrons see. Backstage it is a very different story. Entering the Coliseum via the stage door you pass into a rabbit-warren of narrow dimly lit passages and winding staircases, poky little dressing-rooms with peeling paint and chipped washbasins. In surroundings of near-Dickensian squalor, the grand illusion that is opera takes shape.

In one little cubby-hole, filled with disembodied poly-styrene heads, you will find Eddie Fergusson, the wig magician. Eddie can transform you into a flaxen-headed maiden or a grizzled old woman or anything you might

153

dream of being, just with one of his wigs, while all the time making you roar with laughter with his outrageously camp sense of humour. My Nanan met Eddie once, when she came down to London with my father to see me in *Figaro*. They took an instant liking to each other and chatted together like old friends in my dressing-room before the show. She could not stop talking about him as Dad drove her home the next day and even ventured the opinion that Eddie might be a homosexual. Dad was so shocked by this remark that he nearly crashed the car. He didn't know his mother even knew what the word meant. (Actually, she hadn't until a few weeks before when she had asked me to explain it to her.)

The principal wardrobe department was presided over by the warm, colourful figure of Jean Prentice, known to all as Auntie Jean. In my time at ENO she looked after all the costumes I wore, some of them glamorous, flouncy period pieces like the huge yellow confection I wore as Belle Vivette, others modern and minimal like my black PVC mini-skirt for *The Rise and Fall of the City of Mahagonny*. For *The Cunning Little Vixen* I was transformed into a nineteen-twenties 'flapper' fox, with the wonderful designs by Marida Bjornsen. To help me into these costumes, some of which were more like engineering than clothing, there was Ania, my trusty dresser, parking-meter feeder, bringer of tea, style guru and friend.

I was enormously lucky to be working at the English National Opera at all, but to be there in the mid-1980s was a particular privilege. Lord Harewood had brought together an exceptional array of talent, all of them gifted individuals in their own right, but collectively they formed a magically creative team. Mark Elder, the Music Director, and David Pountney, Director of Productions, were already a formidable partnership. When they were joined by Peter Jonas as Managing Director, something extraordinary happened. He was the final fuel rod placed in a nuclear reactor, the catalyst for a fusion of dynamic creativity that took the arts world by storm. The regime became known as the Powerhouse and with good reason. The whole place sparked and crackled with energy and excitement. The Coliseum became *the* place to be for audiences, directors and performers alike.

Opera had always been seen as being as grand and stately, as imposing and majestic (and, it must be said, old-fashioned) as the houses in which it was so often performed. ENO tried to challenge this image and succeeded. Opera became exciting, sexy, and dangerous. At the time, the work being done at ENO was viewed by many as revolutionary but this wasn't a revolution, it was a renaissance. We felt we were returning opera to its rightful place in popular culture. Opera is not an intellectual affair. When it works well it goes for the guts, not the head, playing on people's strongest feelings. Everybody from the stage hands to the chairman shared the vision, and I felt incredibly lucky and comfortable to be part of an institution that was so democratic. But I still had an enormous amount to learn.

My first official engagement as a salaried member of the company couldn't have been further from Glyndebourne – it was in the unlikely surroundings of Wormwood Scrubs

Prison. I am not quite sure why I was asked to do this particular job – a series of Christmas concerts in London prisons which also included Pentonville and Holloway – though it probably had something to do with me being the new girl. The one hundred or so prisoners and their guards were an unusual audience but an appreciative one. I wanted to give them something light, so I sang a medley from *My Fair Lady* which went down well until I got to 'Wouldn't It Be Loverly', which included the line: 'Someone's head resting on my knee, warm and tender as he can be'. To my embarrassment, there were calls of 'Over 'ere love – I'll give you warm and tender', 'Form a queue lads!' and a few other rather more direct suggestions. The warders were getting very twittery just as George Melly, who was next on the bill, came to my rescue. He immediately began his programme of up-tempo songs with broad and innuendo-ridden lyrics, accompanied by much nodding and winking which soon had them stamping their feet and enjoying themselves, and the warders could relax again.

I was to be eased in gently to the company and my first job was to understudy Norma Burrowes, who was taking the second soprano role of Atalanta in Handel's *Xerxes*. I admired Norma enormously and to be her understudy was a great honour. Sir Charles Mackerras was conducting and the producer was Nicholas Hytner a young man who was relatively new on the opera scene but who was already making a name for himself. I began the process of learning the role – reading the score, listening to recordings of previous performances and, most crucially, trying to get under the skin of the character. Atalanta is in many respects a typical Handel second soprano role, a flirtatious, coquettish younger sister, and great fun to play.

With only a few weeks to go before rehearsals for *Xerxes* began, Norma was forced, through tragic illness, to withdraw. After urgent consultations between Jeremy Caulton and Sir Charles Mackerras, it was agreed that I should be promoted from sausage boy and understudy to take over the role. It was a heavy responsibility, making my debut as a principal soprano in such an important role on what is, literally, the largest theatre stage in the country, but I was fortunate to have such seasoned professionals as Ann Murray and Valerie Masterson on my side. Along with the whole cast, they were supportive and helpful and treated me with the kind of professional generosity which was typical of the Coliseum and which I have never ceased to experience and be grateful for over the years.

It was a wonderfully witty and clever production. The original classical setting had been shifted in time and place from ancient Persia to London's Vauxhall Gardens. There are purists who object to opera being updated from its original setting, just as there are those who hate to hear opera in anything but the language it was written in. I disagree entirely with them. My fundamental belief is that opera works best if it communicates immediately with the audience of the day; in ENO's case this means communicating in English, and using whatever production techniques convey the drama most powerfully. Just as great music is utterly timeless, so are the emotions that opera dramatises. Anger, desire, guilt, grief and joy are passions that transcend barriers of time. The themes of operas written centuries ago are just as relevant today. What could be more contemporary than love, revenge, betrayal and greed?

My next role was very different and even more of a challenge. As a tribute to Sir Michael Tippett on his eightieth birthday, we staged a new production by David Pountney of Sir Michael's *A Midsummer Marriage*. I was to play the part of Bella opposite Maldwyn Davies as Jack. I found myself wearing a blonde wig for the first time and a saucy little costume of pink polka dot shirt, green mini-skirt and fish-net tights. Despite the tights, she wasn't really a tarty character. She reminded me of Marilyn Monroe – incredibly sexy without really knowing it, and very vulnerable. The work is an intriguing allegory of Sir Michael's feelings about post-war Britain. The score is complex and intricate and David wanted to match it with an equally complex production. Some of our audience and, for that matter, some critics, found the production just too much to take in one sitting; to an extent they were probably right. Although opera should be instantly appealing, at the same time all opera has extraordinary depths, and it is possible to see one work twenty times and get something new out of it, to encounter something fresh, on every occasion. For a lot of people, the problem with *Midsummer Marriage* is that they would have needed to see it twenty times just to understand it properly.

Most of the critics readily admitted that they were confused by what was going on. But Uncle Colin wasn't confused. He understood it perfectly. At the time Uncle Colin was a spot welder in Scunthorpe, like his father before him, but that was just what he did for a living – how he fed and clothed his children and put a roof over their heads. His real life was driven by two great passions – natural history and music. He played guitar and saxophone and piano and wanted to go to every concert he could, but modern jazz was his particular love. On top of this he was a keen ornithologist – not just an enthusiast but an authority on birds. He used to present papers to the Doncaster branch of the RSPB. In his middle years he decided that ornithology no longer satisfied his intellectual hunger and he turned his attention to the more esoteric study of moss, on which he became a considerable expert. (In fact, such was his passion that he once had to explain his obsession to a policeman when he was discovered in a churchyard scraping odd substances off a gravestone.)

He and his wife Glenys came to see *Midsummer Marriage* and we went out for supper afterwards. He had understood the production from top to bottom and inside out. He had understood perfectly what Tippett and Pountney were trying to do. He had got every nuance, every detail, every allegory. It made me proud of my family, and more determined than ever to overturn the pompous assumption that opera is too difficult for most people.

Sir Michael came to the opening night, dressed in yellow plimsolls and a bright blue suit, and, very kindly, agreed to take a bow at the end. I was thrilled to be holding his hand in the line up. I performed my curtsey, which I had been taught to do perfectly by Anna Sweeny, and I executed it rather well considering the eighteen-inch mini-skirt I was wearing. He hissed out of the corner of his mouth to me, 'How do you do that?'

I hissed back, 'Do you want me to teach you?'

'Yes.'

'When?'

'Now.'

So in the middle of a tumultuous ovation for him and his work I whispered: 'You put your left foot behind and to the side of your right and you bend your knees and keep your back straight.' He followed the instructions perfectly then promptly fell over.

Later that night Lord Harewood gave a spectacular party at his house overlooking the canal in Little Venice. I wore a little black and white 1960s-style dress and a pair of tights with one black leg and one white leg with piano keys hand-painted on each side by the show's designer Marie Jeanne Lecca. Sir Michael was very taken with these and I think I can truthfully say that I am the only person who has had their leg played by the great man.

The party was noteworthy for another reason too. I had met Peter Jonas a few times before, but this was the first time we had spent more than a few minutes together and I think we both realised that evening that our relationship was destined to become more than professional. He was one of the most attractive men I have ever met, with a combination of good looks, power and enormous vulnerability that I found irresistible. PJ as he was known is ridiculously tall and in his youth was built like a rugby prop forward. A serious illness in his twenties had dramatically and permanently altered his shape so that by the time we met he was spare and rangy, which highlighted his striking bone structure and breathtaking blue eyes.

The attraction between us was palpable and undeniable, though we spent some time trying to deny it to each other and ourselves. It was not a sensible thing for the two of us to become involved. He had just taken over as Lord Harewood's successor and a romance between us would be, at the very least, inappropriate. Months went by but, far from diminishing over time, our mutual desire for a closer relationship became stronger. Our emergence as a couple caused no resentment within the ENO company, or certainly none that either of us was aware of at the time. For a few weeks, admittedly, there was a certain amount of head turning and giggling when I walked into the canteen but nothing more. By and large, people were happy for both of us.

With PJ I saw life from a startling new vantage point. There was a whole world I had only glimpsed through a gap in the curtains; now I walked into it through the front door. I didn't have to scrounge dress rehearsal passes to Covent Garden any more – we went to all the opening nights. I had been to Paris before, but on a coach and to stay in a little backstreet hotel. Now we flew, first class, and were the guests of his old friend Daniel Barenboim or Eva Wagner Pasquier. Lord and Lady Harewood had always shown me great kindness and taken a keen interest in my career, but now I was invited to spend weekends at Harewood House and I learned to call them George and Patricia. That might sound like an easy step to take but you have to remember that my grandmother was a supervisor in a pickle factory; his grandmother was Queen Mary. Despite his ancestry, George Harewood is a modest, approachable and thoroughly unstuffy man with a disarmingly self-deprecating sense of humour. One day we were discussing my birthplace.

'I know Thorne,' he said. 'I was in the Home Guard in Thorne.'

'Were you really?' I said, incredulous. 'Were you Captain Mainwaring?'

'No, no, my dear. I was the Stupid Boy!'

Home life with PJ was very different too. He lived in a post-modernist gem of a house, designed by Piers Gough and filled with modern art. If I answered the phone it could be anyone on the other end – the Minister for the Arts wanting to run some idea past PJ or Carlos Kleiber just calling for a chat. Peter's friends became my friends, and for a year I was Eliza Doolittle to his Higgins – but there was no Lerner and Loewe happy ending for us. This was *Pygmalion* not *My Fair Lady* and in the end our worlds were too far apart for the relationship to last. PJ needed a full-time 'company wife' and that was a role I was not equipped to play. Dazzled as I was by his lifestyle and fond as we were of each other, I knew I had to make my own way in the world. I could not live in his shadow. We parted with enormous sadness on both sides but no hint of rancour. We remain close friends to this day.

There were many people who helped make the ENO such a huge success at that time, like Jonathan Miller, with whom I worked as Zerlina in his production of *Don Giovanni*. I found him unique and idiosyncratic, both as a man and as a producer. I had never met anyone before with his level of charisma and penetratingly analytical mind. Despite his exceptional intellect, he liked to work from a visual perspective, which suited me very well. Before starting any work on an opera he seemed to need an overall image of the shape and colour of the piece. For *Don Giovanni*, he was inspired by the work of Goya and by a statue he had seen in Strasbourg. At the very first meeting of the cast he gave us a fascinating lecture about how he saw the opera. He saw the Don's soul as being utterly dark, with no shred of compassion or feeling. He wanted to express this by making the whole of the production as black as he could make it.

When he began talking about the statue of the Marechal de Saxe as inspiration for the statue of the Commendotore I began to get a little frustrated, as I had no idea what the original looked like. I stuck up my hand like a schoolgirl and explained that I couldn't share his vision as I had never seen the statue or, for that matter, the Goya paintings that he kept talking about. There was a hushed silence, as I naïvely flaunted my ignorance for all to see, but Jonathan was kindness itself and the very next day he brought me a book about Goya and a postcard of the statue. I immediately grasped what he had been trying to convey and, I have to say, so did the rest of the cast who were all eager to have a look at the book and the postcard too.

I was fortunate to have Mark Richardson, one of this country's foremost singer-actors, as Masetto and Jonathan gave us free rein to develop our scenes together as much as possible. I also worked on Zerlina with Phillip Thomas, my old friend from the Royal Academy who was also working at ENO. One of the finest vocal coaches in the business, Phillip is also an exceptionally talented pianist, a wonderful accompanist, outstanding record producer and, most important of all, a loyal and loving friend. He has a unique understanding of the operatic voice. He is able to extract from the music the very essence of the composer's intention, both musical and dramatic. As you might expect from a Welshman, Phillip has a refreshingly basic, earthy approach to opera. He sees better than anyone that the motivation of most characters comes not from the head or even from the heart but from much lower down. Scratch the surface of most operas, he says, and the story is really just about sex. Zerlina, who is one of my favourite Mozart characters, is quite honestly no better than she should be, but none the less interesting for that. During one of our sessions, Phillip remarked that Zerlina was the kind of girl who would be at home behind the bike sheds. This rather brutal summing up of her morals became a kind of shorthand between us. Whenever he wanted me to sound sexier, Phillip would call out, 'More bike sheds, Lesley, more bike sheds!'

If Jonathan's *Don Giovanni* was unremittingly dark, his next production was a complete contrast. Gilbert and Sullivan's works had rarely been seen at the Coliseum (the last time had been *Patience* in 1969) so everyone was eagerly awaiting his version of *The Mikado*. He courageously set it about as far away from Imperial Japan as it is possible to get: Raffles hotel in Singapore between the wars. I played Yum-Yum and the three little maids wore gymslips and carried lacrosse sticks and danced the charleston (taught by the great dancer-turned-choreographer Anthony van Laast).

To begin with I found Yum-Yum hard to get the hang of. Jonathan wanted the three maids to be totally empty-headed, carefree and sparkly; I felt I needed to understand her better, to learn what made her tick. I pestered Jonathan with questions about her motivations until, exasperated, he yelled, 'Oh, do stop trying to be too intelligent. Just sparkle!' I had a bit of trouble with Yum-Yum's voice too. Jonathan knew exactly the accent that he wanted her to have – the clipped, genteel tones of a pre-war Home Counties Englishwoman. In other words, he wanted me to sound like Celia Johnson in *Brief Encounter*. I had never seen the film and wasn't sure what he was talking about but Lady Harewood had the video and she and I watched it together one rainy Sunday afternoon in Yorkshire, sharing a box of tissues, and I learnt to imitate Celia Johnson's accent.

Eric Idle was magnificent as Ko-Ko. His updated (and frequently ad-libbed) Little List was a nightly triumph and included lines like 'Muggers, joggers, buggers, floggers' and 'Girls that tell the stories of the Tories they have kissed'.

One day he came in and sat opposite me in the ENO canteen. 'Hm. I feel funny today, Lesley.'

'Is that the same as me feeling in good voice?'

'Yes,' he replied, and went on to explain that there were some days when he just felt that he could be extra funny. There was no rational explanation, it was just like a sportsman being 'on form'.

Sure enough, at the rehearsal that afternoon Eric demonstrated the truth of this, reducing the whole cast, director and stage crew to helpless mirth. As well as being hilarious, it was extraordinary to watch such technique and timing. In the scene where Ko-Ko has to grovel in apology, he very slowly folded his body from the vertical to the horizontal, and then licked the sole of the Mikado's shoe. When I asked him afterwards, he said that it was spontaneous invention, not planned, just because he was 'feeling funny' that day. Eric taught me about the importance of restraint in a performance. Here was a man who could reduce an audience to uncontrollable laughter just by raising one eyebrow, but he always managed to keep something back, to maintain a distance from the audience that only enhanced the effect.

Apart from a few rumblings from die-hard traditionalists, our *Mikado* was a popular and critical triumph and was brought to an even wider audience the following year when we recorded a version of it for Thames Television.

The English National Opera views presenting opera in English as a major part of its commitment to making opera more accessible. For me the joy of communicating with an audience in its own language, so that the understanding between audience and performer is instant, is unsurpassable. The success of this communication, of course, depends utterly on the quality of the translation. During my years at ENO, the translations available have improved enormously. I can remember, as a student, singing a translation of *Carmen* which was currently in use by ENO but which had been written back in Victorian times. It contained the immortal lines: 'If beauty worships pluck, tonight with any luck, I will get . . . a beautiful young girl.' I thought at the time that it must be possible to do better.

By the time I reached the Coliseum, ENO had realised that translating an opera meant more than turning the original libretto into English and getting it to rhyme in the right places. The words in an opera are at least as important as the music in telling the story and creating the drama on which all theatre depends. Very often, the play or libretto is what inspired the composer to write the opera, so in translation the words must be no less beautiful and dramatic. Opera translation is an incredibly skilful process, and ENO commissioned new translations from the best in the business, people like Amanda Holden, Jeremy Sams and Michael Frayn who totally rewrote *La Belle Hélène* as *Belle Vivette*. It would be impressive enough just to translate original librettos into poetic English, but a translator has to make the words singable, which is a complex task and requires considerable knowledge of the music and the needs of singers.

It had been such a long time since I had sung in Italian that when I was offered the chance to go to Geneva and play Servilia in Mozart's *La Clemenza di Tito*, I decided to seek out my old friend and coach Jane Robinson for some help. Jane had given up her settled, comfortable existence in London some years before and had found a new life in Sicily. She was living in Palermo with her Italian boyfriend in a large and chaotic household of students and artists. Jane and I called them *Il Ragazzi* – the lads. It was bitterly cold in Sicily that February, but I was happy to be away from London for a month and to combine business with pleasure, although my visit got off to an awkward start. I had officially recovered from my breakdown years before, but one lingering effect of it was a self-assumed emotional fragility which those around me indulged. I had grown used to being pampered and coddled and made allowances for. Jane was just the person to put me right. I was twenty minutes late for our first session and she tore me off a strip for bad discipline and unprofessional behaviour. I left chastened and upset. But as I wandered broodingly around the market, I realised that she had a point. I went straight back and apologised. I had needed a kick up the backside and now I felt much better.

We spent the next weeks working incredibly hard and my voice benefited enormously from her attention. In between our sessions we zoomed around the town's winding streets on Vespas, driven suicidally by the *regazzi*, visiting the many mouth-watering markets and all the glorious historical sites in the area. We admired the magnificent Roman amphitheatre and crept nervously round the gruesome catacombs. In the evenings we sat around eating huge and delicious meals and drinking gallons of the rough local wine. One such evening, I overheard a snatch of conversation amongst the boys who shared her house, which illustrated in a simple but startling way the differences between our culture and theirs. They were talking, as young lads do the world over, about a party they had been to and how one of their friends had been so drunk that he had been sick over the balcony. Wouldn't it be funny, said one of them, if in *Don Giovanni*, the maid had come out on to the balcony, not to hear Giovanni's beautiful Mandolin Aria, but to throw up. As the young Sicilian boys collapsed in laughter at this good joke, I wondered just how many centuries it would take before opera became so integrated into our society that a similar group of British lads would refer to a scene in an opera in such a natural way.

Another utterly unforgettable overseas trip took me back to Italy later that year. The conductor Roger Norrington and his wife Kay Lawrence, who was a dancer-turned-choreographer and specialised in baroque dance, invited me to join a small ensemble they were putting together to perform Purcell's *Fairy Queen* for the Il Maggio Musicale Festival in Florence. The plan was that we would perform the opera, in English, in conjunction with an Italian theatre company who would perform *A Midsummer Night's Dream* in Italian. It sounded ambitious to say the least but no one was quibbling with a month in Florence in May on offer, especially as Roger had negotiated a deal that gave us all very generous pay and accommodation in a five-star hotel. It was my first time in Florence and neither the city nor the hotel disappointed. Florence is the setting for Puccini's opera *Gianni Schicchi* from which comes one of my favourite arias, 'O mio babbino caro'. In it Lauretta sings to her father of her love for Rinuccio and of how she will go to the market at Porta Rosa and buy her wedding ring. She threatens to fling herself from the Ponte Vecchio if her father will not permit the marriage. I stood on that very bridge with Puccini's music filling my head and gazed at the dark river Arno swirling below my feet and I walked in the Porta Rosa, browsing amongst the stalls, some of which still sell jewellery. The hotel was on the banks of the river within sight of the Ponte Vecchio and, as I stood at my bedroom window looking straight out over the rooftops to the Duomo, I was in heaven.

As rehearsals began, it was clear that the word 'ambitious' was wholly inadequate to describe the scope and scale of this production. 'Epic' gets closer, though 'insane' is probably more apt. The two works were to be performed in the open air in the Boboli Gardens on two separate stages. The opera and the play were to be somehow woven together so that we would sing *Fairy Queen* in English on one stage, breaking off every so often for the actors on the other stage to continue Shakespeare's version of the story in Italian, on the other. The audience was seated on a gigantic A-frame grandstand between the two stages and, as the action moved from one to the other, they were expected to clamber up to the top and resume their seats on the other side, while gangs of intoxicated stage hands noisily reset the scene on the empty stage. Neither work had been cut and they are both a good two and a half hours long. We never started before half-past eight and the audience and performers alike would stagger home, exhausted and bewildered, at two in the morning.

Posters all over the city announced the event as '*uno spectaculo*!!' and the director, Luca Roncone, was determined to spare no expense to enhance the spectacle. The costumes were extravagantly authentic with enormous farthingales and massive feather head-dresses. There were live bullocks, carriages drawn by plumed horses, hordes of tiny children with sequinned tutus and gossamer wings and monkeys on their shoulders. The birdcage I carried in one scene contained a real bird, which refused to keep quiet however much seed we bribed it with and warbled unharmoniously throughout my biggest aria. We even had Jill Gomez ascending majestically to the heavens in a hot-air balloon.

All this would be a recipe for chaos in any country. With the Italians in charge, it was chaos on a biblical scale. Through this Heironymous Bosch nightmare of a scene wandered our small band of bewildered Brits. As the disorganisation around us descended into madness, we became like caricatures of the English abroad. We stayed calm and professional as production staff (who all seemed to be called Paolo) rushed around shouting and bumping into each other in bursts of frenzied activity before they suddenly downed tools at the crucial moment and took a siesta. One day, to the locals' great surprise and dismay, it began to rain. There was much shouting and arm-waving and tearing of hair until everyone abandoned the stage and retreated to the shelter of the trees to drink wine for the rest of the day. Everybody, that is, except us. We calmly donned our macs and wellies and rehearsed under umbrellas while the director shook his damp head and muttered 'crazy Eenglish' over and over again.

Imagine then our delight when one day, in the midst of the mediaeval madness, we see an ancient, battered bus making its way up the hill to the gardens. On the side of the bus are inscribed the letters that bring comfort to the breast of every expatriate – BBC. We rushed up excitedly to the bus as Russell Harty stepped down, surveyed the scene and enquired, 'What on earth is going on here?' Russell was making a documentary series, travelling on a Grand Tour around Europe and seeking out eccentric Englishmen abroad. We were obviously just what he was looking for so the crew decided to stay, record some of the show and do some interviews.

The night they were due to film, I was running into position when I tripped over the shafts of a bullock cart. I narrowly missed the bullock and avoided falling on to the hot-air balloon which was tethered a couple of feet away but I barked my shins and, worse still, smashed my radio mike. Swearing in whatever language came to mind, I called for the sound engineer (who I had named Acoustico Paolo, to distinguish him from Lumino Paolo, the lighting man, and Rossetto Paolo, the make-up artist) but he couldn't fix it and, of course, he didn't have a spare. All the BBC sound man could come up with was a hand-held mike which we all agreed would rather detract from the authentic baroque feel of the piece so I wedged it down the front of my costume, in the crevice obviously designed for the purpose, and strode back on stage, better endowed than ever. Between scenes, Russell interviewed me in the five-foot-square shed that I shared with Jill Gomez, which served as our dressing-room and costume store. His face was a picture of pink astonishment when I rummaged in my corset and produced the aforesaid microphone, by now very warm and slightly damp, which Acoustico Paolo caressed lovingly before returning it reluctantly to a bemused BBC engineer.

All too soon it was time to return to London where in subsequent months I followed the story of Russell Harty's illness and his brave fight for life. I realised, sadly, that our interview must have been one of the last he made. Like so many others, I felt a deep sense of loss at his passing but I will never forget the brief time we spent together among the pine trees in Florence.

Although retired from the day to day running of ENO, Lord Harewood remained its chairman and continued to devote a great deal of his time and boundless energy to ensuring its continued success. He also maintained an interest in my career and was keen for me to develop my repertoire, not just in operatic roles but in cabaret music. He put me in touch with James Holmes, the Coliseum's resident expert on the genre and we put together and prepared a programme for a recital which Lord Harewood kindly hosted in the Music Room at Harewood House. We called the programme *Classical Cabaret*, the first half consisting of songs by composers such as Britten, Weill, and a selection of Schoenberg's *Brettlleider*. For the second half, we concentrated on the so-called lighter side of the repertoire with works by Gershwin, Porter and Noel Coward. The evening was a huge success and led to Jim and me being offered the chance to perform the entire *Brettlleider* cycle at the Pompidou Centre in Paris. We faithfully recreated the atmosphere of the 1920s – I wore an authentic period dress heavy with beads, and an extraordinary French make-up artist transformed me into Sally Bowles. Our recitals were given at lunch-time in one of the Centre's cafés which had a small performing

NOTES FROM A SMALL SOPRANO

space and which regularly hosted seasons of avant garde music. We played to a packed house of shop assistants and office workers every day and, despite the modernity of the surroundings, took them back in time to the golden age of cabaret, as I sashayed between the tables. Where else but Paris would this have been possible?

Although it is not exactly a household name like *Carmen* or *Madam Butterfly*, Janacek's *The Cunning Little Vixen* is, in many important ways, the perfect opera. The plot is refreshingly straightforward. There are no love triangles or mistaken identities, just the journey of a vixen through life. She is seen to grow from a cub, suffer abuse and captivity, learn to kill, dream of womanhood, fall in love, have and defend her children and be killed. All vulpine life is there and yet, paradoxically, the Vixen is one of the truest portrayals of a woman in opera. (And it has the added advantage of being, unlike most opera, very *short*.) As well as being musically demanding, it is a very physical role – the Vixen is hardly ever off stage and is never still. For me it was a dream of a role. I hoped very much that one day I could play the Vixen, so in 1988 I pleaded to be allowed to 'cover' the role for Anne Dawson. I learnt the role, watched the stage rehearsals in between performances of a revival of *Xerxes* and wished Anne the best of luck for her opening night, which was a well-deserved triumph.

The last performance of *Xerxes*, on Monday 13 June, was followed by a long and liquid party and I spent the next day in bed, dreaming of the two-month summer break I was about to enjoy. On the Wednesday lunch-time the Coliseum rang. Anne Dawson had been taken ill; I was her understudy and there was a performance of *Vixen* that night; how soon could I get there? I didn't have time to feel nervous – I just had to get on with it. I had a meeting with Mark Elder, who was conducting, and we ran through the trickier parts of the score, sorted out the costume (luckily Anne's fitted) and within hours was on the stage. The cast were all wonderfully supportive. Rita Cullis, who played the Fox, literally pushed me around the set when necessary, and John Lloyd Davies, the staff producer, stood in the wings miming instructions and encouragement. Best of all, I had Mark keeping a watchful eye on me from the pit. Mark is not just a brilliant conductor, he is the ultimate singers' conductor. If you have to be in this kind of situation, he is the man to be in it with. It was both the most terrifying and the most exhilarating experience I have ever had in the theatre, but I got through to the end with fewer mistakes than I deserved and a huge sense of relief.

My voice only let me down seriously once in those early years at ENO and that was while I was performing in *The Making of the Representative of Planet 8*, a modern opera by Philip Glass, based on the science-fiction novel by Doris Lessing about a planet whose peace and prosperity is destroyed by an ice age. I played a character called Alsi, who ages in the course of the action from a beautiful young girl to a wizened old woman. I was used to light and happy roles and Alsi was anything but. The music was deceptively difficult but I was determined to do justice to my character and her astonishing emotional journey. Rehearsals were long and draining, particularly when Philip Glass and Doris Lessing were both present, and in my efforts to express

Alsi's drama I pushed my voice much too far. I made it through the London run but was reluctantly forced to pull out of the planned transfer of the opera to Amsterdam. Instead I went to Geneva to take the much smaller role of Barbarina in *The Marriage of Figaro*. I knew a lot of the people in the cast, including Bill Shimmell, from whom I had drifted apart years before, but they were all there with their partners and I felt lost and dislocated so far from home. It was my first real experience of homesickness and I did what any thirty-three-year-old independent woman would do – I called my mum.

'Are you busy, Mum? Can you come and stay for a bit?'

'I had a feeling you'd do this,' she replied. 'So I've got the bus timetable here ready. I can get a bus in Doncaster on Thursday morning and be with you by Sunday night. Will that do?'

'Oh Mum, can't you be normal and catch a plane for once?' I moaned. She was addicted to coach travel, but surely Doncaster to Geneva was a bus-stop or two too far. Twenty minutes later, Mum rang me back.

'Right, dear, the good news is I'll be with you at 9.30 tomorrow morning. The bad news is I have to stay for a fortnight.' I didn't mind one bit.

So Mum flew out to join me – her first time on a plane – and we had a blissful time together. It was a time of great closeness between us which I wouldn't have missed for the world. One day the whole cast went on an outing to the mountains. It was a grey, sunless morning when we got on the funicular railway. The train climbed higher and higher, enveloped in mist, until suddenly, as we neared the summit, we pierced the cloud and emerged into a crystal-clear blue day. Mum quite literally gasped with pleasure at the sight. I realised then that she had never in her life been up any mountain, let alone one as beautiful as this. Her face shone with happiness, like a child on Christmas morning. As we got down from the train and walked up the side of the mountain she flung out her arms as if to embrace the sky. My normally eloquent mother was reduced to repeating over and over again, 'Oh Lesley! Oh *Lesley!*' Then she caught sight of a man further up the track with what appeared to be a tablecloth spread out on the snow to which he was attaching several fine ropes. She stood and watched, first in curiosity, then surprise and finally in utter wonder as he hoisted the contraption on to his back, ran across the snow and launched himself off the mountain. He swooped and glided out over the trees and into the blue beyond, free as a bird. Mum jumped up and down like an excited toddler. 'I've got to do that. I've just got to have a go.' 'Don't be ridiculous, Mum, we're 10,000 feet up and you're fifty-seven years old. Besides, its lunch-time.'

She went very quiet but followed me obediently to the restaurant where she sat with her nose pressed up against the window pane, reluctant to take her eyes off the view, as if doing so might break the spell. As we ordered our meal she finally turned away and looked at me pleadingly. 'Please, Lesley. It's no good. I don't want any lunch. Can I go outside, please?' Not waiting for my reply, she ran back out of the restaurant, leaving me with a dilemma. Should I stay and have lunch with my friends or go and supervise my mother who was running amok out in the snow like a middle-aged Julie Andrews. I decided to risk it for a while, but I wolfed down my *weiner schnitzel* and *gluwein* as fast as I could.

I found Mum sitting on a rock, calmer now, gazing at the peace and majesty of the alpine landscape spread out around her, drinking it in like champagne. We sat silently together, while my friends finished their lunch. As we boarded the train for the return trip, she turned and looked back at the mountain and smiled a deep satisfied smile.

I have always felt that audiences give me more than I give them and this was never truer than at ENO. For every emotion I experienced and shared with the audience, every piece of pain or joy or grief or laughter, they gave me as much if not more back. I sent it out and it came back recharged, which enabled me to go on and do more and more and more. I seemed to draw power from the audience which I didn't know how to control and each character I played, however large or small, just seemed to grow and grow. Sometimes the communication became too strong and in my early and inexperienced years at ENO I was inclined to overdo it. The critics, who were often generous in their praise, noticed this and took me to task for it. And the Chorus, who observe so much, devised a telling nickname for me: 'Lesley Garrett – Never knowingly upstaged'. It took me a long time to harness my relationship with an audience and I only managed it through working with great producers and great artists who showed me, through their own performances, how less is always more.

178

The role in which I finally felt I had learnt to discipline myself on stage was Oscar the page in Verdi's *Masked Ball*. Traditionally he is played as a kind of pantomime character – all tights and tunic and thigh slapping – a bit of light relief. David Alden, typically, saw him very differently. David knows the score of an opera better than any director I have ever worked with. He knows every singer's part and most of the orchestral parts as well. (In an ideal world he would probably like to conduct every opera and play all the roles himself!) He believes that there is no such thing as a single, simple emotion. As every light has its shadow, every emotion has a dark side, and he certainly found the dark side of Oscar. I played him as a chain-smoking, sexually ambivalent hunchback – a cross between Jimmy Clitheroe, Andy Warhol and Quasimodo – the kind of youth who would have pulled the wings off butterflies. The psychological preparation for the role was challenging. I had been used to playing open, exuberant characters but Oscar was emotionally buttoned-down, with a warped, sinister, inner life which I had to explore if I was to make the characterisation work. The physical demands of the role were even greater. I had to sing the part bent over and wreathed in a permanent cloud of cigarette smoke – a vocal nightmare.

At one point in the first act, Oscar has to sit in one of the boxes at the side of the stage, lit by a low follow-spot, smoking as always and observing Gustavus as he sings his aria. One evening, the next-door box was occupied by a group of businessmen who were rather the worse for wear and failed entirely to connect me with the character they had seen on the stage. When my cigarette lighter failed to work, they leant over and gave me theirs, chatting tipsily and offering me a drink, oblivious to the eyes of the rest of the audience turned towards us. The penny finally dropped when I left the box and returned to the stage and they giggled like schoolboys for the rest of the act.

The Princess of Wales came to see the show one evening and came backstage afterwards. A great deal has been written about Princess Diana and by people more eloquent than me. Let me just say that she was not just exquisitely, luminously beautiful, but witty, warm and wise beyond her years.

Chapter 9

Diva!

The ending of my relationship with Peter Jonas left my confidence bruised. I had had enjoyable, fulfilling relationships with a number of men, but deep down I was expecting to marry each of them. That was what I saw as the natural progression of any romance. In terms of finding someone to spend the rest of my life with I had failed miserably and I doubted whether such a man existed. I resolved to give up the quest, not to become a nun, but to concentrate on living my life as I chose. I didn't have to feel lonely just because I didn't have a man in my life. I had a proper job which paid me good, steady money. I had wonderful friends, a loving family, a home of my own and Frank the cat to welcome me into it. What more could a girl desire? I would enjoy the freedom that spinsterhood endowed.

My parents' marriage, which I had watched gradually and painfully disintegrate, had finally ended after over thirty years. My mother had moved out of Red House Farm and left my father there, which seemed appropriate as he had always been the one who had loved the place best. The atmosphere at home had been grim for many years but it was still hard to accept that my mother and father now lived separate lives in separate places.

One day I read a magazine article about the Gower Peninsula and the extraordinary geological feature known as the Worm's Head. It was a part of the country I had always wanted to visit and Mum and I both needed a break, so a few weeks later we set off for Wales. We stayed in the lovely village of Rhosilli, perched above a perfect beach and overlooking the Worm's Head itself. We had no sooner seen this remarkable promontory jutting out into the sea, than we resolved to walk its length. It seemed to be calling us, challenging us to conquer it.

The Worm's Head is nearly a mile long and has several distinct sections, each with its own topography and geological idiosyncrasies. The first section is rocky, pock-marked with little pools and criss-crossed by streams. The rocks are sharp and angular and hurt your feet if you are wearing trainers, as we were, rather than proper footwear. As you walk further along, the rocks become larger and smoother and the landscape takes on a lunar aspect. From there on the terrain becomes tougher, a climb almost, as the gradient steepens, and Mum and I were exhausted as well as triumphant when we finally reached the southernmost tip and could gaze far out to sea, the salty wind stinging our cheeks, already pink from our exertions. The journey back was glorious. We had

The innovative English National Opera poster that changed the direction of my career.

Above Atalanta in
Handel's *Xerxes*, with
Ann Murray.

Left Zerlina in Jonathan
Miller's production of
Don Giovanni with Bill
Shimell as the Don.

Being presented to Princess Diana after a performance of *A Masked Ball* (in which I played the bearded Oscar), with, left, the conductor Michael Lloyd, centre Graeme Broadbent and right, Peter Jonas.

The ENO 'team' in Red Square, Moscow, 1990. Left to right: Gillian Sullivan, Rodney Macann, Eileen Hulse, Christopher Robson, Christine Bunning, Michael Lloyd, Samuel Burkey, Kristine Ciesinski, Malcolm Donnelly, me, Ethna Robinson, Yvonne Kenny (with hat), Ann Murray, Geoffrey Pogson, Menai Davies, Christopher Booth-Jones and John Connell. In front, seated: David Pountney, Peter Jonas and Mark Elder.

Above With 'Eddie Wigs' before a performance of *The Mikado*.

Left Adele in *Die Fledermaus*, wearing what was known as my 'deadly weapons' basque.

Below *The Mikado* with Susan Bulloc Jean Rigby and Eric Idle.

Above Jenny in *Mahagony*.

Right Rose Maurrant in *Street Scene*. In spite of all my work with the dialect coach, one critic said my accent was 'More New Yorkshire than New York'!

Below With Jean Prentice ('Auntie Jean') before a performance of *The Making of a Representative of Planet 8*, me with *fake* aging bosoms and Garfield accessory.

Left *The Love for Three Oranges*, the production in which my husband saw me for the first time.

Opposite page *The Cunning Little Vixen*. It was during this production that Peter and I dashed off to Islington Town Hall to get married.

Below Papagena in *The Magic Flute*, with Benjamin Luxon as Papageno, and tea trolley.

Dalinda in *Ariodante*.

set out as mother and daughter, determined to attempt a difficult walk together. We returned, two independent, divorced women, who had drawn strength from their achievement, strength they had acquired together and could share.

Jill, Kay and I did our best to support both our parents through the pain of their divorce, and the experience, sad though it was, drew the three of us closer together than we had been since childhood. Jill had married John, her childhood sweetheart, and Kay had married Bob. For three sisters separated in age by only four and a half years, we were all surprisingly different in character and looks. Jill is tall, blonde and willowy, down to earth and practical like my father, but one of life's worriers. Kay is her physical opposite, the image of Nanny Wall. Barely five feet tall, she is also the most intelligent with a sharp, darting mind and an innate worldly wisdom that we all rely on. Our much-loved Dad was able to find happiness again with Jenny, who became his second wife, and we have come to admire and value her enormously for the companionship and care she has offered to him and to our families.

Despite the fact that my parents were now living apart, or perhaps because of it, I found I was spending more and more time in Yorkshire. My sisters were both settled near the village of Epworth, just over the border in Lincolnshire and Kay had provided me with two beautiful nephews to spoil. One Saturday morning in the autumn of 1988 Jill and I were strolling down the high street in Epworth, chatting and window shopping, when my eye was drawn to the window of the estate agents. My innate nosiness has always made me fascinated by other people's houses and I have a long-standing affection for that peculiar form of euphemistic English that estate agents use to make even the grimmest of properties sound desirable. We found a particularly fine example of the art tucked away in the corner of the window. There was no picture of the property, which generally signifies that it is too ugly to be shown, and the description involved such words as 'unique', 'potential', 'interesting', which in my book always meant the same thing – a complete dump. Jill and I giggled like schoolgirls as we read on and then one phrase stopped me in my tracks. It read 'in need of tender loving care'. Suddenly I felt sorry for this poor little house. We all need tender loving care sometimes in our lives and I certainly had plenty of it to give.

I dragged Jill into the shop and demanded further details. 'Why don't you go round and see it?' said the agent. 'It's only round the corner.' She handed me a set of keys and gave me directions, which led us down a narrow side street to an old brick wall, overgrown with jasmine. I thought we must have taken a wrong turning, but Jill pointed to an arched wooden door, just visible through the leaves. I tried one of the keys and it turned, reluctantly, in the lock.

Feeling increasingly like Mary Lennox in *The Secret Garden*, I swung open the door and walked gingerly into a Victorian walled garden. It looked like it hadn't been touched for years. The weeds were knee-high but it was clear that this garden had once been loved and tended. Roses rambled unchecked up the trunk of a vast, ancient pear tree, and an enormous, gnarled grapevine had burst out of the greenhouse and smothered the nearby outhouses. I discovered later that the house had once belonged to the local ice-cream seller and the outhouses were in fact an ice-house where he had stored his wares and a stable for the pony and trap from which he sold them. The cottage itself had two bedrooms, one of them tiny, and two rooms downstairs, leading off a substantial and rather beautiful hall. It had been built in the early part of the nineteenth century and it was in a very sorry state. It had wet rot, dry rot, lethal wiring, the roof leaked and half the floorboards were missing. I was right about it being a dump, but it was a beautiful dump and what is more it needed me. I had set out that morning with nothing more on my shopping list than a pair of tights and a new lipstick. I came home with a cottage.

Renovating the cottage turned into a powerfully beneficial and sustaining project. I had very little money to spare after paying for it, but I scraped together enough for the various rots to be dealt with and a new roof put on. The rest, with Dad's help, I did myself. Every time I had a couple of days off work, I would head off to Yorkshire to fill every crack in the old walls, scrape layer upon layer of thick, brown paint off the woodwork and strip blackened old varnish from the floors. I took my time with the decorating, determined that it would be perfect, and spent hours at the Victoria and Albert Museum researching old wallpapers then scouring Homebase for something similar for £4 a roll. The one thing I didn't do was have a telephone installed. My cottage wasn't just going to be beautiful, it would be peaceful too.

In 1989, the Marketing Department at ENO, led by Keith Cooper, the newly appointed Director of Public Relations, came up with a radical new marketing strategy. Most opera company advertising consisted of nothing more than routine announcements of forthcoming productions, placed in serious newspapers and the music press. ENO wanted something more radical – an advertising campaign for the Coliseum itself, something that would capture the eye and imagination of ordinary Londoners, shatter their preconceptions about opera and, perhaps, get them to try it for themselves. Each poster in the new campaign would focus on one person from every department at ENO. There was a box office clerk, a stage hand, someone from management, a producer and me, the token singer. John Stoddart was chosen to take my photograph and he was perfect for the job as he has an eye for sensuality and an ability to elicit it from his subjects. Frankly this guy could make a telephone box look sexy.

My previous experiences of having my photograph taken had involved me having my hair done at my local salon, putting on some make-up, wearing a nice frock and smiling sweetly at the camera. This was a different matter altogether. Professional hair stylists, make-up artists and wardrobe people with armfuls of designer clothes swarmed round me. I was like a little girl with a grown-up dressing up box. I loved every minute of it – what woman wouldn't. I had always loved developing a relationship with an audience and now I found I could have a relationship with a camera too. The whole experience became a performance. I didn't have to be me having my picture taken, I could be anybody I wanted to be. I could be transformed into a character without singing a note, just by putting on the right clothes. One particular outfit caught my eye – a slinky black crepe shift dress with a diaphanous chiffon coat, and in this I was Tosca.

It was the Tosca shots that were used in the campaign, and these photographs of me, draped in black chiffon, my head flung back, with an expression of indefinable ecstasy, appeared overnight on posters in every tube station in town emblazoned with the slogan 'She makes music theatre'. Rather than publicising individual productions, it would make people aware of the company itself and what it stood for. The posters certainly got noticed. Karl, the stage hand, became an instant pin-up and was interviewed by the *6 o'clock News*. He received mountains of fan mail and offers of modelling work. I got noticed too in some unexpected quarters. Offers began to flood in, some good, some bad, some just plain peculiar.

I had been at ENO for five years when I reached what I later saw as a crossroads in my career.

Robert Slotover asked me to go and have lunch with him at Montpelier Square. He was a very fine cook and business lunches often took place around his kitchen table. Sometimes there would be a number of guests, this time it was just the two of us as there were work offers to discuss.

'Now, Lesley, about your ENO contract . . .'

Here we go again, I thought. Robert was always keen for me to take more work in Europe. Opera is a truly international business and singers are very much expected to ply their trade all over the world. I had been under contract to the ENO for five years and although I had taken time off to perform in Italy, Paris and Geneva a couple of times, and had toured with ENO in Russia, Robert felt the time had come for me to spread my wings more, leave ENO and seek my fortune further afield. Every year, when my contract came up for renewal, Robert would counsel me to take the opportunity to leave and work elsewhere and every year I resisted. I was working with such phenomenal people – Sir Charles Mackerras, Mark Elder, Nicholas Hytner, Jonathan Miller – how could it possibly be better anywhere else?

'You know how I feel, Robert. I'm more than happy where I am.'

As I pleaded my well-rehearsed case, my eyes wandered over the table, spread with the remnants of lunch and piles of paper needing our attention. One letter, all but hidden at the bottom of the heap, had an arresting heading – the magical initials BBC.

'What's that one?' I asked, stopping in mid-flow and pointing. Robert laughed.

'Oh, this will amuse you. They want you to do some variety show. Bruce Forsyth or something.' He placed the letter dismissively back in the pile and carried on extolling the delights of Prague.

'Hang on a minute. I'd like to see that.'

I read the letter. The producer of the forthcoming *Bruce Forsyth Christmas Special* had seen my poster and wondered if I would be able to do a guest spot on the show. A fee was mentioned – I had always thought the BBC were mean with money. As Robert looked on, bemused, I checked my diary. 'I'll do it. It looks like fun.'

It was fun, too. I was entirely new to this kind of work but I could not have wished for a kinder and more skilful tutor than Bruce, who made my first day of television recording a joyful and happy occasion. The only unpleasant part of the experience was the dress that I was given to wear to sing 'All I Ask of You' from *Phantom of the Opera*. For reasons best known to themselves, the wardrobe department saw me as a Laura Ashley kind of girl and kitted me out in a hideously unflattering purple confection. Bruce declared that it made me look like an exploding blackcurrant and took personal charge of finding me a sexy little black number to change into for the finale.

Another person who saw the posters was Reynald da Silva, co-founder of Silva Screen Records, a small independent record company that had carved out a niche in the market producing albums of film soundtracks. Silva Screen were about to make a record with Dave Willetts, the fine singer who had so triumphantly carried off the difficult task of succeeding Michael Crawford in the title role of *Phantom of the Opera*. Dave wanted to do a couple of duets from *Phantom* on his record and they were looking around for a suitable female voice to accompany him. I was more than happy to agree as I had seen *Phantom* more than once and was a great fan of the music. I caused quite a stir when I turned up for the first recording session, all five foot four of me in my size 10 black leather mini-skirt and bomber jacket. Everyone had been told that an opera singer was coming and, despite my picture being plastered all over the Underground, they were still expecting some huge and difficult prima donna. I found that there was no need to make any adjustments to my vocal technique to sing Lloyd Webber's music, only to the style in which I sang.

It is a mistake to equate so-called 'lighter' music with vocal simplicity. For instance, 'If I Loved You' from *Carousel* is one of the most difficult songs that I sing – far harder than most Mozart at least. The great musicals were written for classically trained lyric voices. Lily Pons, Grace Moore, Deanna Durbin all had classical training. In terms of their technique, they were no less opera singers than I am. In particular, Julie Andrews, who I have admired since I was a small child, has a classically trained, full-throated lyric voice.

Reynald da Silva saw me on the Bruce Forsyth show and figured that if an opera singer could appear on a peak-time TV variety show, then she could probably sell a record or two. He offered me a recording contract and I set to work planning my first album with Ren's partner, James Fitzpatrick. James and I took to each other instantly. He is a Northerner too, though from the wrong side of the Pennines, and though outwardly shy is at heart an intensely jolly person. Rosy-cheeked above his extravagant beard, he looks like he should be a roadie for Guns 'n' Roses. He and Ren had run a record shop before they moved into the recording industry and he had an encyclopaedic knowledge of all kinds of music gained from listening to thousands of records. He claimed to know nothing about classical music other than knowing what he liked and I was genuinely and totally ignorant about the process of making a record, but over the years we developed a rapport which led to an exchange of knowledge and skill. James understands better than anyone I have ever worked with the potential of music in the middle ground between classical and popular, and my potential to perform and record that music.

With Silva Screen's background in film music and mine in opera, it seemed natural to combine the two for my first album. We chose arias which had been used in the sound-tracks to recent films, such as Dvorak's 'Song to the Moon' from *Rusalka* in *Driving Miss Daisy* and Musetta's 'Waltz' from *La Bohème* which had been heard in *Moonstruck*. I was pleasantly surprised at just how many classic arias had made their way into films. There was no money to spare on another singer, but I managed to include 'Dome Epais', the 'Flower Duet' from *Lakme*, by doing the duet with myself, so to speak, thanks to the magic of double-tracking. This aria had become very well known and popular through its use in a British Airways commercial, but it qualified for inclusion because it had apparently been used in the film *Someone to Watch Over Me*.

The albums I have made have played a crucial part in my career and have enabled me to bring music to a wider audience than would ever be possible on stage. But I find it hard to create a performance in the clinical, anonymous surroundings of a recording studio. For me, singing and performing have always been one and the same thing, and learning to express what a piece of music is saying without having someone to express it to has been difficult for me. Nevertheless, recording can be a happy time, if for no other reason than that it involves spending hours in a room with a bunch of people who are not just skilled professionals but great fun to be with.

Making an album is an expensive business and time is a precious commodity. A trumpeter dropping a mute or a conductor's baton hitting a music stand is enough to turn a stressed producer or engineer into a gibbering wreck.

On the last day of recording my first album, a mysterious, intrusive squeak could be heard every time I sang. Mike Ross-Trevor, my ever-patient, ultra-professional sound engineer thought it might be a wobbly music stand. Every member of the orchestra was commanded to move their stand six inches to the left and we tried again. Still the noise was there – maybe it was the orchestra's chairs. Everyone shuffled two inches to the right and started playing again. I came in on cue and watched Mike tearing his hair out at the control desk. The squeak just wouldn't go away. Suddenly, I had a hunch and rushed into the control room. Clasping Mike's head to my chest, I took a deep breath. 'Is that what you heard?' I asked him. 'Yes,' he replied, blushing as he recovered his composure. 'But why is your chest making that noise?' The culprit was my new bra, made to measure at vast but worthwhile expense by Rigby & Peller, the Queen's corsetieres. It was a miracle of engineering and very comfortable to wear but the underwiring obviously needed some oiling. I went into the ladies', removed the offending garment and did the rest of the session bra-less and squeak-free. It has become a ritual now for Mike to ask me before every recording, 'Have you got the right bra on?'

We called the album *Diva!*, after the film of the same name whose hit aria 'Ebben Ne Andro Lontano' was our title track, and subtitled it *A Soprano at the Movies*. The cover design was simple – we used the John Stoddart photo that had recently graced the Underground. The picture raised a few eyebrows but it seemed to me to be much more appropriate to the musical content than the covers of most classical recordings. Scenes of grazing sheep, a soprano sitting in a cardi by a roaring fire, a conductor self-consciously reading a score (you mean he hasn't learnt it yet?) – why were those kind of images being used to sell any kind of classical music, let alone opera? What have they got to do with powerful human emotions? I wanted people to know that inside this small perspex box was music that could make your senses reel – music that could change you for ever.

Chapter 10

And This is my Beloved

Live opera is such a powerful medium because it is multi-sensory – it grabs the attention of both the eye and the ear. On one memorable occasion at ENO, we made a tongue-in-cheek bid for the audience's noses as well. Prokofiev's *The Love for Three Oranges* is a glorious adult pantomime, a surreal fairytale full of wild grotesque characters. The plot involves a melancholy prince who, in his quest for the elusive gift of laughter, encounters wicked witches, scheming magicians and crazy courtiers until finally he finds his true love (me, in a knee-length, platinum blonde wig) inside a giant orange. It was a production brimming over with visual and musical jokes, and to heighten the audience's fun each ticket came with a scratch 'n' sniff card, to be used at appropriate moments in the action. Who said opera had to be relevant?

Half-way through the run of *Love for Three Oranges*, my friends Imogen Cooper, the pianist, and her husband the photographer, John Batten, rang me to say that they were coming to see the show.

'We're bringing a friend of ours. He's ever so nice, Lesley. Can we bring him round after the performance? Perhaps we could take you out to supper?'

My heart sank into my boots. I knew they were trying to be kind and I was sure that any friend of theirs was bound to be good company but their motives were as obvious as they were well meant. I was being set up.

'Sorry, John,' I replied, 'thanks but no thanks. I'm not interested and, besides, I'm too old for blind dates.'

I hung up feeling guilty but determined. I was an independent woman with the career I had always wanted. I had a flat, a car, a cat and my beloved cottage and anyone who thought that I needed a man to make my life complete could jolly well think again. Having held extensive auditions, I had already come to the conclusion that my Mr Right did not exist and I was weary of the procession of Mr Wrongs that well-intentioned friends brought to my door. Imo rang a few days later to let me know that the friend couldn't come after all, so they were bringing their local GP who was a big opera fan. I was hugely relieved as I conjured up an image of a tweed-jacketed, pipe-smoking old buffer. No threat there, obviously.

The show seemed to go particularly well that night and my spirits were high as I sat in my saggy old candle-wick dressing-gown with my hair pinned up and my face covered in cold cream. 'Come in!' I yelled and span round to greet my friends and their guest. Then I saw him. The 'eyes across a crowded room' thing is such a cheesy old cliché, but that's just what it was. No heavenly choirs, no violins, no thunderbolts. It was much more down to earth than that, much deeper and more real. It wasn't so much a feeling of attraction (though he was – and still is – devastatingly good-looking), more a sense of recognition, of coming home. What an exquisite irony. Here I was, a confirmed, card-carrying single girl gazing into the eyes of a man I knew would be my husband. I discovered later that Peter had also made up his mind about me that night. 'I was sitting watching an opera with some friends,' he later related, 'and my wife stepped out of an orange.'

I suppose we must have been introduced and I think we had some kind of conversation, but I honestly cannot remember what either of us said. I had learnt that his name was Peter and I knew that I was going to marry him. That was all that mattered. As John and Imo bundled Peter out of the room so that I could change before supper, other girls from the cast rushed in eagerly. 'Phwoah, Lesley! Who was that gorgeous man?' 'Blimey, he's a bit of all right!' 'Whatever happened to the doddery old doctor?' I remembered to my horror that all I had brought to change into was a hideous, shapeless, woollen dress. High necked and long sleeved, it looked like something out of *Little Women*. 'Help me, girls!' I groaned. 'I've got nothing to wear.' They fluttered around me like maids in a harem, offering scarves and jewellery and lipstick, anything to give me a bit more allure.

We ate at a lively little Italian restaurant in St Martin's Lane where Peter and I kept up a constant gabble of conversation, while John and Imo looked on indulgently, thrilled and a little surprised that their match-making had been so instantly and obviously successful. We talked like old friends who had been apart for decades and needed to catch up on their news. We talked about opera, medicine, politics, food – we covered everything.

Two days later I drove up to Yorkshire to spend Christmas with my family. I greeted my mother with the words:

'I've found him, Mum. I've found the father of my children!'

Peter was all I could talk about or think about over the holidays and I must have bored them to tears, telling the story of our meeting over and over again to anyone who would listen. My diary has always been a business-like document, recording nothing more than day-to-day appointments. When I recently looked back at the entries for the first week of 1989 I found that the whole page looked like a fourteen-year-old schoolgirl's rough book. Peter's name was written in every margin, encircled in a heart. All I really wanted to do was come back to London and see him again. John and Imo arranged another meeting, this time at their house, and at the end of the evening Peter asked me to have lunch with him. He took me to a Thai restaurant in Islington where we discovered we shared a passion for hot and sour soup. The soup that afternoon was the hottest and sourest either of us had ever encountered and we both spent the rest of the meal with our eyes streaming and sweat pouring off our brows. After coffee he took me back to see his flat in a converted church.

'You will stay, Lesley, won't you?'

'Yes, of course I will.'

'You do know what I mean, don't you?'

'Oh yes.'

I had never been so sure of anything in my life. We had spent only a few hours in each other's company since we met, but I had no doubts. Pausing only to pack my worldly goods and scoop up Frank, I moved in.

The only fault that I could find in Peter was that he wasn't a Yorkshireman, though he wasn't that far off. He had been born and brought up on a farm near Spalding in Lincolnshire, and, by a phenomenal coincidence, his maternal grandmother had been born in Wath upon Dearn, where my grandfather came from. Like me, he had nurtured a childhood dream. Mine was to sing, his was to become a doctor. Also like me, he had had to struggle to fulfil his dream. Unable to get into medical school, he had gone to university in London to study psychology which he enjoyed but always regarded as second best. After three years, with a psychology degree in his pocket, he finally obtained a place to read medicine and started at the bottom again. General Practice had always been his aim and when he qualified he found a traineeship at a large, modern practice in north London where one of the other partners was Rachel Miller, wife of Jonathan Miller with whom I was working at the time. Peter had spent his twenties in unwedded bliss with Linda, a lawyer whom he had met at university. Their split in 1983 was amicable and since then he had concentrated on enjoying his life, working hard at his new job as a partner in a leafy suburban practice and indulging his passion for opera.

Misty-eyed as we were, I think we both realised that it was the timing of our meeting that had been perfect. We were not just right for each other, but ready for each other. If our friends were concerned at our headlong rush into life together, they did their best to conceal it. I think everyone could see how happy we made each other. We both had a lot of new people to meet; there were large families and armies of friends to be introduced to and be sized up by. Peter was delighted to be mixing with musicians and I was fascinated by all the doctors I now found round our dinner table – I even met my first brain surgeon. It was heartening, if a little daunting, to see just how loved Peter was by so many people. He came to the Coliseum whenever I was performing and watched from the wings, chatting to the stage crew and becoming an honorary member of the ENO family.

I think he was surprised, at first, at how noisy backstage theatre life is before a performance. As well as the banging and crashing of sets and props being moved, there is a constant buzz of chatter from the small army of people that the staging of an opera requires. As curtain up draws closer, the tannoy emits ever more urgent commands. 'Flymen to the Flies!' It is not a reference to any Peter Pan antics about to take place, nor is it an injunction to gentlemen cast members to adjust their dress. It is the cue for a gang of burly men to ascend to the fly tower above the stage from where they raise and lower the backdrops on huge ropes. Peter was enchanted by this strange new world, though he misunderstood some of its terminology. One night, on the way home he said to me, 'I do think it's nice that the less experienced members of the cast get an extra five minutes to practise.'

I explained, gently, that the call he heard at 7.25 every evening, 'Beginners on stage, please!', meant that it was time for everyone in the first scene to head for their positions.

In any career there are milestones, points at which the road to success changes and takes on a new character, events which alter for ever the route you are taking. With the benefit of hindsight, I can identify many such milestones. The one that stood out most clearly at the time was my appearance at the Last Night of the Proms in 1990.

Mark Elder had been invited to conduct the Last Night that year and asked if I would like to join Ann Murray, who was the principal soloist, in the 'Flower Duet' from *Lakme* and the traditional finale of 'Rule Britannia'. Naturally, I said yes. It has always been the most enormous honour to be invited to sing at the Albert Hall on the Last Night of the Proms and I was thrilled at the prospect of sharing such a stage with Ann, whom I had admired for so long. As the day crept nearer, however, my nerves began to twitch. The Albert Hall is a very big place and accommodates a very large number of people who are all intensely knowledgeable about music. What is more, the event is televised and broadcast all over the world. The more I tried to calculate just how many people I might be singing to, the more terrified I became. I devoted every spare moment when I wasn't rehearsing or performing *The*

Magic Flute to working on the duet, which is a tricky piece, with either Joy or Mark.

With six weeks to go I suddenly realised I had nothing to wear. The only evening clothes I had were slinky little cocktail numbers or sedate 'oratorio wear'. I ran to Auntie Jean in the wardrobe department. 'Auntie Jean, I need you to make me a new frock,' I pleaded. 'For the Last Night of the Proms!' 'Oh my dear gawd!' was all she could reply until she had had a sit down and a nice cup of tea. When she recovered her composure we set off down to Berwick Street to choose some material. She decreed that I needed something that would catch the light, I decided that, as *Lakme* has an Indian setting, the style should be like a sari. Berwick Street, a little by-way in Soho, is lined with shops selling nothing but mile upon mile of dress fabric. In one such emporium we found just what we were looking for – a material called Liquid Gold. It was soft and light and shimmered like a humming-bird's wing. It was also sensationally expensive, but I paid up and blew almost my entire fee for the job just on the fabric.

As summer drew to a close and my Big Day edged closer, the crisis in the Gulf was in the forefront of everyone's mind. The moral certainty with which the country had gone to war in the South Atlantic seven years before had been undermined and concern about Saddam Hussein and his motives was overlaid with doubts about the ethical issues involved in Britain waging war so far from her own shores. A fortnight before my Albert Hall debut, Ann, Mark and I gave what we understood to be a promotional interview to Michael Owen of the *Evening Standard*. After a few innocuous questions about what it felt like to be singing on such a unique occasion and such like, Michael asked Ann and me a topical, but hypothetical, question. If the situation in the Gulf were to worsen in the next few days and lives were to be lost, on either side, how would we feel about singing such ostentatiously patriotic songs as 'Rule Britannia' and 'Land of Hope and Glory'? We fielded the question as diplomatically as possible, with stock answers about keeping music and politics separate, and Michael let us off the hook.

Mark was not so fortunate. Asked the same question, he was pressed for a more direct answer. He replied, quite simply and honestly, that if hostilities did begin, he hoped it would be possible to discuss with the BBC whether or not it would be proper to continue with the programme or whether alterations should be made. The ultimate responsibility for any such decision would obviously lie with the BBC and not with the conductor. Michael Owen persisted and, under his insistent, niggling interrogation, Mark agreed that if English forces were, indeed, under fire on the Last Night, the *automatic* inclusion of all the traditional songs might seem ill-timed and inappropriate. A few days later, just a week before the concert was to take place, the interview appeared in the *Evening Standard* under a sensationalist headline which implied that Mark was 'standing by to cancel the programme'.

Outraged by what appeared to be Mark taking a personal stand on such a sensitive issue, the BBC removed him from the concert that same day. The order for his dismissal came from John Drummond, though there were rumours that the impetus for it was political rather than corporate and came from much higher places. This was far from being an end to the matter and over the following week the issue of why he had been sacked became a *cause célèbre* and was hurled round national and international newspapers. I was so angry at the injustice that had been done to such a dear friend that I resolved to withdraw as well, in protest, but Mark would have none of it and not only persuaded me to carry on but continued to give me last-minute coaching for my performance.

Andrew Davis, who was Principal Conductor of the BBC Symphony Orchestra, took over at the last minute, as he was obliged to do. I had been nervous about the occasion for weeks, but I had been comforted by the thought that Mark would be there. Now that I was on my own, the nerves became pure terror. I became hell to live with, lurching between grouchiness and hysteria, but Peter's patient love for me never faltered as he and Mum gently coaxed me towards my big moment. At the last rehearsal, all I could think of was the sheer size of the Albert Hall. How could my voice possibly fill such a vast space? Why didn't they just stick to tennis tournaments?

When I walked out on to the stage on the night, the space was filled with thousands upon thousands of people. I had never seen so many human beings gathered together in one place before and I didn't dare let myself think about the untold millions watching me on TV. My legs were like jelly and my heart pounded in my chest and then the silence was broken by a single, shrill wolf-whistle. This isn't a concert hall, I told myself, it's a building site. Then a balloon popped, the sound echoing round the vast auditorium, and I thought, it's not a building site, it's a party – just a great big party and Ann and I are doing a turn, just like I used to back home in Yorkshire. My nerves evaporated and I relaxed. The hard work of the *Lakme* duet over, it was time for 'Rule Britannia'. I had practised and practised at it for weeks, working on some extravagant ornamentation with Mark and Noel Davies, the Coliseum's Ornament King. I set my feet firmly on the stage and thought 'Rule Britannia' – I'll give them a broadside! I sang my ornaments for all I was worth, up and down my arpeggios, pinging out the top Cs. As we went for the rousing encore, I realised that I wasn't just singing, I was entertaining. This was what I had done on Saturday nights in our little cottage in Waterside, what Nick Grace had sarcastically accused me of wanting to do – I was entertaining the troops and I just adored it. I came off the stage with applause ringing in my ears knowing that I had achieved something I was born to do and that I had to keep on doing it.

Peter and I spent the first anniversary of our moving in together in Geneva where I was playing the second niece in Tony Palmer's production of Britten's *Peter Grimes*. I had been lonely and homesick last time I had worked in Switzerland and I knew it would be ten times worse this time if I were living by myself in a soulless rented flat. Peter solved the problem by arranging for me to stay with Linda (his 'previous dancing partner' as he puts it) and her husband Simon who lived just over the border, in France. This may seem like a rather odd arrangement but it was an absolutely delightful time for me. To say that Peter and Linda had remained friends was, for once, the complete truth, and she and Simon swiftly became my friends too. Linda was pregnant with their first child and as I watched her swell and blossom I realised how much I yearned for a child of my own. My assertion that in Peter I had found the father of my children had hitherto been little more than a metaphor for how right our relationship felt. Now, despite my increasing age and the dire warnings of doctors about my dodgy kidney (which Peter had, admittedly, dismissed as 'a load of tosh'), I wanted a real, live baby.

Peter Grimes was not a happy experience for any of the cast. Tony Palmer was not an easy man to work with – perhaps he was intimidated by the fact that many of the cast had played their roles elsewhere and had arrived with them clearly defined. The cast was almost entirely British apart from Grimes himself who was played by Jan Blinkoff, a Dutch tenor. The chorus scenes in *Peter Grimes* are among the most difficult in the whole of opera, even for a British chorus used to singing in English, and, despite heroic efforts, the Geneva chorus found the challenge too great. If the rehearsal period was tense, the opening night was catastrophic. We had a beautiful and ambitious set which involved a section of the stage lifting up to form a hut. That night, the elderly stage manager forgot to give the cue which should have alerted a technician to remove the securing bolt from the hut, before the hydraulic mechanism was switched on. We watched and listened in horror as the hut, straining against its moorings, thrust its way upward, taking a large section of the stage with it. The air was filled with the terrible sounds of metal grinding on metal, wood splintering and Tony Palmer wailing like an injured beast in the wings. While Jan did his best to keep the scene going, a stage hand bravely got underneath the hut to try to secure it but lost his footing and was badly injured. During the extended interval, as we discussed whether it was safe to continue, the chorus had a union meeting and the Swedish set designer headed for the airport and the first plane back to Stockholm. In the end, the hut was winched back and we carried on, avoiding the ragged, gaping wound in the stage.

When my three-month contract in Geneva finally came to an end, we came back the long, slow way, driving across France in my ancient Fiat Panda. The spring weather was glorious and the French countryside as captivating as ever.

'Perhaps we should have a party when we get back,' I suggested. 'To celebrate finding each other.'

'Let's not have a party,' proposed Peter. ' Let's have a wedding.'

I found a free week in my diary, between performances of a revival of *Cunning Little Vixen*, and we planned a small, informal wedding. I had no need of the fairytale trappings of church and long white gown this time. We were married in the unprepossessing surroundings of Finsbury Town Hall in Islington, sandwiched into a fifteen minute slot in the nuptial production line. I wore an eye-catching summer dress patterned with bright blue and red irises and a large white hat. John and Imo, naturally, were our witnesses and there were only eight other guests. Afterwards, we all went to lunch at our favourite Swedish restaurant, Anna's Place, where the owner's father, who had once baked for the King of Sweden, presented us with a spectacular wedding cake of profiteroles piled high and decorated with a cloud of spun sugar.

Two dear friends, Anthony and Penny Costley-White had offered us their beautiful nineteenth-century farmhouse for the week as a wedding present and we set off, still in our wedding finery and covered in confetti, directly from the restaurant to Paris. We took the overnight train and pulled into the tiny station at Vindrac, near Toulouse, at seven in the morning. We stepped out into a crystal-clear blue day, fresh with dew and as bright and inviting as a glass of champagne. The farmhouse was exquisitely beautiful and we spent our first week as man and wife in a languid haze of sunbathing, swimming and exploring. We walked in the cool green woods where wild orchids carpeted the ground, rambled around the mediaeval village of Cordes and shopped in the local market for cheese and bread and fruit. We were in paradise.

Our actual wedding had been a very intimate affair, but we made up for it when we got home. Determined not to miss anybody out, we had three huge parties, one for Peter's family and their friends in Lincolnshire, one in my cottage for the Garrett clan and, biggest of all, a party for our London friends in Islington. We invited everybody we could think of. After all, I thought, they won't all come. As the days went by, more and more people wrote and phoned to say how delighted they were that we had finally done the decent thing and, of course, they would be delighted to come and, by the way, could they bring the children? The flat was minute – how could we possibly squeeze them all in? In the end, over 150 people came to celebrate with us that Sunday morning, filling the sitting room to bursting point and spilling over into the tiny kitchen where I was struggling, helped only by Maria, my cherished Spanish cleaner, to keep up with the demand for champagne and smoked salmon bagels. Some of the guests were old friends of mine, some I hardly knew and I got into such a tizzy that I could barely remember which was which. I have a terrible feeling that at one stage I attempted to introduce Jeremy Isaacs to his own wife and then forgot both their names.

My cottage in Epworth was no longer a bolt-hole, a private escape from the world. It became a shared delight, a phone-free haven for weekends and a base from which I could introduce Peter to the land of my birth. It was on one of these weekend trips that fate was to play another of her tricks. I had been playing Musetta in *La Bohème* and the last night had been very exciting. Eric Clapton was in the audience, which gave me a real buzz as he had been my hero for years – not just for his skill as a musician, but for the courageous way he has fought his private demons and his honesty in speaking about them.

We left the theatre and headed straight for Yorkshire, looking forward to a quiet couple of days on our own. In the early hours of the morning, as we came off the motorway only a few miles from Epworth, we met another car travelling at high speed the wrong way around a round-about and collided with it, head on. My seat belt saved my life, but I was knocked unconscious for a minute or so and came round hearing Peter yelling, 'Get out of the car! Get out now!' as smoke billowed ominously from the bonnet. But I could barely breathe, let alone move. My chest felt as if someone had taken a battering ram to it. The passenger door was jammed so Peter hauled me, screaming in agony, across the driver's seat and on to the grass verge. I could not speak, but it was clear from the way I was clutching myself where the pain was coming from. Terrified that I had ruptured my liver, Peter knelt down beside me, blood pouring from a wound to his leg, and anxiously felt for signs of internal bleeding. A police car miraculously appeared and one officer called for an ambulance while the other doused our engine with foam. Having reassured himself that my liver was probably intact, Peter left me with a policeman and limped off to help give first aid to the passenger from the other car until the ambulance arrived to take us all to Doncaster Royal Infirmary. I was poked, prodded, X-rayed and declared to have nothing much wrong with me. Peter's knee was patched up and we were discharged after a few hours, dosed up with pain-killers.

We hobbled back to London the next morning and within days I was back at work, rehearsing Adele in Richard Jones's production of *Die Fledermaus*. The pain in my chest did not go away as the hospital had assured me it would. In fact it got worse – I felt as if I had been laced into an over-tightened straitjacket. I could breathe enough to live, but not enough to sing. I was sent to see the ENO company doctor who ordered more X-rays. They showed that I had, in fact, broken my breastbone and cracked several ribs. Dramatic as this sounded, I was assured that no treatment was required. The bones would mend in time and until they did I should rest as much as possible – some chance! Peter was less convinced, and spent several days thrusting my X-rays anxiously at every medical friend and colleague he could find. The response was always the same – fascination at the overdeveloped anatomy of my chest and reassurance that no permanent damage was done.

Back at work, I struggled through most of Adele's part, though the famous 'Laughing Song' was anything but a laugh for me and try as I might, I could not reach the top note at the end of the audition aria – it just hurt too much. Richard and I put our heads together and decided to revive an idea he had suggested to me weeks earlier. At the end of the aria, as Adele left the stage, she would do a quick strip-tease, baring her bottom to the audience to distract them from the lack of the final note. This attention-grabbing device aptly suited the coquettish Adele. It said every-thing about her character – sexy, audacious, immature and contemptuous of authority. The production was already full of spectacle. Instead of a traditional maid's costume I was dressed in a Madonna-style conical bra and fish-net tights. There was a chorus line of sequin-clad, high-kicking dancers, a real horse, a pantomime gorilla in a tutu (played with extraordinary zoological accuracy by one of the cast of the film *Greystoke*), a live poodle and an electric cat which zipped along a wire at the front of the stage.

The curtain had barely risen on the first night before the poodle had chased, attacked and dismembered the cat, leaving it a tangle of fizzing metal and wires in the wings. As the cast carried on regardless, an apoplectic stage manager could be heard on the backstage tannoy screaming, 'Christ! The dog's savaged the cat! Dog handlers to the stage immediately please! For heaven's sake don't let the horse see the gorilla!' I think I can be forgiven for believing that my little light-hearted flash of buttock would pass unnoticed amongst all this. I was certainly unprepared for the reception it received in the press the next morning. The papers, particularly the tabloids, went into a feeding frenzy. The headlines screamed 'Opera Star Les Bares Her Arias' and 'Pop Take-off By Opera Star' (this was in *The Times*, believe it or not, *and* they managed to spell my name wrong). It amused me that my bare bottom was supposed to have been so shocking to Princess Alexandra and Norma Major, who had both been in the audience. Neither lady had ever given me the impression of being the kind of delicate creature who would swoon at a glimpse of naked flesh and when I met them both after the show they were not in the least offended. The prudery of the tabloid press, especially that section of it which makes a living out of sleaze and smut, never ceases to astonish me.

By the time the fuss died down, I was out of the eye-catching basque and into a simple, demure cotton frock for my next role as Rose Maurrant in a revival of Kurt Weill's *Street Scene*, which is set in a New York tenement in the 1930s. Weill himself described this work variously as his 'Broadway opera' and a 'dramatic musical'. It contains elements of both traditional opera and musical theatre (including a show-stopping dance number that had been performed in the original 1989 production by a young Catherine Zeta Jones). Rose is shy and inexperienced, dreaming of life beyond the narrow immigrant community in which she lives with her family, until family tragedy forces her to leave her home and her sweetheart and find the strength to make a life of her own. The specific setting in time and place was so crucial that I was determined to master the New York accent the part required. I was helped a great deal by Kevin Anderson, the American tenor who played my boyfriend, Sam, but I was never confident that I had got it quite right and one critic referred to my accent as 'New Yorkshire'. Ironically, I made my first visit to New York only days after *Street Scene* finished.

Contrary to what some people think (I was once described in the press as 'as publicity shy as a charging rhinoceros'), I do not crave publicity for its own sake. On the other hand, if interviews need giving and photographs need taking in order to promote a record or a new opera, then I'm happy to oblige. My work is all about reaching out and communicating to people. If the press want a picture, I'll smile; if they want a quote, I'm their girl. The power of the media was brought home to me most vividly on my first ever trip to the USA. *Diva!* was selling very respectably in America and Reynald da Silva arranged for me to go there to undertake a coast-to-coast promotional tour.

In New York I was placed in the capable hands of Yusef Ghandi, Ren's American partner, and I discovered that he had organised a packed schedule of press and radio interviews. Yusef is a delightful, charming and funny man – a one-man publicity dynamo who had contacts everywhere. Together we travelled the length and breadth of the country, talking to newspapers, TV and radio stations, anyone in fact who was prepared to listen to me. We were met with great warmth and courtesy wherever we went and nowhere more so than in St Louis. Jim Connett who ran KFUO FM, the local classical music station, was incredibly kind to me and I spent a whole morning as a guest on his show, chatting to him, taking calls from his listeners and enjoying myself hugely. By the time we reached Los Angeles I realised what a popular and powerful medium radio is in America. One day I was interviewed by a delightful presenter called Bonnie Grice and I spoke in general about my attitude towards classical music and my album in particular, mentioning the fact that I was going straight from the studio to the local record store to sign copies. When I arrived there, less than an hour later, 200 people had turned up to meet me.

Back in New York, Yusef had managed to wangle me on to a spot on a local TV show, singing four arias from *Diva!* – 'Song to the Moon', 'O Mio Babbino Caro', 'Voi Che Sapete' and 'And This is My Beloved'. I was thrilled as twenty minutes of music was practically my own show. What is more, the programme would be recorded at the Steinway showrooms just off Broadway, a wonderfully prestigious and glamorous venue – thank God I had packed a posh frock! I turned up at the appointed time and got my first shock of the day. The pianist they had promised to provide appeared to have been scooped up from a downtown dive. He was enthusiastic and could sight-read perfectly but he could play in only one style, a style that could best be described as honky-tonk. The notes were all more or less in the right place but the rhythm and arrangement were entirely his own.

The second disappointment came in the shape of a harassed young producer: 'Gee, Miss Garrett, this sure is a shame, but it seems like we only got a four-minute slot for all these nice numbers. We really don't wanna lose one of 'em. D'ya reckon you could do us a medley, honey?'

To my eternal shame, I was so desperate both to be on American TV and to please these charming people, I said yes.

The honky-tonk piano man came into his own and cobbled something together. It was more of a mongrel than a medley, with Dvorak segueing uncomfortably into Mozart, which led straight into Puccini with barely time to draw breath, the whole thing ending appropriately with three bars of a Broadway show-stopper. But it only lasted four and a quarter minutes, and that was what was wanted.

By the time I came home I was exhausted and I had a very busy year coming up. I was to record another album for Silva Screen, and was looking forward hugely to working with the great Ken Russell in the title role of Gilbert and Sullivan's *Princess Ida* which he was scheduled to produce at ENO in the autumn, with my old sparring partner Nickolas Grace playing my father. We decided to celebrate Peter's fortieth birthday with a whole month off, staying at Anthony and Penny's house in France, where we had spent our honeymoon. Friends came out to join us and we had a magical time, recovering from the nagging effects of the accident and recharging our batteries. One morning in the third week of our holiday I got out of bed and was horribly sick. I knew instantly and instinctively that Peter had an unexpected extra birthday present. When we came home it was confirmed that I was indeed pregnant.

Carrying on working while pregnant posed few problems at first. Far from making singing difficult, pregnancy suited my voice very well. I felt grounded and centred and at peace, and I found I could sing better than ever. It also made me feel incredibly sexy. It had already been agreed that the cover of my next album, *PriMadonna*, would be another glamorous shot by John Stoddart, but the photograph that we came up with was racier than we had originally envisaged. I couldn't find a dress that fitted me properly and my body was by that time a very odd shape so I wrapped myself in a piece of deep purple silk, slipped on a pair of shoes with heels so high I could never have stood in them let alone walked, draped myself upside down over a piece of exceptionally uncomfortable, but very beautiful, modern furniture and yelled at John, 'Go for the legs!'

Not everyone was as thrilled at our news as our family and friends were. The Opera Planning Department at ENO reacted with dismay and Ken Russell was furious. I had rung him up to tell him the good news, assuming that he would be able to work round my condition somehow. He was, after all, notorious for his liberal interpretations of classic texts. 'I'm pregnant!' I yelled down the phone to Ken who was in a muddy, windswept field in the depths of the countryside, filming *Lady Chatterley's Lover*. 'That's OK isn't it?' 'No it bloody isn't OK,' he screamed back.

'Princess Ida's a self-confessed man-hating virgin, you silly tart!' Even he couldn't get away with her being seven months pregnant. The solution was found in a nifty bit of role-swapping with my friend Rosemary Joshua who had been cast in a revival of Jonathan Miller's *Don Giovanni*. She would do Princess Ida and I would take Zerlina, if Jonathan would have me. He was ecstatic at the prospect of an expectant Zerlina – it made perfect sense to him. He had always been troubled at why she should marry 'that idiot Masetto' – now it was obvious that it was a shot-gun marriage. It also pleased him that seducing a pregnant woman would make Don Giovanni himself look even more of a monster.

The only person for whom my pregnancy was a problem was poor Christopher Purves who played Masetto. During Zerlina's aria 'Beat Me, Beat Me' (*Batti, Batti*) he was obliged to pick me up, and as the weeks went by and I got greater and greater with child we were all afraid he would herniate himself during the performance.

Those of us who campaign for the demystification of classical music gave a resounding cheer when Classic FM was born in September 1992. Here at last was a radio station that accepted what I had always known – there are millions of people in this country who love classical music but who don't feel they have to sit alone, in a quiet, dark room to listen to it. For months before its launch, there were mutterings in certain quarters of the press. It couldn't be done, they sagely agreed, no one would listen to it. When the first set of listening figures was published, it was clear that it had tapped a vast well of demand. Still its detractors protested; perhaps it could be done, but now they declared that it shouldn't be done. To play an aria rather than a whole opera, a movement rather than a symphony was deemed heresy; to tell a joke or play a jingle between the two was the ultimate blasphemy. But the public, the real people, had the last word – they re-tuned their radios in droves, responding to the enthusiasm of the presenters who actually seemed to be enjoying the music they were playing rather than showing off their erudition. The press enjoyed making snide remarks about the mispronunciation of some names, but so what? I was teased for weeks as a student at the Royal Academy after talking about 'Mantovani's Vespers'. If Henry Kelly could combine two of my great loves, classical music and horse racing, in one radio show then he was all right by me. I had only one reservation about the new station and I expressed it forcefully to Michael Bukht, their programme controller, when I bumped into him at an industry do only weeks after they went on air.

'You've got these fantastic jingles, Michael, played on all the different instruments of the orchestra, but where is the greatest instrument of them all, the human voice?'

'Good point, Lesley. Thanks for the offer,' he replied. 'Would next week suit you for recording some for us?'

And that is how I came to spend an afternoon at Joe & Co, having great fun recording the Classic FM signature tune in an enormously diverse range of styles. Some of the versions were written by Paul Hart, some of them I just made up on the spot. The question I am most frequently asked in my life is, 'Do you get a royalty on those jingles?' and my answer is always a proud and resounding 'NO'. They are more than welcome to a few free Garrett twiddles.

On New Year's Eve 1992, with two weeks to go until my baby was due, Peter and I went to one of Mark and Mandy Elder's legendary parties. Peter Jonas and his new wife Lucy were there, as were David and Jane Pountney, David Alden, John and Imo and the whole of the ENO gang. We drank gallons of champagne, ate far too much sherry trifle and played party games until two in the morning when we staggered merrily home and collapsed into bed. When I woke up a couple of hours later, I blamed my queasiness on the sherry trifle and continued to do so until I noticed that the stomach ache was not constant but coming at regular intervals. It finally dawned on me that I was having a baby. There was no point in waking Peter who would be too hungover to be of any use so I got up, packed a suitcase, cleaned the flat from top to bottom and waited for morning. Peter finally surfaced at about 9.30 and found me in the spare bedroom on my hands and knees, frantically trying to remember my breathing exercises.

'What are you doing, Lesley?'

'I'M HAVING A BABY! WHAT DOES IT LOOK LIKE I'M DOING?'

My cool, calm, professional GP of a husband, who had delivered countless babies, many of them on bathroom floors, went into a complete tail-spin and demanded we go to the hospital there and then. I made him wait for a bit, but eventually gave in and allowed him to drive me to University College Hospital. Peter had trained at UCH and was determined that his child should be born in his alma mater. I was more than happy with the choice as the experience and skills of its staff are second to none. They have a policy of encouraging mothers to make a genuine choice about the way their baby is to be born. If you want to give birth in a paddling pool full of tepid water, that's fine by them. If you want to have a go at the birthing stool (a peculiar contraption that looks like a mediaeval instrument of torture) that's fine too. If you want to do it swinging from a chandelier they would be glad to help (though you'd have to provide your own chandelier, this is the NHS after all). On the other hand, if, like me, you want nothing but to put yourself and your baby in the hands of the doctors and midwives and every bit of technical wizardry science can come up with, no one at UCH will make you feel the slightest bit guilty about it.

We needn't have hurried – the baby certainly wasn't going to. Towards evening we turned on the TV and I realised I had forgotten that I was on the box that night – in a recording of Weill's *Street Scene* that had been made earlier in the year. I was singing in hospital too, as I had discovered that the best way to cope with contractions was to sing arpeggios through them. After twelve hours of arpeggios, however, I was getting very tired and in need of help, which arrived, like the answer to every girl's prayer, in the shape of an absolutely divine Hawaiian anaesthetist – tall, dark and handsome and bearing *drugs*. With an epidural administered and heaven knows what other jolly stuff floating round my bloodstream I was perfectly content and sent Peter out to get some food – poor thing hadn't eaten all day. No sooner had he set off to scour Tottenham Court Road for a chip shop than trouble began.

The monitors I was hooked up to showed that my baby was in distress and a decision was taken to perform an emergency Caesarean section. The most capable team I have ever come across, in any walk of life, now surrounded me. Nurses, midwives, anaesthetists, obstetricians all swarmed around, calmly but with obvious urgency and wheeled me towards the operating theatre, with me protesting weakly through a drug-induced mist, 'Can't we wait for my husband . . .' Peter arrived back in my room with a mouth full of greasy hamburger to find it deserted. He thought for one terrible moment that I had died but then common sense got the better of him. He established where I had been taken and ran hell for leather along a maze of dark corridors in the bowels of UCH, grabbed a gown and mask and, in a wonderfully operatic gesture, burst through the swing doors at the very moment of his son's birth.

Jeremy (as we had already decided to call him) was a very funny colour, on account of having the cord wrapped four times around his neck and body. But by the time he had been sucked out, cleaned up and wrapped in a blanket he was fine – blond, peaceful and perfect in his father's arms. It was all Tom Jones's fault, of course. We had been to see him in concert in Croydon only two weeks before and I had bumped and ground with the best of them to 'It's Not Unusual'. Poor Jeremy must have been thrown around so much he got himself trussed up like a turkey. (I had drawn the line at throwing my knickers on stage, but only because

I was so ashamed of the kind of underwear eight months pregnant women are obliged to wear.)

I was wheeled back to the ward as *Street Scene* drew to an end on BBC2. 'Good old Mummy,' said Peter to his new-born son, 'trust her to take a curtain call in two theatres at the same time.'

We had recognised, some time before Jeremy was born, that our little flat was just too small for a family and had been trying to buy a proper house in a leafy suburban street closer to Peter's work. We had sold both our flats but had been gazumped at the last minute on the house. I returned home with Jeremy in the knowledge that we had to vacate the place in ten weeks' time. In sheer desperation we bought the next house that came on the market, but it turned out to be perfect and, by a rather spooky but delightful coincidence, only a few doors away from John and Imo, without whom we would never have met. Seven years and several bouts of the builders later, we are still there.

I was due to go back to work just twelve weeks after Jeremy was born, singing the soprano solo in Haydn's *Creation* in the Royal Festival Hall with the great Willard White. I had taken to breast-feeding like a duck to water. At last I realised why I had been given my ridiculously ample chest. Jeremy was perfectly content with the arrangement, though he was threatened with drowning at every meal. None of my clothes fitted me and whilst Peter's shirts were fine for slopping about at home, they were hardly appropriate as stage wear. In desperation, I looked up 'dress hire' in the yellow pages and rang the first number I found which, by a happy accident, turned out to be that of

Andrea Galer, a marvellously talented woman who not only created her own range of clothes but was also a costume designer for TV and films (she had just finished working on *Withnail and I*) and hired out frocks as a side-line. She came up with the perfect solution for me – a full, shot silk skirt and an exquisite Indian jacket, embroidered all over with plants and insects.

Being away from Jeremy for the day was, however, tricky as I needed to express milk frequently if I was to avoid copious and embarrassing leakage. The *Creation* was a minefield for me, littered as it is with references to milk and fecundity and general overflowing. I went on stage with my bra stuffed full of padding, but I still had to dash to my breast-pump in the interval, closely followed by Willard, eager to assist in, or at the very least witness, this unusual operation.

In April I returned to ENO as planned, to prepare for Handel's *Ariodante*, but I was suffering from an acute case of Nappy Brain. I wasn't depressed, just tearful and distracted and utterly unable to concentrate for more than thirty seconds at a time; I barely knew a crochet from a quaver. *Ariodante* was not the easiest work to come back to. It is a very, very serious opera. David Alden didn't have to look very far for the dark side of this piece because Handel had already written it. The second soprano role of Dalinda is not the light relief that Handel more frequently wrote and I more frequently played – the naughty younger sister or the flighty shepherdess. She is a maid, but not in the Adele or Damigella mould at all. Dalinda is neurotic and vulnerable, desperate for love and

obsessed by the powerful sexuality of Polinesso (played by
Christopher Robson). Ann Murray played Ariodante, who
represents everything that is good; Polinesso is pure evil.
Chris Robson is mesmeric on stage, with an extraordinary
capacity to generate warped and disturbing energy, drawing
the rest of the cast into a twisted, dangerous world. The part
could have been written for him. Our rehearsals together
left me physically and emotionally drained.

'What have you been doing today?' Peter would absent-
mindedly enquire when I staggered home. 'I've spent the
afternoon being raped over the back of a chair by a
counter-tenor,' was my reply for days on end. It was an
exhausting part to play, not least because of the harrowing
emotional journey my character made from her innocence
at the beginning, through violence and degradation to
the last scene when she sits, broken, on the floor and
is comforted by the man who truly loves her. Every time
Paul Nilon, playing the sensitive Lurciano to perfection,
enveloped me tenderly in this scene my tears were real
and unforced.

I was feeling like a human being again, albeit a very,
very tired one, as Jeremy had still not slept for more than
two or three hours at a stretch, night or day. I was enjoying
being back in harness when, one morning, yet again, I
got up and was terribly sick. It must be something I've
eaten, I thought. It wasn't, of course, I was just pregnant
again. After the initial shock died down, Peter and I
were delighted at the prospect of another baby, but we
were, nevertheless, slightly embarrassed by it. Our friends'
congratulations were tempered by concern for my health

and we were the subject of much ribald comment, with Peter being taken aside by colleagues who offered to show him diagrams of what had caused my condition and how it could be prevented in future. I was just gloriously happy to be pregnant again. It is probably a good thing I didn't meet Peter earlier or I would have ended up with fifteen children.

This time around, no roles had to be recast or reinterpreted to fit in with my pregnancy, just a bit of Auntie Jean wizardry with my Rose Maurrant costume for another run of Kurt Weill's *Street Scene*. My bump did appear undisguised, though, on a couple of distinctly non-operatic stages. I was delighted to be asked to take part in the 1993 Royal Variety Performance at the Dominion Theatre. Andrea Galer made me a beautiful dress – a sort of sexy mediaeval number with a high waist, slashed sleeves and a train, with a slit up the front to reveal a bit of leg. I am as star-struck as the next person, so it was wonderfully exciting to share a dressing-room with Ruth Maddox, Alexandra Bastedo and Lulu. I was enormously impressed by Lulu's professionalism. My preparation for the performance was limited to a quick ten minutes of scales as a warm-up. She practised non-stop, repeating phrases over and over and over again until she was confident her performance would match her own exacting high standards. Waiting in the wings, sandwiched between The Village People and the Bee Gees and surrounded by a gang of Muppets, I calmed my nerves by remembering that we were all there to do a turn, just as my family had always done. The audience was different, but the principle was the same.

With a cast of hundreds and dozens of different acts, the show is a logistical nightmare and there is bound to be the odd technical hitch. It was just my luck that it was my turn when the gremlins struck. I was supposed to wait behind a glitter curtain while Cilla Black introduced me then, as the curtain rose, walk to a stand mike at the centre of the stage. On the night, the curtain missed its cue and by the time it finally went up, the orchestra were half-way through the introduction to 'I Want to be a Prima Donna'. High heels and pregnancy notwithstanding, I ran down the stage and hit my spot, breathless but in time, just.

Later, when I came off stage, the director took me aside: 'What was all the running for, Lesley? The band would have done a play till ready.'

'What's a play till ready when it's at home?'

He explained that the orchestra would have repeated the last couple of bars of the introduction until I was in position and gave them the nod that I was ready to sing.

'Blimey! I wish we had that at the Coliseum,' I replied, 'but Mozart doesn't do Play Till Readies.'

My next appearance on TV was in the even more unlikely setting of *Top of the Pops*. Esther Rantzen had asked me to appear on her programme *Hearts of Gold* to sing the Bach/Gounod 'Ave Maria', accompanied by Amanda Thompson, a talented thirteen-year-old pianist from Keighley who, despite being tragically struck down by leukaemia, was a one-girl fund-raising phenomenon. What Amanda didn't know until after the show was that a record was made of our performance and put on sale in aid of the Malcolm Sargent Cancer Fund for Children.

The record sold so well that we made over £150,000 for the charity and made it to Number 16 in the pop singles chart. We were invited to appear on *Top of the Pops* which was a dream I had never expected to come true. I was absolutely huge by this time and felt very out of place amongst all the lithe, trendy teenagers in the audience, especially as 'Ave Maria' was a far cry from the music they were used to hearing. My backstage remark that I felt and looked like Mama Cass was greeted with blank stares from the young production team, none of whom had a clue who I was talking about. But the kids were wonderfully open-minded, listened with rapt attention and applauded us enthusiastically.

My last public engagement before the baby was due was singing Handel's *Messiah* with Christopher Robinson and the City of Birmingham Symphony Orchestra and Chorus. The *Messiah* probably means more to me than any other piece of music. I was suckled on it, weaned on it, cut my teeth on it and I fervently hope to die at a very ripe old age singing it. Despite his encyclopaedic knowledge of opera, Peter is a newcomer to oratorio and had never heard the *Messiah* sung until that evening. It didn't take him long to understand what a joy he had been missing. As the choir reached 'For unto us a child is born', Peter and I found each other's eyes. His were bright with pleasure and tears, and I realised I was crying too.

I went into labour on 31 March, the very day my baby was due, and it was the first time I have ever been on time for anything in my life. But after hours of hanging around in hospital with absolutely nothing happening, we were ignominiously sent home again, to my husband's acute embarrassment. I spent the next day desperately keeping my legs crossed and praying that my child wouldn't be saddled with a birthday on April Fool's Day. I was so exhausted by the following day that Chloe was also, like her brother, delivered by Caesarean section, expertly performed by my consultant Anthony Silverstone. Her arrival, joyful as it obviously was, was tinged with sadness. The following morning I was told that my grandfather, Arthur Garrett had died, four hours before her birth.

He had been in hospital in Doncaster for a while, recovering from a stroke, but no one had thought his life was in danger. The night before his death, one of the nurses had learnt that I was his grand-daughter. 'Gosh,' she had exclaimed, 'Lesley Garrett's the most famous opera singer in the country.' Grandad had sat bolt upright in bed and rounded on her: 'The world, young lady, she's the most famous in the world.' They were his last words.

Chapter 11

———•———

Soprano in Red

With two children under fifteen months old and two full-time careers Peter and I found out the meaning of hard work. Jeremy had still not slept through the night once and Chloe showed no signs of being any different. I don't know which was worse, the nights when they both woke at the same time, leaving us shuttling frantically from one cot to another, or the ones when they took it in turns and there was barely time to get back to sleep again before the other one woke. If anyone had told me when I set out on the great adventure of parenthood that it would be possible to follow a busy singing career whilst permanently, chronically deprived of sleep I'd have said they were crazy. But for six years the only undisturbed nights I was to have were when I was working away from home or when, desperate for proper rest before a big day, I guiltily took myself off to Joy's spare room for the night.

When Jeremy was tiny, we managed with part-time help,

but with two babies and my work schedule getting more and more crowded, we finally had to be realistic and employ a full-time nanny. For months, friends had been telling us that Alison Tullett was available and should be snapped up while we had the chance. Alison was something of a legend in our north London suburban village. She had arrived from Cornwall in 1986 as a fresh-faced teenager, with no fancy certificates but abundant wisdom and common sense, to work for a local family. She stayed with them for five years (which was in itself something of a record around here, where nannies are known for their itchy feet). Popular with mothers and nannies alike, her help and advice were often sought with fractious babies and obstreperous toddlers. 'I'm not getting anywhere with this potty training business,' one mother would grumble to her friend over coffee. 'Why don't you send him over to Alison for a couple of afternoons? She'll sort him out.' Alison changed our lives beyond measure. Firm but infinitely patient, practical but never dull, and Jeremy and Chloe adored her from the start.

Even with Alison's help, life was a constant juggling act. As well as trying to balance the demands of home, husband and children with my work, the work was becoming more and more complicated. Making records, performing in gala concerts and on television, all of which had been side-lines to my day job at ENO, were claiming a growing share of my energy and time. One day I would be dolled up to the nines in a photographer's studio, fussed over by hairdressers and make-up artists, the next I would be rolling around a dusty rehearsal-room floor pretending to be a prostitute, or I might be sitting on a train heading for heaven knows where, trying to remember what I was supposed to be singing that night and hoping I had packed my heated rollers. Sometimes, if I was lucky, Peter would travel with me, acting as a combination of chauffeur, sound and lighting advisor, dresser, PR man and security guard.

One evening, at home, after a particularly chaotic day, Peter turned to me and said, 'What would you rather be doing? Singing Gilda in Bologna?'

He was right, as usual. This was the career I had chosen for myself. If I had followed a more traditional path, I could have been on the international circuit by now, singing a few well-chosen roles in opera houses around the world, flying in for a couple of weeks' rehearsal, doing six performances and flying out again. Aside from the fact that it would bore me rigid, I could never have coped with being away from Peter and the children for so long and so often.

Yet something had to be done to bring some kind of order to the chaos. Robert Slotover, my agent, had felt for some time that he and his team did not have the necessary experience of the world of television and commercial concert promotion, so he brought in a specialist in the field to look after my affairs. Diane Hinds, young, feisty and bursting with energy and ideas, had worked as a plugger for Silva Screen, and was completely at home with record companies, concert promoters and the press. Diane took control of all my other engagements while, at home, my friend Caro Bradford struggled valiantly with a mountain of paperwork and the ceaseless demands of getting me (and, it sometimes seemed, more importantly, my dresses) to the right place at the right time with the right music.

Since my appearance with Bruce Forsyth, I had done a number of bits and pieces of TV work, ranging from pre-senting a Joshua Bell promenade concert to duetting with Frank Bruno on a Saturday morning children's show and taking part in the world's shortest opera on *Record Breakers* – I was rapidly becoming the BBC's rent-a-soprano. The next programme I was offered was a much bigger project. *Jobs for the Girls* was a new series starring Pauline Quirke and Linda Robson. The brainchild of producer Nick Handel, it involved the girls learning to do various unfamiliar tasks, like dog handling and photo-journalism.

My programme would involve them learning to sing 'Rule Britannia', with me as their guide, and performing it on stage with me at an open air concert at Kenwood House. Pauline and Linda were extraordinary. As open and genuine and funny as the day is long, they have known each other for years and have an infectious rapport. They both admitted to being more daunted by this challenge than any of the others in the series, but they put their hearts and souls into it. They took singing lessons from a professional teacher, had some practice with a choir, took advice from their friend and *Birds of a Feather* colleague Peter Polycarpou about stagecraft and even went to see Dame Kiri te Kanawa for some tips. By the time the three of us went round to see Stanley Black, who would conduct the concert, to do a proper rehearsal, the girls' singing had improved immeasurably. Pauline, particularly, had really hit her stride.

'You're really getting the hang of this,' I said to her. 'How are you doing it?'

'Well,' she replied, 'I suppose I'm acting being a big opera singer. Once I'm in the role, the voice seems to come with it.'

She was right, of course, and I have borrowed her technique more than once since. Now, when I am called upon to sing arias that are really designed for a bigger, stronger voice than mine, I go on stage and pretend I am Jane Eaglen. It works a treat. Linda found the whole process much harder, which only heightened my admiration for her determination and courage.

The last part of our preparation was to organise suitable frocks and we were told David Emanuel would design these. Wow! David had first attracted public attention when he and his then wife Elizabeth designed Lady Diana Spencer's wedding dress.

We met David in the Lanesborough hotel at Hyde Park Corner, where he kept a room in which he would see new clients. The three of us turned up straight from a recce on Hampstead Heath, looking decidedly less than our best, and were ushered into a sumptuous apartment, where David, looking suave and impeccable, stretched elegantly on a *chaise longue* surrounded by his latest collection. David is the most charming man one could possibly meet, but the interview got off to an uncomfortable start as he tried to find out what kind of dresses we were looking for.

'Now, Pauline, tell me, what is your idea of evening wear?'

'Er, well, David,' Pauline replied, uncertainly, 'jeans wivout 'oles I s'pose.'

David swallowed hard and sharpened his pencil while we shuffled our feet awkwardly. Pauline was heavily pregnant at the time and, as I knew from my own experience, finding a dress that flatters a bump, is comfortable to sing in and looks glamorous is a tall order. There and then David sketched a beautiful diaphanous design in deep blue chiffon, slit up the front to show off her legs.

'Blimey, Paul,' joked Linda when she saw the drawing, 'you'll have to shave your legs to wear that!'

'Only the fronts, Linda, only the fronts.'

For Linda, he drew a silver and white fairytale of a dress, in a fabric as soft and light as a cobweb. When it came to my turn, David looked me up and down, as if puzzled by my appearance. I guessed what he was thinking – I had grown used to being regarded in this way.

'It's all right, David,' I said, 'I know what you're thinking. You were expecting someone BIGGER weren't you?'

David blushed fetchingly and admitted he had assumed there would be rather more of me to deal with. Some opera singers are built on a grand scale, but I am not. At nine stone soaking wet, I am a Small Soprano. Mentally amending his estimates of the amount of fabric it would require, David got on with designing my dress. With the other two girls in blue and white and 'Rule Britannia' as our song, there was no question but that my dress should be red. Actually, dress is quite the wrong word. What David drew for me was, at the very least, a gown. It was Cinderella's ball gown as imagined by every six-year-old girl. All we had seen was a few hasty sketches on paper but we already knew that our dresses would be perfect and beautiful and we absolutely had to have them to keep. We ganged up and presented the BBC with a united front. If they wouldn't throw the frocks in as part of the deal then we weren't playing.

I had been smitten when I saw the first rough sketch. When I got my hands on the real thing I fell in love. It wasn't crimson, it wasn't scarlet, it was Red. It was the most inexcusably gorgeous, glamorous and romantic dress I had ever seen, let alone worn, not to mention being exquisitely made and fitting me like a second skin. Strictly speaking it wasn't a dress at all, as it came in five separate parts. First there was the voluminous, stiff petticoat made up of layers of tulle. On top of that went a skirt of the softest silk taffeta which swooshed and rustled as it went over my head and fastened at the back with hooks and eyes (this is couture, remember, no zips for David Emanuel). The bodice was in matching silk, boned into shape and decorated across the front with hundreds of twinkling sequins. Down each edge of the bodice were eyelets through which were threaded laces which had to be pulled tight like a Victorian lady's corset before the bodice and skirt were finally secured together with yet more concealed hooks and eyes. Two sets of delicate, frothy, hand-made silk roses were attached to form the straps of the gown and a sequinned tulle stole completed the extraordinary ensemble.

On the night of the Kenwood concert David was on hand with his team of wardrobe mistress, hairdresser and make-up artist to make sure we all looked our very best, as well as doing justice to his creations. I was just as nervous as Pauline and Linda, but all three of us knew that, at the very least, our dresses made us look a million dollars. I learnt the important lesson that looking good isn't just a matter of vanity. If you look good you feel good, and if you feel good you sing good. However well I sang, though, the girls were the stars of the show. I already knew that they were game for anything and prepared to work incredibly hard at the tasks the series set them. On stage, what they lacked in vocal technique that night they more than made up for in guts, enthusiasm and determination to do more than their best. We all three of us came off stage knowing that something special had been achieved and were touched to find that Dame Kiri had sent us all champagne to celebrate.

I had enjoyed working on *Jobs for the Girls* so much that I was keen to do more TV work as soon as possible, whether it involved singing or not. When I was offered the job of presenting a BBC children's educational programme about life in Roman times, I jumped at the chance. It didn't seem to me that it would be very difficult. All I had to do was wander round various sets, dressed in an approximation of Roman dress, talking about aspects of Roman civilisation. On the day, however, I was disconcerted by the amateurism of the production. The script was, to my mind, poorly written, the crew didn't seem to know what they were doing and, worst of all, the actors I was working with hadn't a clue. One man in particular, who was supposed to be playing a lion in a scene about gladiators, insisted on wandering moronically around the set, making inane comments, interrupting the action and generally making a thorough nuisance of himself. I could not understand why I was the only one bothered by his behaviour but, being relatively new to TV and not wanting to make a fuss, I gritted my teeth and put up with his antics until the final scene in which I was supposed to be explaining about Roman food. The wretched lion turned up yet again and tipped an entire bowl of spaghetti right over my hair. I was appalled at his lack of professionalism but it was vanity which overcame my last reserves of patience, and I turned on him in fury, only to see him remove his lion's head and reveal himself as Noel Edmonds. I had been Gotcha'd. I suppose I was expected to laugh at this point or, at the least, show stoic acceptance. Instead, I let out a blood-curdling yell and, grabbing great handfuls of the cold, slimy spaghetti, stuffed them forcefully down the front of Noel's lion costume.

I have always thought it was a crying shame that there is so little classical music on television. The BBC transmits the Proms, of course, but I sometimes wonder if they feel that lets them off the hook for the rest of the year. There are occasional broadcasts of whole operas on BBC2, but not on a regular basis. Music of any kind, for that matter, is hard to find at peak time on the main channels. Gone are the days when singers such as Val Doonican and Nana Mouskouri hosted Saturday evening shows, attracting enormous audiences and showcasing a wide variety of music, including regular appearances by classical entertainers such as James Galway and John Williams. We can all have a good laugh when we see excerpts from these old shows, but only because the production style now looks so old-fashioned. It was always a dream of mine to find a way to bring good music back on to mainstream television and I was fortunate that one man who agreed with me was Michael Leggo, then Head of Light Entertainment at BBC Television. Following my appearance on *Jobs for the Girls*, Michael made me a fantastic offer – a one-off, hour-long TV special. It gave me the opportunity to sing, and talk about, a wide range of music, introduce and sing with guests like John Hudson and Jason Howard, and experiment with dance and visual imagery to enhance the impact of the music.

The process of recording the programme was an education for me and the production team. There was much to learn about the mechanics of television – knowing which camera to look at, how to use an autocue effectively, how to move around the set properly. Michael, who produced the show himself, and his assistant Emma Cornish found out very quickly the needs and limitations of a singer. I was used to rehearsing an opera for weeks and weeks, but in television you only have a few hours to create something which in many ways is technically more difficult. When I make an album we record two or three arias in a session. To make the entire show we had only two days and I had to sing twelve extremely contrasting pieces in a very short space of time, and I had to do them over and over and over again while camera angles were checked and sound levels sorted out. There were guests to incorporate as well, and costumes had to be matched to each section of the programme (David Emanuel made this part easier by making me a beautiful cream dress and coat which could be adapted, through ingenious use of scarves and detachable bits and pieces, from sexy to serene and back in seconds). The first day of recording ended at midnight and, as I sat in my dressing-room, tense and drained, I broke down in tears. I could not imagine how I was going to cope with another day like that one. But the next day I felt back on home territory. There was a live audience in the studio – real people for me to sing to and who bore me up and carried me through.

Only hours after the TV show, which we had decided to call *Viva La Diva*, was finally completed, I set off for a recital tour of the USA exhausted and voiceless. Thankfully, my beloved Phillip Thomas was coming too, as my accompanist, and we flew to Detroit together, communicating in sign language. When we arrived I went straight to bed and stayed there, fast asleep for most of the time, for two days. When I finally emerged, I was refreshed and ready to perform again, though I already missed my children dreadfully and two whole weeks without them was going to be very hard indeed. Yusef had planned our tour meticulously and I fitted in another round of radio interviews and record signings in between performances. By the time we reached St Louis I was acutely, agonisingly homesick. I yearned so much to hold my children again that my arms ached. We performed in the Sheldon Theater, a stunningly lovely building, designed in a simple Shaker style. The audience was large and welcoming, Phillip was happy because the piano was a particularly good one, everything should have been perfect. But by the time I got half-way through Tchaikovsky's 'None But the Lonely Heart', the music was so moving and the lyrics so poignant that I was unable to hold back my tears. As the final notes ebbed away I began to sob. I levelled with the audience: 'I'm so sorry, but today is my little girl's first birthday and I'm missing it. I just so want to be home.'

Half the audience clapped and the other half reached for their hankies, while I cleared my throat, sipped some water and took a fresh hold. I gave them a rousing rendition of 'I Want to be a Prima Donna', to remind myself of why I was there and finished the recital to a thoroughly undeserved standing ovation. Our last stop was Los Angeles, where we played at the Henry Ford Theater, a dilapidated old building sitting neglected and overlooked amongst the glitz and sparkle of Sunset Boulevard. With its bare lightbulbs, peeling paint and radiators hanging from the walls, Phillip and I felt completely at home – it was like an ENO set from the 1980s. On the long plane journey home from California, I could think of nothing but my family, how much I had missed them and how I never wanted to go away from them again.

Although I got to keep my beautiful red gown, I was obliged to keep it under wraps for six months until the TV programme went out. Just as soon as the embargo was lifted, I rushed to show it to my record company who immediately arranged for Kate Garner to take some publicity shots of me wearing it.

Every moment I had it on, my whole body wanted to dance and Kate encouraged me to frolic in the studio to my heart's content. The photographs she produced captured this feeling astonishingly well – they sang out with energy and movement. There was an air of *fin-de-siecle* gaiety about them that started musical bells ringing in my head. Silva Screen were equally enthusiastic about the photographs, and James Fitzpatrick instantly recognised the musical connection. This was the embodiment of operetta, of Offenbach and Lehar and Strauss. From these connections between a dress and a musical era was born my fourth album. What else could it be called but *Soprano in Red*.

The dress didn't just inspire an album and provide a name for it, it created an image, a trademark, a symbol which was instantly recognisable. Even when I wasn't performing I was haunted by the image of the soprano in the red dress. One summer, when Jeremy and Chloe were about three and two years old, I was struck down by an attack of acute nostalgia and decreed that we should have a Proper British Seaside Holiday. I inveigled my mother, my sisters, their husbands and children and assorted in-laws and cousins into joining us in St Ives for a week of family fun. Every morning, a regiment of Garretts would troop down to the beach, armed with buckets and spades, balls, bats and boats, and establish base camp with windbreaks and deckchairs, while the children, entering into the territorial spirit, dug trenches in the sand around us and defended them against marauders. One particular morning, after an hour or so of particularly heavy trench-digging, a cry went up from the children: 'Chips! We want chips!'

It was only half-past ten, but I'd long abandoned the quaint north London notion of only fruit between meals, so I trudged off to the nearby café and returned laden with chips and sauce, and steaming mugs of tea for the grown-ups. As I doled out the rations, a flock of huge, ravening seagulls appeared above our heads, dive bombing us, squawking and pecking at chips and children alike. As

I flailed around, swiping at the birds with a rolled-up copy of *Opera* magazine and yelling at them to bugger off while trying not to pop out of my bikini top, I was approached by a woman apparently oblivious to my predicament.

''Ere, are you 'er what sings in that red frock?'

'Oh God,' I thought, 'she's going to want me to autograph her beach ball.'

'Why aren't you in the South of France?'

Why indeed, thought Peter, sinking deeper into his deckchair and weeping silently.

Everywhere I sang, the dress went too. So much of a trademark did it become that promoters would request, sometimes tentatively, sometimes quite forcefully, that I wear it, not just for the concert itself, but to the after-show parties that almost invariably took place for sponsors and local dignitaries. It was made perfectly clear that everyone, audience and sponsors alike, would be disappointed if the dress failed to put in an appearance. I was normally happy to oblige, though there could be problems.

The skirt is six feet across and, although light as air, is stiff and very difficult to manoeuvre – it seems to have a mind of its own. Orchestras would have to be rearranged on stage just so I could get on and off without knocking over music stands and getting tangled up with the cellos. The production team at *The National Lottery* were aghast at my request for a dress rehearsal before the show. 'Who does she think she is?' they must have been muttering to themselves, until Caro explained that we meant it quite literally. If they wanted the dress, then it would have to be rehearsed or they were running the risk of me getting stuck in the doorway or bits of the set being sent flying on live TV.

All David Emanuel's dresses are the product of extraordinary craftsmanship, which is just as well because I subjected mine to terrible punishment. However hard I tried to remember to pick up my skirts as I walked from dressing-room to stage, it got filthy dirty every time I wore it and spent more time at the dry cleaners than it did in my wardrobe. David grew so tired of replacing the sequins that we finally gave up and put diamante beads in their place. Transporting the thing was a nightmare in itself as it occupied three separate boxes, which was a struggle on trains. Porters were bemused at why I should be carting around these huge cardboard boxes and treating them with such solicitude when they weighed so little they could have been empty.

Whenever I travel around the country I always prefer to go by train. This is partly because I'm inclined to car sickness, partly because trains are more convenient if I need to work on a score or learn some words, but mainly because I just love the railways — they are in my blood. Everyone likes to moan about bad experiences with trains and I suppose I have had a few myself, but on the whole it is a great way to travel. Dear old British Rail once came to my rescue when I was returning from the Malvern Festival where I had been singing Berlioz's 'Nuits D'Ete' with William Boughton and the English String Orchestra. There was no buffet car on the train, but I was desperately thirsty and I had brought no water with me. I do have to drink rather a lot of water, not just for my voice but because of my wonky kidney, so I asked the guard if they had any drinking water on board. The next thing I knew, the train ground to an unscheduled stop at an isolated signal-box and a brimming glass of mineral water materialised from the signalman's private supply. I wonder if my father ever had to provide this level of service to passengers? I have even been afforded the honour of having a train named after me – not any old train, mind – the Lesley Garrett is a Eurotunnel shuttle!

Even packed in its boxes, the dress would always need ironing when I reached my destination and unless a dresser could be found for this thankless task, or a willing stage manager could be pressed into service, I had to do it myself. 'Does Miss Garrett have any special requirements?' concert organisers would ask politely. 'A banana, a bed and an ironing board,' was Caro's standard reply.

We only ever had one real disaster with the dress and that was when I sang in Sheffield at a benefit concert for Vivien Pike's Cantores Novae and other youth choirs in the city. The blasted thing was returned from the cleaners only minutes before I left to catch the train from St Pancras. Half an hour before I was due on stage I unpacked the boxes and found, to my horror, that the special red laces which secured the bodice were missing. The situation seemed hopeless until I remembered that the choir and orchestra were made up of young people. Just down the corridor in their dressing-room there must be hundreds of pairs of trainers. I walked on to the stage like a crab, trying to hide the grubby white criss-crossing down my back and sang the first section of the programme standing to attention. I could hear the choir and orchestra tittering behind me, so in the end I came clean with the audience, allowed them a good chuckle at my expense and carried on as if nothing untoward had happened. I was keen for the show to be a success, as it was important to me not only to help raise money for the choirs, but to pay tribute to Vivien, my first singing teacher. The highlight of the evening for me was performing 'We'll Gather Lilacs' with her, the first and only time we have ever sung together in public. In case you are wondering, I did return the shoelaces, autographed at the owner's request.

Outdoor concerts posed even greater challenges. At Radley College in the summer of 1995, I discovered to my horror as I popped out of my portakabin to spend a pre-concert penny, that the dress was too wide to fit into a portaloo. I crossed my legs for the first half of the show, while the organisers rigged me up a tent and a bucket for the interval. How glamorous can you get! Of course, open air events are always at the mercy of the weather. If it is too cold no one can play, if it is too damp the tuning on the instruments goes crazy. Even a hot, sunny day can make life difficult. I remember doing a concert for the Chester Festival when it got so hot during the afternoon's rehearsal that the violins began to melt – not the players but the instruments themselves, or at least the varnish on them. We ended up rehearsing with a gang of helpers holding umbrellas over the orchestra to shade them from the sun.

Despite these complications I absolutely love this sort of concert. At their best they are a quintessentially English form of popular entertainment – an eccentric cross between Glyndebourne and a Sunday School picnic. Music becomes the focus for a day out for the whole family and what worthier backdrop can there be than the grandeur of a stately home or the natural beauty of a park. I've sung in some stunning locations such as the grounds of Cardiff Castle, Hampton Court and Greenwich Park, but also in some odder ones like a golf course in Devon, a floating pontoon at Henley, and Ascot Racecourse (yes, of course, I did a couple of 'My Fair Lady' numbers there).

Naturally, there are those who sneer, who feel that an audience cannot appreciate music if they are sitting on a rug or in a deckchair with a glass of wine in one hand and a smoked salmon sandwich in the other, with children playing around their feet. They can sneer as much as they like, it sounds like heaven to me. However relaxed and comfortable an audience is, people will always give their attention to the music if it is good enough. When I sing I find it all the more satisfying that audiences listen to me out of choice, not because of concert hall etiquette.

Open air events are also a marvellous way of singing to very large audiences, although one of the largest audiences I have ever encountered was not at a concert but at a recording of a special edition of *Songs of Praise* in the unlikely location of the brand new Court Number One at Wimbledon. I sang the first verse of 'The Day Thou Gavest Lord Has Ended' to a packed crowd and was then supposed to lead them all in the rest of the hymn. To my shame, I wasn't watching the conductor properly, misjudged the gap between the verses and brought in 9,000 voices two whole bars too early. My embarrassment was heightened by the fact that when 9,000 people start to sing, they, like a

With my singing teacher and great friend, Joy Mammen,
after the Last Night of the Proms.

Right With Jeremy, Peter and Chloe, in our garden, training Jeremy to use the mobile to say 'Sorry, Mummy's in a meeting.'

Left Bruce Forsyth, with me in the frock he called 'an exploding blackcurrant'.

Below With my old friend Nick Folwell, third from right, Roy Castle and the rest of the BBCTV *Record Breakers* team.

Right With my mother outside the
RAM after receiving my fellowship.

Below Nanan Garrett at my
wedding party.

ROYAL ACADEMY OF MUSIC

With Pauline Quirke and Linda Robson, before and after the Kenwood concert, the first outing, for 'that dress': 'There will be 8,000 people out there tonight, but don't let that worry you.'

MISS LESLEY GARRETT
for
KENWOOD HOUSE CONCERT

'FLAME'
RED SILK TAFFETA

TULLE STOLE

ALL SPRINKLED
WITH SEQUINS &
DIAMONTE
RUBIES

DAVID
EMANUEL
COUTURE
© COPYRIGHT

With LOVE
DAVID x

Above left At St Andrew's Church, Epworth, with Phillip Thomas and Canon Derek Brown, at a recital in aid of the church restoration fund.

Above right David Emanuel's sketch for the red dress.

Right At the Althorp concert Ania had to summon help to get me from dressing room to stage through the mud.

Previous page
With guests on my TV
show: Bryn Terfel, Darcy
Bussell and Michael Ball.

Right Performing the 'Cat
Duet' with Lily Savage on
her show.

Below With Desmond
Barrit and Jonathon Pryce
after the Hollywood Bowl
My Fair Lady.

Left With my Dad
in Tim O'Sullivan's
portrait taken for
The Sunday Times
'Relative Values'
article, 1997.

Below Rosina
in *The Barber of
Seville* at ENO,
1998, with dear
Donny (Gordon)
Sandison.

supertanker, need a long time to stop. I had to stand on my dais, silent and blushing, for a full two minutes before the last voice finally faded away and we were able to try again.

If there is one thing more enjoyably and eccentrically British than a concert in a stately home, it is a day out at the cricket. I have loved and followed the game since I was a tiny child and I still find watching it the most perfect form of relaxation. People who have yet to understand the true delights of cricket are inclined to make jokes about the game being slow, but to my mind they have got it wrong. Cricket, especially test match cricket, is not slow, it is very, very slow; and that is precisely why I like it so much. A cricket match is about the only chance I get to allow my brain and body to settle to a gentler pace. Of course, slow doesn't have to mean boring. I often draw a parallel between listening to Wagner and watching a Test Match. Both contain some extraordinarily exciting moments, but you have to wait patiently and for a long time to catch them. In the meantime, the build up is an essential part of the experience.

In 1987 my mother and I were both at Lords to watch Yorkshire win the Benson & Hedges cup. Mum was at the Nursery End with a crowd from the Yorkshire supporters' club and I was at the Pavilion end with Peter Jonas and his old friend Martin Campbell-White. It was the most exciting match I have ever been to, as the outcome depended on the very last ball. The scores were dead level, but Yorkshire had lost fewer wickets and Jim Love, facing the last ball, had to do no more than stay in for our side to win. As Davis delivered the final ball and Love stood his ground, Mum and I waved and beckoned frantically to each other and then, simultaneously, ran towards the pitch, arms outstretched like Cathy and Heathcliff until we met and embraced victoriously amongst a vast crowd of other invading Yorkshire men and women.

Despite the fact that Jeremy Isaacs was General Director of the Royal Opera House and I was a principal soprano at the English National Opera, we never let any sense of rivalry get in the way of our longstanding friendship, which was based as much on a love of cricket as our shared background in the arts. Jeremy often received glitzy invitations to Lords and I would tag along with him (frequently, to his dismay, in jeans and a T-shirt). I was usually the only woman in the box (though once I was fortunate enough to spend the afternoon sitting next to Rachel Hayhoe-Flint), and I would generally be regarded with a certain amount of suspicion until it became clear that not only did I know my silly mid-off from my square leg but could quote Darren Gough's averages by heart. One particularly vivid cricketing memory is of the glorious afternoon I spent in Will Wyatt's box at Lords in 1995 watching the MCC play the West Indies. I sat in companionable silence next to Ludovic Kennedy, turning from time to time to the little TV set at the back of the box which was kept turned on so we could see the action replays. During a break in play, I was happily chatting to Jeremy Paxman about the respective merits of Fred Truman and my grandad when a voice came from the TV uttering the time-honoured phrase: 'Ladies and Gentlemen, we interrupt this broadcast to bring you an important news item.' It was announced that the Prime

Minister, John Major, had, quite unexpectedly, resigned as Leader of the Conservative Party. The room erupted in a frenzy of excitement and speculation and Paxman dashed off at high speed with his mobile phone already clamped to his ear. It only took Ludovic, Jeremy Isaacs and me a moment or two to weigh up our order of priorities and we resumed our seats before we missed too much of the match.

John Major won the subsequent leadership election and I was able to tell him this story when I met him in person. I have never voted Conservative in my life and, to my shame, I had expected a dull, grey, banal man, like his *Spitting Image* puppet. I could not have been more wrong. He was witty, knowledgeable, charming and disarmingly sexy. I was invited twice to Downing Street to receptions for representatives of the arts world and, in October 1995, we had the considerable honour and pleasure of being the Majors' guests at Chequers. Peter and I set off, late as usual, in our trusty old Peugeot, armed with our invitation to a reception and dinner in honour of President Chirac of France. Peter had planned our route days in advance, but I was in charge of map reading and we found ourselves driving along a narrow hedge-lined Buckinghamshire lane with no idea where we were or even if we were going in the right direction. We stopped the car while I pored intently over the map. I felt Peter's hand reach out towards me.

'It's all right, darling, I think they've found us.'

Looking up, I saw standing in front of us two large, unsmiling men in flak jackets carrying machine guns. A helicopter hovered overhead and behind us were two more members of the security forces on motorbikes. Heaven knows where they had come from – we had not passed a turning or seen a soul for miles.

'I think the tax disc's out of date,' whispered Peter, panicking.

'Show them the invitation,' I hissed back, but it was not necessary. Our car had obviously been identified long before and our welcoming committee knew precisely who we were. Our car was escorted to Chequers and we parked in front of the house, self-consciously squeezed between the Daimlers and Range Rovers, and went in to find ourselves in a large and elegant room containing the entire French and British Cabinets and their wives with a sprinkling of the great and the good from the arts establishment. The Majors greeted us warmly and I felt more at ease in our grand and historic surroundings. We were a railwayman's daughter and a farmer's son, but the Prime Minister was a Brixton boy and proud of it. If he could feel at home here, as he quite obviously did, surrounded by hundreds of years of British history, then so could we.

The glamour and grandeur of Chequers was a far cry from the starkly simple room at the London Welsh Association headquarters where I rehearsed my next opera. *The Rise and Fall of the City of Mahagonny*, though also composed by Kurt Weill, was in stark contrast to *Street Scene*. Where *Street Scene* was heart-warming and uplifting, *Mahagonny* was an operatic setting of Berthold Brecht's cynical vision of the ultimate capitalist city. Anything goes in *Mahagonny*, a city founded by three criminals on the run. Drinking, gambling, sex and murder are the life-blood of the place – the only sin is to have no money. My character was Jenny, a prostitute, and I mean a prostitute. She was not a good-time girl or a tart with a heart – Jenny was hard-bitten, cynical and tough. Our producer, Declan Donellan, the celebrated founder of the Cheek By Jowl theatre company, was keen for us to breathe real life into a cast of very difficult characters, and put us through hours of rehearsal.

It was a fascinating and rewarding process but a gruelling one, physically and emotionally. Performances were hard work too. *Mahagonny* contains a lot of dialogue, which can put a strain on the voice and the part of Jenny required a hard edge to my singing. June 1995 was hot and the stage at the Coliseum was like an oven, while my dressing-room, equipped with an antiquated and temperamental air-conditioning unit, was bitterly cold. On the last night, towards the end of the first act, my voice suddenly stopped working. It felt as if I had a frog in my throat so I coughed but that only made it worse. The rest of the cast stood, appalled and helpless as I croaked to the end of my song. As the curtain went down, I rushed off stage squeaking, 'Someone call my husband! Get Peter for me, now!' My colleagues crammed into my dressing-room, offering sympathy, advice and all manner of obscure remedies from their own emergency kits. There were strange-tasting oriental infusions, lozenges obtainable only from an obscure Swiss pharmacist, throat sprays from America ('everyone at the Met uses this stuff'). I tried them all, gratefully, though I was amazed at the level of hypochondria amongst these other singers. Being married to a doctor, I'm lucky to have a paracetamol at the bottom of my make-up box. Alas, none of the miracle cures worked for me.

Dennis Marks, the General Director of ENO, was kindness itself and offered to hold the show while they sent for the understudy, Helen Kucharek, who was at home, forty minutes away. I decided to have a go at the second act, reminding myself that Lotte Lenya, who had made the croak into an art form, had been the first singer to play this role. I found some bits of my voice that would work, I ducked and weaved, employing every vocal trick that Joy had ever taught me. The rest of the cast were marvellous. Whenever one of them could take my line they did. Peter was already in the wings when I came off stage at the end, as calm and reassuring as I was frantic with worry. Through the wonderfully efficient medical old pals' network he had already found the name of the best larynx man in town. There was no need to panic any more; we would get it all sorted out in the morning.

He was true to his word and the next day I had an appointment at the Royal National Throat Nose and Ear Hospital (I liked the way they got the order right) to see Mr David Howard. I had been in rude vocal health for so long that my larynx had not been examined for years. The last time, the doctor had put a little mirror in my mouth and told me to say 'Aaah'. The technology had obviously moved on a bit since then and Mr Howard's room was lined with high-tech machinery. Before he looked down my throat, he sprayed some magical concoction into my nose to open up my nasal passages. That was a revelation in itself, as I had not realised just how congested my sinuses were. Then a minute fibre-optic camera was passed down into my throat to take pictures of my larynx, pictures that showed that I had ruptured a capillary at the base of my larynx which had flooded the right-hand side with blood and left it bruised and swollen. Dramatic as this sounded, it was actually very good news. It would heal perfectly well with rest. Mr Howard was much more concerned with how I had got into this state in the first place and sent me to see Phillipa Ratcliffe, who headed the Speech Therapy department.

It was generally agreed that I had been harming my voice, not through singing but through speaking and I spent many a long hour with Phillipa learning how to support my speaking voice, just as much as I do my singing voice. She also gave me a long list of dos and don'ts to keep my voice healthy. Some of these were easy to adhere to, some less so. Drinking more water was straightforward, drinking less tea was harder, but I did cut down a lot. Remembering not to shout benefited me and my children who found me wagging a finger at them much less intimidating than my normal exasperated yell. Staying away from smoky environments, avoiding fizzy drinks and not speaking in a crowded place all sounded feasible enough in isolation, but a visit to the pub for a pint of beer had, alas, become a three-fold sin.

In order to keep their voices healthy, all singers have to judge very carefully the amount of work they do in any one year. Unfortunately, this means I have to turn down a great deal more than I accept, including many requests to sing for charity. Nevertheless, I do try to help when possible, and one offer I certainly could not refuse came, personally, from Sir Ian McKellan. He telephoned my home one day while I was out, giving Peter a bit of a shock, and asked if I would be prepared to take part in a gala evening at the Albert Hall in aid of Stonewall. I rang him back to agree and asked who else would be on the bill. Among the other glittering names was a personal favourite – Lily Savage.

'Any chance of me and Lily doing a duet?' I asked.

To my amazement, Lily (or more accurately, her alter ego Paul O'Grady) agreed. The choice of duet was easy. It had to be Rossini's 'Cat Duet', a hilarious parody of soprano rivalry and perfect proof that opera can be uproarious fun. Although I sent Paul a tape of the duet and he said he had learnt it, it was not until the afternoon of the show itself that we finally got together to rehearse. I quickly realised, and Paul admitted, that he had picked out from his part just the notes he could sing. With Phillip at the piano, we worked out a way for me to fill in his gaps, came up with a few extra cadenzas for Paul to make fun of and knocked our turn into shape in just half an hour. We were as faithful to Rossini as it was possible to be. All his notes would be sung, just not necessarily by the person he had intended nor in the octave he had originally imagined.

It didn't take me long to realise that I was in the presence of real comic genius and I was perfectly happy to be his straight man. On that night any doubts I had ever had about having fun with opera were dispelled. The audience loved us. They laughed hysterically throughout the duet and when it was over they rose to their feet, clapping, cheering and stamping. I have never known an ovation like it before or since and announced to myself (and, as it happens to the entire audience – I forgot I was wearing a microphone):

'Sod Covent Garden!'

Chapter 12

——◆——

The Possible Dream

Soprano in Red had been my most successful album yet, staying in the classical charts for months on end and winning the *Gramophone Magazine* Award for the Best Selling Record of 1996. It seemed natural and fitting to follow it up with an album devoted to music directly descended from the European operetta tradition. The early years of the twentieth century saw a migration of musical talent, from Europe to the United States. Much of this talent came from the world of operetta, with the arrival of composers such as Romberg, Herbert and Weill. Weill transferred his work from Berlin to Broadway but many of the others found work in the movies. Thus Gershwin, Kern and Porter were the American heirs of Offenbach, Lehar and Sullivan. As well as being an opportunity to sing some wonderful music, the album, which we called, appropriately, *Soprano in Hollywood*, gave me the chance to pay an indirect tribute to sopranos such as Lily Pons and Grace Moore. In the

1930s, they made the transition from opera house to silver screen, and gave pleasure to millions. Now, sadly, they are often forgotten in the annals of opera. Silva Screen were kind enough to commission David Emanuel to make me another dress to wear for the album cover. It was the most delicate shade of dusky pink, with a wide black silk sash and matching elbow-length gloves. Strapless, close fitting and divinely elegant, it captured the sophistication of the golden years of Hollywood quite perfectly. I was pleased with the record and it attracted a lot of favourable reviews, but its content and style stirred up controversy among the music world's purist pigeonholers.

The classical chart had existed quietly for years alongside its more well known pop sister, but the increase in awareness of classical music, encouraged by Classic FM, ensured that it now became a prominent marketing tool. Somebody, somewhere, of course has to decide what is and is not classical music and *Soprano in Hollywood* was deemed to have failed the entry tests. This was a frustrating situation for Classic FM as well as for me. If my record was not deemed to be 'classical' enough it was awkward for them to play it. A rickety compromise was achieved by establishing yet another chart, to be termed Crossover (I hate that word – it sounds like a bra) into which was dumped all the recordings that couldn't be fitted into the Classical or Pop categories, alongside the increasingly popular and lucrative 'Best of . . .' and 'Greatest Ever . . .' compilations. In one particularly bizarre week in January 1997, Bryn Terfel and I each had an album in both charts. We were joined in the crossover listings by Jacqueline du Pre and John Williams and by two collections of Christmas carols in the classical ones. Faced with this kind of Alice-in-Wonderland logic, I decided to stop worrying about what is and is not classical music and get on with recording and performing the kind of music I care about and that people want to listen to.

Despite my reluctance to spend too long too far away from home, I simply could not pass up the opportunity to sing in a gala concert at the Sydney Opera House. It is not simply a breathtakingly beautiful building, it makes a powerful statement about the city and its people. A young, energetic, confident nation has chosen to build, as its defining architectural landmark, not a cathedral or a skyscraper or a statue, but an opera house.

One day, during a lunch break in rehearsals, I was standing in a queue in the Opera House canteen, when I heard a small, diffident, but familiar voice behind me.

'I don't suppose you remember me, Lesley, but . . .'

I turned around and found myself face to face with Anna Sweeny, my movement teacher from what seemed like centuries before. I threw my arms around her and we spent a magical hour reminiscing about the old days at the Royal Academy. Before we parted I persuaded her to give me an impromptu refresher course on my curtseying technique. The red dress had always been a challenge to curtsey in and although it now hung in well-earned retirement in my spare-room wardrobe, its lovely silk roses tired and wilting, David Emanuel had made me a blue version to replace it.

Joy came to Australia, too, and after my concert we travelled around for a few days. We drove up the glorious, sun-drenched Hunter Valley, sampling wine from more vineyards than I dare to remember. All the way I watched out of the car window like an eager child, hoping to catch a glimpse of the wildlife I expected to be roaming the countryside. I failed to see a kangaroo, let alone a koala, but I did spot a kookaburra in the branches of a gum tree, so I came home well satisfied.

Back in London, there were difficult decisions to be made. My management arrangements had been working well enough over the busy years as my career developed. Robert was in overall charge at Allied Artists and oversaw my opera career. For years he had harboured dreams of me branching out on to the continent, but finally came to realise that ENO and motherhood had put paid to any ambitions he might have had on that score. The breadth and variety of my career seemed perfectly natural to me, but I was now working in two very different worlds, one commercial and one artistic, each with very different ways of doing business. Despite everyone's best efforts to keep both halves working together, cracks began to appear which made it painfully clear that it was time to consolidate and to appoint a manager with expertise in all the areas I was now involved in. I parted company with Allied Artists and put myself in the capable hands of Patrick Voullaire, a delightful, gentle and capable man with years of experience in all aspects of music management, who I already knew well as the agent of my friend and regular conductor, Peter Robinson.

Caro, too, decided this was a good time to make her escape (she had come in for a morning two years earlier to sort my fan mail into piles and somehow got stuck) and devote more time to her husband, Bob the brain surgeon, and their two daughters. In view of the amount of travelling I was now doing, it made sense to replace her with someone who was free to come with me wherever I went and I managed to persuade Ania, my old dresser from ENO to take me on. Six feet of patient Pole, Ania is the ultimate PA. She combines to perfection the roles of travelling companion, wardrobe mistress, secretary and minder. No detail ever escapes her attention. With her at my side, I know that everything will run like clockwork. Apart from the singing, I can delegate everything to her — she can have the nervous breakdowns for both of us.

Ania is very much a town girl. Her idea of heaven is to live at least five floors up in the centre of a big city. She likes pavement beneath her feet, grass confined tidily behind railings and anything with more than two legs locked safely away in a cage. Her idea of hell is the situation we encountered when I sang at the Memorial Concert for Princess Diana at Althorp House. It had been raining persistently for thirty-six hours when we arrived at Althorp and saw the enormous stage set at the bottom of a slope in a natural amphitheatre. By the time the audience began to arrive the whole area had been turned into an ocean of mud. It made Glastonbury look like a day at the beach. It didn't bother me too much — I was brought up in the country — but Ania simply doesn't do mud. She cowered in our caravan, shaking her head in despair, looking at the floaty white dress I was planning to wear, then at the mud outside and back to the dress.

In the end, she plucked up courage to venture out and commandeered a burly security guard to carry me on to the stage. Despite the rain, the audience enjoyed the show and I was honoured to be part of it. The concert was, as Lord Spencer had planned, poignant and moving but never sombre or sad. It was an apt memorial to a young woman whose warmth and compassion touched the hearts of millions and whose untimely and violent death shocked the world.

Being under contract to ENO required me to give them first call on my time. This was right and proper, but by the middle of the 1990s it was becoming increasingly difficult to do. Scheduling concerts, TV shows and making records – with all the promotional work that those activities involved – around the demands of opera required more and more compromises on both sides. Moreover, and more painfully, I began to recognise that I belonged to a bygone era at the Coliseum. Peter Jonas, Mark Elder and David Pountney, the Powerhouse generation, had long since departed. I felt I had become a remnant of another age, an anachronism, possibly even a dinosaur. I belonged to the company with my heart and soul but deep down I knew I would have to let go.

ENO had an equivalent predicament. They had no wish to see me leave, but every role I played was one fewer role to be offered to a younger singer whose career they were committed to developing, just as they had developed mine. I knew that casting me was becoming a problem for the company and I feared that there would come a time when this might become an embarrassment. The dilemma was resolved, fortuitously, by the retirement from the ENO board of Richard van Allen and the recommendation by Lord Harewood that I be invited to take his place. To be offered a seat on the board was an enormous privilege in itself but to take Richard's seat was an indescribable honour. The timing could not have been more perfect. As a member of the board, I was obliged to resign from my contract, but I would maintain the close link with the company that was so dear to me. What is more, I would still be offered roles as a guest artist. I would still be able to walk through the stage door, hang up my dressing-gown in the dingy dressing-room, be part of a team creating magic from words and music and step out on to that immense stage in front of the greatest audience in the world.

As a new member of the board I had a lot to learn, but the other members, and especially the chairman, John Baker, were patient and helpful. I attended my first meeting as an observer, which was just as well, for I found some of the terminology baffling. The phrase 'corporate revenue' kept cropping up, so I scribbled a note to my neighbour Russell Willis Taylor. 'What's corporate revenue?' The piece of paper was passed back. Underneath my question she had written, 'I think we need to have lunch.'

Funding for opera in this country is a highly controversial subject and one that arouses strong emotions. I make no apologies for believing passionately and wholeheartedly in public funding for the arts, just as I believe in promoting the widest possible accessibility to the arts. ENO has a desire, as well as an obligation, to present to the public work of the highest standard and also to offer a wide range of opera

– from Monteverdi through Handel, Puccini, Gilbert and Sullivan and Weill to Michael Tippett and Philip Glass. We could fill the house every night and balance the books with ease with three-month runs of *La Bohème* or Jonathan Miller's *Mikado* but that is not what we are there for. Just as a public library must stock Proust alongside Catherine Cookson, so any opera company worth its salt must offer something for every taste. To do all this and to do it well costs money, lots of money.

Budgeting and financial control are a perfectly proper part of the process of staging opera. The discipline they impose can be to the artistic benefit of the production. But the system of funding under which we currently operate sometimes feels as if it was invented by Lewis Carroll in a particularly playful mood. Detailed plans for a year's work have to be drawn up and published before the grant for that year is announced. Despite the management's best efforts at prudent forecasting, the grant, when it is finally announced, is never enough to cover the costs of the planned seasons and the plans have to be scaled down, publicly, to fit the budget. This puts the company in the position of appearing to complain endlessly about not getting enough money when, in fact, if we just knew how much money would be available we could cut our coat according to the cloth.

I didn't need to join the ENO board to discover how much of a preoccupation money is in running an opera company. I had spent years watching pennies being saved and corners being cut. A set consisting of a single lightbulb and a chair begins as interesting minimalism, but

THE POSSIBLE DREAM

can become a cliché and wind up being an irritation to
performers and audiences alike. Some productions were
just not amenable to the slimming-down process they
needed to undergo to be viable. One instance of this
that was particularly sad for me personally, was Dennis
Marks's plan for a new production of *My Fair Lady*. For
a few short weeks I believed I might be able at last to play
Eliza on the London stage. But of course it was not to be.
There was no point in doing the show unless we could do
it at least as well as the original West End production, let
alone the film, and to do that would have been way beyond
ENO's means.

The nearest I was to come to playing Eliza again was
when I was invited by John Maurceri to perform a selection
of songs from *My Fair Lady* in a series of concerts of
film music he was conducting as Musical Director of the
Hollywood Bowl Festival. Jonathan Pryce played Professor
Higgins and Desmond Barritt was Doolittle, stepping in as
a late replacement for Bob Hoskins who got a Better Offer
at the last minute. If I felt a twinge of disappointment at
missing my chance to work with Bob, it vanished as soon
as rehearsals began. Desmond's Doolittle was beautifully
sung and brilliantly acted and he was an absolute joy to
work with.

For once, Peter was able to come with me to Los
Angeles, so we mixed business with pleasure, finding plenty
of time before and after work to lounge around the pool of
our outrageously luxurious hotel on Sunset Boulevard and
indulge in some intensive retail therapy on Rodeo Drive.
We even spent a day at Universal Studios, bravely and

enthusiastically sampling all the rides (we managed Back
to the Future four times in a row).

Hollywood was everything I had imagined it would
be, and then some. Everything seemed bigger, brighter,
more beautiful than it had any right to be. We received
the full star treatment and I have to admit I loved every
minute of it. The day of the first concert dawned as fresh
and sharp as Californian orange juice, so it felt strange to
spend the morning in the warm sunshine brushing up my
expertly coached Cockney, but there is absolutely no point
in singing Eliza without getting the accent right. I had
been working hard at it for weeks and was determined my
vowels would be in tip-top condition. In the afternoon, a
limousine the length of a small street drove me from the
hotel to the arena where I was greeted by the extraordinary,
magical sight of my name in huge lights over the entrance.
I had come a long way from Thorne Grammar School
and the little typed, hand-duplicated programme (Price
3p) which had given me my first billing in this role.

The glamour of the occasion was heightened by the
frequent appearance backstage of Jonathan's film star pals
who came to wish us well. Alas, I missed Pierce Brosnan's
visit (I had cold cream all over my face at the time and I
wasn't going to let him see me like that!), but I did catch
Catherine Zeta Jones who was kind enough to remember
me from her ENO days and recalled her time at the
Coliseum with obvious affection. Later that evening, I
stepped out in my blue Emanuel gown on to a stage that
would have seemed huge had it not been dwarfed by the
vastness of the arena itself. I had been awed by the scale

of the place during rehearsals, but while I was backstage getting dressed 18,000 people had arrived, swarming up the staircases and filling every single seat. Nothing could have prepared me for the sight of so much excited, expectant humanity. It made the Royal Albert Hall look like my front room. In such a massive space, applause is not heard as a single sound. It comes in a wave, like the noise of rain falling on the distant mountainside of seats, growing louder as it pours down, coming closer and closer. I walked to the front of the stage feeling like a very small soprano indeed, but as I hit my spot a gloriously uninhibited Californian in the front row leapt to his feet waving his arms, swinging his hips and cheering 'Wear that dress, baby, wear that dress!!' After such a welcome I could not fail to feel relaxed and at home.

Jeremy and Chloe are gratifyingly blasé about seeing me on TV and on the stage at concerts, but the idea of me singing at the Hollywood Bowl sent them into a lather of excitement. One of their all-time favourite videos features Tom and Jerry at the Hollywood Bowl and every time they watch it (which is often, and generally at 6.30 on a Sunday morning) they squeal with delight and point at the screen: 'Mummy's sung there! Mummy's sung there!'

My five-year contract with Silva Screen Records came to an end in the summer of 1997 and I was faced with a painful choice. Silva Screen were more than happy to re-sign me, but they knew, and I was forced to admit, that for my career's sake it was time for me to move to a larger company. I joined BMG in September, in time to record my sixth solo record, *A Soprano Inspired*. Just before I left Silva Screen I took a case of champagne round to their offices in Camden Town and spent an emotional afternoon bidding farewell to Ren, James and their staff. I thanked them for their bravery in taking me on in the first place, their faith in my potential and their support for me over the years. 'I may be moving to a bigger company,' I told them all, 'but it cannot possibly be a better one.'

I had barely become accustomed to a new record company when I discovered I would need a new manager, too. Patrick Voullaire, who had looked after my affairs so smoothly and effectively since Allied Artists days, broke the news that he could no longer carry on. As a widower with a young son, he felt he needed to spend more time at home, which I quite understood. However, he promised not to leave me in the lurch and undertook to stay on until he could find me a new manager with whom I felt comfortable. This gesture was typical of Patrick's thoughtfulness, generosity and integrity and I knew I could rely on him to find me the right person. Before long he heard on the grapevine that Louise Badger, who had been General Manager of the BBC Symphony Orchestra for six years, was looking for a new direction for her career. Patrick arranged for us to meet and I was instantly and profoundly impressed by her calm, confident manner and her clear and orderly mind. On top of this, she had vision, ambition, and a delightful sense of humour. Most important of all, she was willing to take me on. Patrick had performed his last task for me impeccably.

I spent most of 1998 being shadowed by a camera crew

from *The South Bank Show* who were making a profile of me for their coming season. I felt very honoured to be the subject of such a prestigious programme, but rather intimidated by the prospect of meeting and being interviewed by Melvyn Bragg. He was, of course, utterly charming, gracious and disarmingly shy, and as a pair of northerners we got on famously. The producer, Nigel Wattis, and the production team became like a second family as they trailed around after me, filming a cross-section of my year's work.

They came with me when I returned to ENO for the first time since I came off contract and on to the board. It was a wonderful opportunity to show off the theatre which had been my artistic home for so many years, and to make some serious points about the relative cheapness of a night at the opera compared to a day at the races or an afternoon watching football. I was even caught on camera complaining bitterly about my costume for *The Barber of Seville*. It was supposed to be reminiscent of a 'distressed doll'. It looked to me like a frock with holes in it. I took a film crew up to Yorkshire to meet my dad who had a wonderful time showing off and telling embarrassing stories about my childhood. They even followed me to Barbados where I was giving a couple of concerts (a tough job, but somebody had to do it!). As if being paid to go to Barbados wasn't enough, my visit coincided with the arrival of the England cricket team and I managed to escape for a blissful afternoon of cricket in the sunshine. The final piece of filming took place in the summer in Harrogate where I was to be Artist in Residence for the Festival, performing in a series of three concerts – a musically varied gala, and two recitals, one of classical material the other of cabaret. The morning I arrived, a national newspaper published an article about me by a well-known opera critic. I don't know what I have done to offend this gentleman but he obviously saw it as his duty to belittle and insult every area of my work in such sneering, condescending terms that my family, friends and fans, who normally take a sensibly detached view of the press, rose up in my support. I have always hoped that I respond well to reviews. When the critics are kind then I am pleased that I have given at least one person pleasure. When they are harsh I listen to what they are saying and take their comments to heart. On this occasion, though, the criticism hurt and hurt deeply, because of its implications for so many other people. By insinuating that I was a second-rate singer, he seemed to suggest that the opera houses that employed me, the conductors I worked with, the company that produce my records were also second rate. Worst of all, he implied that the millions of people who buy my records and come to my concerts must also be lacking in musical taste or discernment.

Peter, wise and practical as ever, helped me to see things in perspective.

'You know he's wrong, love,' he said to me one day. 'We all know he's wrong. Just get back out there and show him.'

Basically, just as my mother had done years before, he told me to spit on my hands and take a fresh hold.

I went into rehearsals for my new BBC series determined to use the experience we had all gained in making *Viva La Diva* to improve on the way television deals with classical music and to show viewers that it is not something that need be mystifying or frightening or difficult. We had lined up a superb selection of guests from many different areas of the entertainment world who would join me in interpreting music that was special to me in a variety of different ways. Gary Barlow came and performed with me his own arrangement of a Chopin Etude, displaying a gratifying disregard for sartorial convention by doing so in jeans and beaten-up trainers. Darcey Bussell danced her own breathtaking sensual interpretation of the Seguedille from *Carmen* on a set the size of a handkerchief. I had met Darcey years before when she and I presented the award for Best Millinery at the British Fashion Awards. It was one of the stranger jobs I have been asked to do and Darcey and I had made an odd-looking couple – she pencil slim and me hugely pregnant with Chloe, but we had taken an instant liking to each other, and it was worth the long wait to work together again.

Lily Savage, fresh from our success at the Stonewall Gala, agreed to appear with me again and we sang a version of 'Three Little Maids from School' from the *Mikado*. Our third maid was Patricia Hodge, the exquisitely lovely and talented actress who was wonderful fun to work with. The contrast between Patricia and Lily was superficially extreme – one refined and stylish, the other outrageously vulgar and loud. Look more closely though and you can see that the character of Lily is a creation which requires extraordinary subtlety. Every gesture is acutely observed, every nuance of voice or mannerism captured with consistent perfection by Paul O'Grady.

The guest who had the greatest challenge of the series was probably Michael Ball, who gamely agreed to sing Papageno to my Papagena in the famous duet from *The Magic Flute*. I have always thought Michael would be wonderful in the part of Papageno, as Schikaneder, the great actor/singer of Mozart's day had been. He proved me right, singing quite beautifully and with true Mozart style.

One of the disappointing side-effects of my decision to confine my operatic career to this country after the children were born was that I had never sung with a real live Italian tenor. I have performed with some outstanding tenors in my time, but nothing can ever quite match the thrill of performing Italian opera with a real live Italian tenor. With Andrea Boccelli I finally fulfilled that dream. I was initially nervous of working with Andrea as he is completely blind. Would it be politically incorrect of me to mention it? Would it look odd if I didn't? It was, of course, crass and unnecessary of me to worry. He was a singer who happened to be blind and a very fine singer at that. His lack of sight simply wasn't an issue. We sang 'O Soave Fanciulla' from *La Bohème* which I had sung before in concert but which contains a rather exposed and nerve-wracking top 'C' at the end. Andrea gave me such confidence that I soared up to that note and was able to hold it longer than I had ever done before.

If I had to pick one highspot of the series, though, it would probably have to be performing the duet from *Porgy and Bess* with the great Bryn Terfel who is without doubt the greatest baritone alive in the world today. Bryn's talent and artistry are matched by his Welsh charm, and his warm generosity gently envelops all who have the good fortune to work with him. We did have one technical hitch in our duet, however. My microphone was, as usual, concealed in my hair and Bryn, towering a foot above me, found he was singing not only into his own mike but mine as well. Singing with one Bryn Terfel is daunting enough. I felt as if I was singing with two of him, which was a very tall order indeed. We ended the last show in the series quietly and reflectively with 'Goin' Home', the song based on the Largo from Dvorak's 'New World' Symphony, accompanied by the Grimethorpe Colliery Band.

'Goin' Home' was an appropriate end to the TV series because within days of completing the recording, I was back at ENO to start rehearsals for *The Barber of Seville*. I had always been rather sceptical about Rossini's operas and I definitely didn't have any burning ambition to play Rosina. *The Barber of Seville* had always seemed just too frothy for me. I am as fond of froth as the next woman but it needs to be on top of something more substantial. Phillip Thomas convinced me to give Rosina a try, however, and persuaded the talented conductor Mark Shanahan to take it on as well. Phillip oversaw the musical preparation for the production, coaching Mark and me and writing some extra ornamentation and cadenzas to add some top to my part (Rosina is generally regarded more as a mezzo role than a soprano one). Working with my old friend Gordon Sandison as Bartolo, I realised that although it is a mercilessly funny piece, there was pathos to be found in this opera after all, especially in the touching scene when Bartolo finally has to accept that he is no longer the great seducer of his youth. Gordon and I were by far the oldest members of an otherwise very young cast and we were painfully aware that the others saw us as elder statesmen. Watching the delightful and talented Clare Weston playing Bertha I was poignantly reminded of myself nearly twenty years before, starting out on my operatic career under the watchful eye of Valerie Masterson. I was determined to put every ounce of effort I could muster into this production. I had been accused of being a second-rate singer and I needed to prove, to myself if nobody else, that it was not true. In the end, the critics did us proud. Rodney Milnes, whose views I am not alone in respecting enormously, gave us a particularly favourable review in *The Times*.

The psychological hurdle of *The Barber of Seville* over, it was time to set out on my first ever concert tour – not just a series of dates at the same time of year but a proper tour in the 'if it's Tuesday it must be Nottingham' sense. Over the years I had been looking for ways to improve on the traditional format of the classical gala concert. I was very much aware that pop concerts had changed out of all recognition over the twenty-odd years I had been going to them. The days when a group could get away with standing in a line on a stage and strumming their way through their greatest hits had disappeared long ago, due, in large measure, to the advent of pop videos which presented the public with a new, dramatic, visual dimension to the music which they expected to find in live performances too. At its best, a pop video is a tiny but wonderful piece of musical theatre. The grandness and spectacle of opera seemed to have been an inspiration for the lavish productions which became a required part of the pop and rock scene, and yet classical performers, me included, were still standing immobile in front of an orchestra on an otherwise bare stage, singing their arias and walking off again. It seemed to me that it was high time for a more modern approach and I began to experiment with lighting, movements and enhancements to the sound – challenging some people's preconceptions of what a classical concert should be like.

Many of the changes I made came about by accident. I had never planned to go on stage in a huge red frock, but I wore it because it was the most beautiful garment I have ever owned. I soon discovered, though, that it enabled me to stand out on a stage, making me seem closer to the audience. Speaking directly to an audience, welcoming them and introducing the orchestra and my songs is something else that came about initially by accident. Concert audiences were expected to know about the music they were going to listen to, or if they didn't to consult the programme notes discreetly to find out. Soloists were a pair of tonsils in a motionless torso – to hear them speak would somehow break the spell. At one concert in my early gala career, however, there was a mix-up over the programme. I had planned to sing, and brought the music for, Dvorak's 'Song to the Moon'. The printed version had me down as singing something completely different. The conductor, very apprehensively, asked me if I would be prepared to make an announcement about the change – just a few words would do. When the time came, nervous though I was, I realised that a few words wouldn't really do at all. There was no point in the audience listening to me sing this aria if they had no idea what it was about, so I launched into an off-the-cuff explanation of how Dvorak's opera *Rusalka* concerns a water spirit who inhabits a magical pool and who falls in love with a prince who comes to swim in her. Being a sensible water spirit she realises immediately that there is a major barrier to their relationship. After all, he is a handsome prince and she is a pond. So, in the absence of any nearby relationship counselling service, she turns to her one true friend, the moon, to intercede on her behalf. The story got a laugh, which was something else that wasn't supposed to happen at classical concerts, and afterwards, when I chatted to members of the audience, they told me how much they appreciated having operatic arias put in context for them.

I always make a habit of talking to the audience after the show if I possibly can. I like to know not just whether or not they enjoyed themselves, but whether they could hear properly from where they were sitting, did they like what they heard, was there enough variety in the programme? Very often people would suggest new songs for me to sing. Some of them were songs I had never heard of or thought of, though more often than not they were songs I remembered singing around the piano as a child. I started putting together a wider range of material, adding numbers by Rodgers and Hammerstein and Lerner and Loewe to balance the Handel and Mozart. Some people think that songs from musicals are ill-suited to an opera singer's voice, and it is true that they can sound gruesome if sung in an 'operatic' style, but there is no need for that to happen. As the great singers of the 1930s and

1940s demonstrated, it is just a matter of having a flexible technique. I don't sing Puccini in the same style as I sing Handel, so singing Hammerstein is simply a question of finding the right style.

I am lucky enough to be able to work regularly with some of the best orchestras around, notably the BBC Concert Orchestra and the Northern Sinfonia, and to have them conducted by my own Musical Director. I have known Peter Robinson ever since I joined ENO, where he was Mark Elder's Assistant Music Director, and we worked together on *The Mikado*, *The Magic Flute* and *Cosi fan Tutte*. As well as being a marvellous conductor, he is a wonderfully sensitive coach and he has an incredibly deep knowledge and understanding of music. What I most value in Peter is his innate thoroughness. He is meticulous in the extreme in his preparation for concerts; without him I might be tempted to turn up and busk it. Firm and commanding on the podium, off it he is quiet, gentle and extraordinarily kind and I value him as much as a friend as a conductor. As a team, we are greater than the sum of our parts. The benefits of working with a regular team of people are enormous. If I am going to sing eighteen songs and arias, I can't rehearse them all fully on the day or I would have no voice left by the evening. Now that Peter and I know what we are doing, and are using the same orchestra for each series of concerts, we no longer have to start from scratch.

The 1999 concert tour went well and as it came to an end I experienced a deep and intense sense of relief and offered up a heartfelt grateful prayer. My latest operatic role had been well received by critics and audiences alike, my latest album had 'gone gold' in two weeks, every single ticket for my tour had sold before I had even packed my suitcase, and the television series which I hoped would bring the music I loved so dearly to a wide and new audience had been recommissioned.

Keeping clear of colds and flu is an irritating but necessary part of any singer's life. With two children now at school and a husband who spends his day ministering to the mucoidal masses, I am exposed to more than my fair share of germs. I try not to be obsessive, but when the diary is full of important work that a bad cold or sore throat could threaten, I find myself hugging more and kissing less. When Peter caught a particularly nasty bug and passed it on to the children just before I was due to go on tour, I resorted to wearing a surgeon's mask around the house. I was probably over-reacting, but it made me feel I was doing my utmost to stay healthy and it gave the kids a good laugh. At the end of the tour my diary was delightfully and deliberately empty for a while. My only commitment was a promotional visit to Paris. The plan was for me to do three days work there after which Peter would join me for a long weekend of peace, Pouilly-Fuisse and passion. On the train to France I felt that I was coming down with a sore throat. It was annoying to be ill now, but at least the bug had waited for a more or less convenient moment. By the time Peter arrived I was feeling distinctly under the weather but I was not going to let a virus spoil our precious time together. We spent a glorious day at Versailles and ate an early dinner in a restaurant in Montmartre. We shared a *chateaubriand* and while Peter toyed with some sorbet I demolished a rich and delicious pot of chocolate mousse. That chocolate mousse was my undoing. Back in our hotel I rapidly became very ill indeed. I spent more of the night in the bathroom than the bedroom and the next morning, though my stomach was calmer, my throat was agony.

We came straight home to see John Rubin, my new consultant at the Royal National Throat Nose and Ear Hospital. He was appalled when he saw the inside of my throat this time. He was looking not at a sore throat but a seriously injured one. The mild infection I had taken to Paris had made the tissues inflamed and sensitive. Eight hours of non-stop vomiting on top of this had quite literally burnt my larynx. I was ordered to spend at least two days in total silence and then rest my voice as much as possible until it healed. Only a few years before, this situation would have seemed desperate. I would have panicked, it would have been the end of the world. But such was my new confidence in my medical back-up team that I was able to relax and know that I would get better.

All was well again with my throat by late spring, in time for me to set off for a concert and recital tour of the Far East. We had a blissful family holiday in Thailand on the way but after two carefree weeks the time came for Peter to return home with Jeremy and Chloe and for me to make my way to Korea without them. Leaving the children is always hard. However often it happens, however big they get, I know I will never get used to it. Leaving them for three weeks and having to say our farewells in Bangkok airport at 1.00 a.m. was horrible. If they are at home when I say goodbye they are secure and comfortable and distracted by the competing attractions of videos and Lego, so I'm lucky if I get a last hug and a wave. On a bleak and frightening airport concourse, hollow-eyed with tiredness they became distraught at my departure, clinging frantically to my legs and weeping piteously. If I had looked Peter in the eye as he pulled them gently away from me I know I would never have gone through with it. I stared at the ceiling to keep my own tears from falling as he ushered them towards their plane, waiting until I knew they were gone before I made my way, miserably, to my flight.

Flying into Seoul at night was a breathtaking experience. It is a place where the lights never go out and the congested traffic never stops, so at night the streets are lit up like a Christmas tree with bright strings of red and white. It was a compelling, futuristic nightmare vision of a city, excitingly, frighteningly foreign. There were many other English faces in Seoul at the time, though, as the Queen was there on her first ever state visit to Korea. My hotel was full of trade delegations, busy forging new contacts and reinforcing old ones. The press always seem to report royal visits overseas as a round of tree-planting, present exchanging and displays of native dancing. What I realised in Seoul was how important such visits are to our international reputation and trade and how fantastically hard the Queen works promoting our interests. The first date of my tour was a concert organised by the British Council as part of the royal visit. It was an honour to perform in front of Her Majesty and particularly on that day, as it was her birthday. As a surprise, it had been arranged for me to sing 'Happy Birthday' to her, accompanied by a choir of forty tiny Korean children.

The children had been rehearsing for months for their big moment and sang beautifully, though they found the English words very difficult to get their mouths round. The Queen seemed genuinely moved by our tribute and I am sure I saw her reach into her famous handbag for a hankie at the end.

As well as Korea, we visited Taiwan, Malaysia and Japan, treated everywhere with unfailing courtesy. The audiences at my concerts were appreciative in a self-contained, inscrutable way, although I was never sure how much English was understood and whether they laughed at my jokes out of mirth or politeness.

Despite being well looked after by my team of Phillip, Ania and Louise, I still found homesickness impossible to conquer. I knew perfectly well that Jeremy and Chloe had calmed down within minutes of boarding the plane home, but the scene in the airport was something I would never forget. By the end of the three-week tour, I had made a decision. From now on, overseas trips would somehow have to be scheduled for the school holidays. I would go anywhere people wanted me to go, but only if the children could come too.

I flew home to a rapturous and tearful welcome from Jeremy, Chloe and Peter and upsetting news from Dad. His mother, my Nanan, had been unwell and suffering from some worrying symptoms. She had seen a specialist while I was away and now the worst had been confirmed. She had cancer, and it was terminal. There was no question in the minds of the family of her going into hospital. If she was going to die, she could at least die at home, cared for by those who loved her. My father, his brother Fayne and sister

Arleen, and my cousin Julie all took turns to be with her. Doncaster Social Services department arranged for teams of nurses to visit her three times a day, seven days a week, tending to her needs with exceptional skill and kindness and making her as comfortable as they could. My sisters and I visited her as often as we were able, and I was grateful for the chance not just to help with her care but to enjoy her company while there was still time. It was obvious to us all that she was desperately ill. Her body seemed to be fading away and her sight began to fail, but her spirit remained indomitable to the very last. The agonies and indignities of her situation were borne not with resignation but with exceptional courage and characteristic humour. She died on 11 September with her children at her side and peace and laughter in her heart.

In that summer of 1999, Millennium fever was already taking hold. When my generation were children, we often wondered what we would be doing in the twenty-first century. I was good at sums and worked out that I would be forty-five years old in 2000, which is very old indeed when you haven't reached double figures yet, but beyond that I had no idea what the future would bring. By my teens I had formed a dream of a life spent singing for other people's enjoyment. To have achieved just that would have been enough. Instead, I have been blessed with a career that has given me more pleasure than it is possible to describe. I know what I will be doing in the year 2000: I will make another TV series, release another record, teach the children how to tie their own shoelaces and celebrate my ninth wedding anniversary. Beyond that, who can tell? I shall probably have to accept that I will never play Eliza Doolittle on the West End stage, but I still have other dreams. Maybe my horse will win the Grand National, maybe I'll finally become a member of the MCC, maybe I can persuade Tom Jones to have a go at Don Giovanni. Maybe they will turn the Millennium Dome into a People's Opera House and give free tickets to everyone prepared to open their minds and enjoy themselves. If they did, I'd be the first one on the stage.

Epilogue

———•———

A small suitcase sits on my living-room floor. Its deep red leather is scuffed and worn, its hinges dull and rusted. The handle, mended once too often with string and sticky tape, hangs limp and useless. The suitcase looks forlorn and out of place on my carpet, a long way from its home beneath Nanan's bed. But that bed is gone now, cleared like the rest of her things from the little house in North Eastern Road, and Dad has sent the case to me.

I lift the bulging, battered lid slowly, tenderly, hoping to catch a last breath of my grandmother's scent as it opens. But instead there is just the musty smell of damp newsprint as dog-eared magazines, and sheaves of old press clippings spill and tumble to the floor. Underneath are fat albums of photographs, envelopes full of postcards and letters, concert and opera programmes. Thirty years of reviews, from *My Fair Lady* to *The Barber of Seville*, are all here. Dated and annotated in Nanan's careful, spidery hand and stored lovingly away, this is my life.

Acknowledgements

My grateful thanks to Rupert Lancaster at Hodder & Stoughton who enticed me into this project in the first place and who, with my old friend Caro Bradford, guided me unerringly throughout its writing with boundless patience, wisdom and good humour. Without their kindness and encouragement, this book would quite simply never have been started, let alone finished.

Thanks also to Mum and Dad, Jill, Kay and the rest of my family for putting me straight on the details of my early life and Joy Mammen, for twenty years of memories, tea and laughter.

I would also like to thank my agent, Louise Badger, for all her help in so many ways, and my assistant Ania, for wading through mounds of old papers and just being there.

Thanks also to the many other people who have helped me with research into the dustier corners of my life; Jane Livingstone at ENO for her assistance with names and dates from the Coliseum archive, Bill Rafferty for all his wonderful work in tracking down sometimes very elusive photographs for the book, and all my other colleagues and friends who have had their brains picked for obscure facts and figures over the past year. I would like to offer my sincerest apologies to all

285

those whose roles in my life story have, through lack of space, been omitted or have ended up on the cutting room floor.

Last but not least, thanks to my husband Peter, for reading every word of the manuscript, giving me wise advice and remembering all the best stories.

The author would like to thank the following for kindly granting permission to reproduce the following photographs—

Picture Section 2: page 3, reproduced with the kind permission of The Haddo House Choral and Operatic Society. Page 4, both photographs reproduced with the kind permission of Wexford Festival Opera. Page 5, both photographs reproduced with the kind permission of the Buxton Festival. Page 7, reproduced with the kind permission of the Welsh National Opera. Page 8, copyright Guy Gravett.

Picture Section 3: page 1, copyright John Stoddart. Page 2, copyright Bill Rafferty. Page 3, bottom, copyright Sue Adler. Page 4, page 5, page 6, all photographs copyright Bill Rafferty. Page 7, top left, top right and bottom, copyright Bill Rafferty. Page 7, centre, John Batten. Page 8, copyright Bill Rafferty.

Picture Section 4: page 2, copyright © BBC. Page 3, top, John Batten. Page 4, copyright © BBC. Page 5, inset, copyright David Emanuel. Page 6, copyright © BBC. Page 7, top, copyright © BBC. Page 8, top, copyright Tim O'Sullivan, 1997. Page 8, bottom, copyright Bill Rafferty.

Every effort has been made to trace all copyright holders, but if any have been overlooked, the author will be pleased to make the necessary arrangements at the first opportunity.

Index

LG refers to Lesley Garrett

287